Größere Gegner gesucht
Stronger Opponents Wanted

WITHDRAWN-UNL

Dietmar M. Steiner/Sasha Pirker/Katharina Ritter

Größere Gegner gesucht
Stronger Opponents Wanted

Kulturbauten im Spannungsfeld von Politik – Medien – Architektur
Cultural Buildings Caught Between Politics – Media – Architecture

Herausgegeben von / Edited by Architekturzentrum Wien

Birkhäuser – Publishers for Architecture
Basel · Boston · Berlin

Herausgegeben von / Edited by Architekturzentrum Wien

Konzept / Concept: Sasha Pirker, Katharina Ritter
Redaktion / Editorial work: Katharina Ritter
Mitarbeit / Assistance: Claudia Czesch, Kerstin Gust, Michael Hammerschmid,
Constanze Röthel, Markus Jung (Übersetzung aus dem Holländischen)

Übersetzung aus dem Deutschen ins Englische /
Translation from German into English: Elizabeth Schwaiger, Toronto
Übersetzung der Einleitung von Dietmar Steiner und des Beitrages über
das MuseumsQuartier aus dem Deutschen ins Englische /
Translation of the introduction by Dietmar Steiner, contribution about the
Vienna Museum Quarter from German into English: Kimi Lum, Wien

Graphik / Graphic design: Thomas Kussin, Gabi Schuster, Erik Turek für buero 8, Wien
Font: Frutiger Condensed
Gedruckt auf / printed on 115 gm² Profistar / Printed on 115 gm² Profistar

A CIP catalogue record for this book is available from the Library of Congress,
Washington D.C., USA

Deutsche Bibliothek – CIP-Einheitsaufnahme /
Cataloging-in-Publication Data
    Grössere Gegner gesucht: Kulturbauten im Spannungsfeld von Politik – Medien –
    Architektur = Stronger Opponents Wanted / hrsg. vom Architekturzentrum Wien.
    Dietmar Steiner; Sasha Pirker, Katharina Ritter. [Übers. aus dem Dt. ins Engl.:
    Elizabeth Schwaiger; Kimi Lum] – Basel; Boston; Berlin: Birkhäuser, 2001
    ISBN 3-7643-6463-7

This work is subject to copyright. All rights are reserved, whether the whole or part
of the material is concerned, specifically the rights of translation, reprinting, re-use of
illustrations, recitation, broadcasting, reproduction on microfilms or in other ways, and
storage in data banks. For any kind of use, permission of the copyright owner must be
obtained.

Mit freundlicher
Unterstützung von /
With the kind support of

© 2001 Birkhäuser – Publishers for Architecture
P.O.Box 133, CH-4010 Basel, Switzerland
Birkhäuser is a member of the BertelsmannSpringer Publishing Group
Printed on acid-free paper produced from chlorine-free pulp. TCF∞
Druck / Print: Konkordia, Bühl

.KUNST
bundeskanzleramt

bm:bwk

STADTPLANUNG WIEN

Printed in Germany   ISBN 3-7643-6463-7   9 8 7 6 5 4 3 2 1

Inhalt/Content

Geschichten von
Sasha Pirker und Katharina Ritter
Vorwort Dietmar M. Steiner
Essay MuseumsQuartier Wien
Melanie van der Hoorn

Stories by
Sasha Pirker and Katharina Ritter
Preface Dietmar M. Steiner
Essay MuseumsQuartier Wien
Melanie van der Hoorn

Größere Gegner
gesucht!

Wir bewundern spektakuläre neue Architektur, wir delektieren uns an Plänen und brillanten Photos, wir beschreiben die einzigartigen Überlegungen und Intentionen berühmter Architekten. Aber haben wir uns jemals damit beschäftigt, wie all diese Landmarks wirklich entstehen? Welchen Einflüssen sie während der Planung ausgesetzt sind? Der Architekt hat eine Vision, er zeichnet einen Plan, und dann wird gebaut? Diese naive Vorstellung wird uns ständig von den Medien vorgespielt – als gäbe es ihn noch, den omnipotenten Fürsten, der befiehlt und bezahlt. Architektur, wenn sie entsteht, ist in der heutigen Demokratie das Ergebnis eines unberechenbaren Prozesses. Diesen wollen wir in dieser Publikation erstmals anhand von anschaulichen Fallstudien dokumentieren. Wir sehen sie als „Lesebuch" mit spannenden Geschichten, begleitet durch erläuternde Abbildungen.

Architektur als bewußtes Zeichen, Architektur im politischen Auftrag, Architektur im Diskurs der Öffentlichkeit und der Medien. Dieses Dreieck der Interessen – Architektur, Politik, Öffentlichkeit – hat das am Ende jeweils gebaute Ergebnis eigentlich zu verantworten, wobei die Interessen naturgemäß unterschiedlich sind und auch jeweils eine andere Gewichtung in den Auseinandersetzungen haben. Die Architektur hat bei öffentlichen Kulturbauten ein natürliches Selbstdarstellungsinteresse. Die Politik, genauer die gewählten Politiker als Auftraggeber haben dieses Instrument erkannt und wissen es zu benutzen. Die Öffentlichkeit schließlich – als Bürgerinitiative oder als Strategie der Massenmedien – findet dabei eine willkommene Gelegenheit der Agitation. So eskaliert die Debatte über das „stolze" Projekt, das von allen Seiten bedrängt, letztendlich aber doch realisiert wird. Deshalb das leicht sarkastische Motto: „Größere Gegner gesucht!"

Dieses Buch steht für sich und hat dennoch eine Vorgeschichte. Seit Mitte der achtziger Jahre wird in Wien ein Kulturprojekt auf dem innerstädtischen Gelände des sogenannten Messepalastes, der vormaligen kaiserlichen Hofstallungen, diskutiert. Ein zweistufiger Wettbewerb fand statt, der 1990 entschieden und von den Architekten Ortner+Ortner gewonnen wurde. Dem folgten sieben harte Jahre heftiger öffentlicher und medialer Debatten und ständig neuer Raumprogramme. Ausgehend von dem Wettbewerbsentwurf der Architekten, ist ein vollkommen überarbeitetes und letztlich neues Projekt seit 1998 im Bau und wird im Jahr 2001 eröffnet werden: das MuseumsQuartier Wien, einer der größten Kulturbezirke der Welt.

Das Architektur Zentrum Wien, seit 1993 eine der kulturellen Institutionen des Museumsquartiers Wien, hat im Herbst 1999 erstmalig dieses Projekt präsentiert. Angesichts der sowohl langwierigen als auch schwierigen Entstehungsgeschichte war allerdings an eine konventionelle Ausstellung nicht zu denken. Wir entschlossen uns zu einer

6

Stronger Opponents Wanted!

We admire spectacular new architecture, we delight in plans and brilliant photos, we describe the inimitable reflections and intentions of famous architects. But have we ever considered how all these landmarks actually come to be? What influences they are subjected to during planning? Does the architect have a vision, draft a plan, and then construction begins? This naïve notion is constantly being presented to us by the media – as if he still existed, the omnipotent prince who commands and pays. Architecture, provided it comes to be, is in today's democracy the result of an unpredictable process. In this publication we would like to document this for the first time, using case studies to illustrate our thesis clearly. We see this anthology as a "storybook" full of exciting (hi)stories accompanied by explanatory illustrations.

Architecture as a conscious sign, architecture that serves political interests, architecture at the centre of public and media debate. This triad of interests – architecture, politics, public sphere – is in effect responsible for the building that results in the end. A tug-of-war, where the interests vary, of course, and each has a different weight within this contest. In public cultural buildings architecture has a natural interest in its own image. Politics, or more precisely, the elected politicians as clients have recognized this instrument and know how to use it. And finally, the public seizes upon the project as a welcome opportunity for agitation, be it through civil action committees or mass media campaigns. In this way the debate escalates over the "proud" project, which is subjected to pressure from all sides but ultimately ends up being realized. Hence our motto with a faintly sarcastic undertone: "Stronger Opponents Wanted!"

While this book can stand on its own, it does have a history that leads up to it. In Vienna a debate has been going on since the mid-eighties about erecting a cultural project on the grounds of the so-called Messepalast – formerly the imperial stables – which is situated in the middle of town. A two-stage competition was held in 1990, which the architect duo Ortner & Ortner won. This was followed by seven years of grueling public and media debates accompanied by constantly changing spatial programmes. Departing from the architect's winning competition design, a completely revised and essentially new project was drawn up, which has been under construction since 1998 and is scheduled for inauguration in 2001: the Vienna Museum Quarter, one of the largest cultural districts in the world.

The Architektur Zentrum Wien, one of the cultural institutions within the Vienna Museum Quarter since 1993, presented this project for the first time in autumn 1999. In view of its long drawn-out and difficult genesis, however, a conventional exhibition would have been unthinkable. We decided on a new form of architectural exhibition: the

neuen Form der Architekturausstellung: Der Erzählung von Geschichten, genauer: Entstehungsgeschichten. Das Ziel war, den „lokalen Skandal" der Entwicklungsgeschichte des Museumsquartiers in einen internationalen Zusammenhang und Vergleich zu stellen.

Im Zuge der Recherche dieser Geschichten stellte sich heraus, daß die öffentlichen Debatten rund um die Entstehung des Wiener Museumsquartiers durchaus mit anderen „Schicksalen" wichtiger öffentlicher Kulturbauten in Europa vergleichbar sind. Das angesprochene Dreieck – Architektur, Politik, Öffentlichkeit – ist für sie alle gültig, aber mit jeweils anders gewichtetem Schwerpunkt. Das Wirken dieser Kräfte ist unbestritten; entscheidend und spannend sind aber die agitativen Muster, die dabei von den handelnden Gruppen und Personen eingenommen werden.

Bei den ausgewählten Beispielen haben wir uns bewußt auf europäische Projekte konzentriert. Die Rolle der handelnden „Parteien" sind in den USA oder Japan gänzlich anders. Konflikte entstehen beispielsweise in den USA vornehmlich durch einzelne Lobby-Interessen, von einer wirklich handelnden Politik kann dagegen kaum gesprochen werden. Der Entstehungsprozeß der Architektur des 20. Jahrhunderts in Europa beruht dagegen auf einer sehr starken Einflußnahme der Politik. Minister, Bürgermeister, Stadträte: Die Geschichte der modernen Architektur hätte ohne ihre verantwortliche Mitwirkung nicht stattgefunden. Neu hinzugekommen ist die Rolle der Medien und der öffentlichen Meinung. Ihre Macht hat in der zweiten Hälfte des 20. Jahrhunderts dramatisch zugenommen. Heute wird die Debatte um ein neues Projekt mit einem politischen Beschluß kaum je beendet, sondern meist erst eröffnet. Politik steht heute mehr denn je in Abhängigkeit von einer veröffentlichten Meinung, nicht selten motiviert von spezifischen Medieninteressen. Dieses ist auch die wesentliche neue Dimension im öffentlichen Bewußtsein für engagierte neue Architekturprojekte.

Dennoch beginnen wir mit einem außereuropäischen Beispiel, dem Sydney Opera House, das bis heute als Opernhaus unvollendet ist. Erstens handelt es sich um eines der bedeutendsten Symbolbauwerke des 20. Jahrhunderts. Seine identitätsstiftende Silhouette dient noch immer bei vielen Symbolbauten als Vorbild und Argumentationshilfe. Es gibt kein Bild Australiens, das ohne die Skyline der Sydney Opera auskommt. Sie ist das herausragendste Beispiel dafür, daß die Architektur des 20. Jahrhunderts neue und zeitlose architektonische Symbole schaffen kann.

Der zweite Grund aber war, daß die komplexe Geschichte der Sydney Opera und das dramatische Scheitern ihres jungen Architekten Jørn Utzons – erst durch jüngste Recherchen vor allem durch Françoise Fromonot und Daryl Dellora – wieder neu in das Bewußtsein der Öffentlichkeit gebracht wurde. Die Geschichte dieses Projekts ist so spannend und unglaublich zugleich, daß wir nicht auf sie verzichten wollten. Gleichzeitig führt sie zurück zu den Wurzeln einer Moderne, die so eindringlich den Architekten als unermüdlichen Sucher, als Schöpfer neuer Räume und Entdecker neuer Techniken benötigte.

In der öffentlichen Wahrnehmung steht lediglich das großartige Bild

storytelling, or more precisely, the telling of stories of genesis. The goal was to place the "local scandal" of the Museum Quarter's developmental history in an international context and provide international comparison.

While researching these stories it became clear that the public debates surrounding the genesis of the Vienna Museum Quarter were by all means comparable with the "fate" of other major public cultural buildings in Europe. The aforementioned triad – architecture, politics, public sphere – applies to all of them, but to a different extent in each case. It is uncontested that in each case all three forces are at work, but what is crucial and exciting is the agitative patterns assumed by the groups and persons actively involved.

This selection of examples is deliberately focused on European projects. The role of the actively involved "parties" is completely different in the USA or Japan. Conflicts in the USA, for instance, arise mainly from clashing interests of the individual lobbies; one can therefore hardly speak of political force as an actor. By contrast, in Europe political forces have exercised a powerful influence on the process of architectural realization in the 20th century. Ministers, mayors, city councillors: the history of modern architecture would not have taken place without their participation. There is the role of the media and public opinion, whose power increased dramatically in the second half of the 20th century. Today a political decision rarely marks the end of a debate on a new project, but rather tends to initiate the debate in the first place. Politics is today, more than ever, dependent on a publicized opinion that is often motivated by specific media interests. This is also the essential new dimension emerging in the public consciousness, which will determine challenging new architecture projects in the future.

In spite of all this, we begin with a non-European example, the Sydney Opera, which has yet to be fully completed as an opera house. First, because it is one of the most important symbolic architectonic examples of the 20th century. Its identity-giving silhouette still serves as a model and precedent for many symbolic buildings. There isn't a picture of Australia that gets by without the skyline of the Sydney Opera House. It is the most prominent example of the architecture of the 20th century creating new and timeless architectonic symbols.

The second reason, however, is that the complex story of the Sydney Opera House and the dramatic failure of its young architect Jørn Utzon has – only recently and above all through research by Françoise Fromonot and Daryl Dellora – been reintroduced into the consciousness of the public. The history behind this project is both so fascinating and unbelievable that we didn't want to leave it out. And at the same time it also leads us back to the roots of a modern age that so urgently needed the architect as an indefatigable seeker, as a creator of new spaces and discoverer of new technologies.

The public's perception is dominated by the great image of this building. It wasn't until Jørn Utzon was commissioned to draw up guidelines for the future renovation of the Opera House on the occa-

dieses Gebäudes im Vordergrund. Der tragischen Geschichte des unvollendeten Werkes wurde aber erst mit der Beauftragung Jørn Utzons für die Erstellung von Leitlinien im Hinblick auf zukünftige Renovierungen des Gebäudes anläßlich der olympischen Spiele Sydney 2000 Rechnung getragen.

Die nächste Station – obwohl eine beträchtliche Zeit dazwischen liegt – markiert eindeutig das Museum Mönchengladbach des Architekten Hans Hollein. Kein Kulturprojekt in der Zeit zwischen Sydney und Mönchengladbach konnte eine vergleichbare Aufmerksamkeit auf sich ziehen. Das Museum Mönchengladbach war weltweit das erste Projekt, das einer neuen Museumsarchitektur besondere öffentliche Aufmerksamkeit bescherte. Holleins Museum hat im Übergang von den siebziger zu den achtziger Jahren des letzten Jahrhunderts den kulturindustriellen Typus einer architektonischen Landmark neu interpretiert und begründet. Das Projekt wurde in den siebziger Jahren als damals typisch bürgernahes Stadtteilzentrum geplant. Doch in der Folge wurde auch erstmals die Rolle und die Macht von Direktoren und Kuratoren neu definiert. Der Direktor Johannes Cladders konnte nur mit seinem Wunscharchitekten Hans Hollein seine Vision für dieses Museum verwirklichen und setzte dieses Projekt politisch durch.

Ohne Mönchengladbach, so bekannte der Architekt Frank O. Gehry, wäre ein Guggenheim-Museum in Bilbao nicht denkbar gewesen. Nicht nur im Sinne der Freiheit des Architekten eine einzigartige Landmark zu schaffen, sondern auch im Hinblick auf die Initiative und Unterstützung seitens der verantwortlichen Museumsdirektoren und Projektmanager.

Dennoch haben wir Gehrys Projekt nicht in die Sammlung dieser Geschichten aufgenommen, da genau diese Konstellation heute eine neue Realität geschaffen hat. Das inzwischen sogenannte „Bilbao-Syndrom" wird in Zukunft dem hier thematisierten Dreieck eine neue Gewichtung verleihen. Doch davon später.

Zuvor erregte die Welt noch das Projekt des Louvre in Paris. Als ein Beispiel der Grands Travaux in Frankreich verdeutlicht dieses Projekt auf sehr anschauliche Weise die politischen Strategien der jeweiligen Staatspräsidenten, architektonische Wahrzeichen zu schaffen. Historisch war der Louvre das erste öffentliche Museum der Welt. Dessen Neugestaltung folgte allein der Macht und Vision eines einzigen Politikers, François Mitterrand, der dieses Projekt von I.M. Pei – mit geradezu monarchischer Potenz – gegen alle medialen und politischen Widerstände durchsetzte.

Ein gänzlich anderes Beispiel ist das spektakuläre Monument des Postmodernismus in Groningen. Hierbei ging es weniger um die Architektur als solche als vielmehr um eine Standortfrage, die massive Proteste der Bürger hervorrief. Wieder war es der Museumsdirektor, der unterstützt durch einflußreiche Politiker, sein ambitioniertes Konzept für ein Museum durchsetzte, wobei die Rolle der Politik die eines Vermittlers darstellte – zwischen dem Anliegen der Bevölkerung auf eine unverbaute Sicht auf die Altstadt und dem Anliegen der Architektur, ein postmodernes Monument zu schaffen.

Das Kultur- und Kongreßzentrum Luzern von Jean Nouvel fällt dabei

sion of the Sydney 2000 Olympic Games that this unfinished work was given its proper due in this unfortunate story .

The next stage – although many years later – is marked undoubtedly by the Mönchengladbach Museum, designed by the architect Hans Hollein. No cultural project between Sydney and Mönchengladbach was able to attract comparable attention. The Mönchengladbach Museum was the first project worldwide that gave special public attention to an example of new museum architecture. In the transition from the 1970s to the 1980s, Hollein's museum re-interpreted and established the cultural industrial type of an architectonic landmark. The project was planned in the seventies as a typical district centre of the time with an emphasis on public access. But then the role and power of the directors and curators started to undergo redefinition. The director Johannes Cladders was only able to realize his vision for this museum by working hand in hand with the architect of his choice, Hans Hollein, with whose help he managed to push this project through politically.

Frank O. Gehry has admitted that the Guggenheim Museum in Bilbao would have been unthinkable without the precedent set by Mönchengladbach. Not only in the sense of the architect's freedom to create a unique landmark, but also in reference to the initiative and support of the museum directors and project managers responsible. Nevertheless, we chose not to include Gehry's project in this anthology of stories because precisely this constellation has created a new reality today. What has come to be known as the "Bilbao Syndrome" will in future lend a new meaning to the triad of interests discussed here. But more on that later.

The next project to capture the world's interest was the Grand Louvre project in Paris. As an example of the "grands travaux" in France this project clearly demonstrated the political strategies each president employed in creating architectonic landmarks. Historically the Louvre was the first public museum in the world. Its restructuring is due to the power and vision of a single politician, François Mitterrand, who persisted with this project designed by I. M. Pei against all media and political opposition with what can only be described as monarchic authority.

A completely different example is the spectacular monument to postmodernism in Groningen. Here it was less the architecture than the question of the location that incited massive public protests. Again it was the museum director who with the support of influential politicians pushed through his ambitious concept for a museum, where the role of politics represented that of an arbitrator – between the public's interest in an unspoiled view of the old part of town and the interest of architecture in creating a postmodern monument.

The Culture and Convention Centre Lucerne by Nouvel diverges slightly from this pattern. In Switzerland the political picture is marked by an institutionalized democratic practice based on direct democracy. In order to carry out a project on a certain financial scale approval of those entitled to vote is necessary. After the complicated history leading up to the event, the star architect was finally used as a market-

leicht aus der Reihe. In der Schweiz wird das politische Bild durch eine institutionalisierte demokratische Praxis, auf Basis einer unmittelbaren Demokratie, geprägt. Um hier ein Projekt einer bestimmten finanziellen Größenordnung durchzuführen, bedarf es der Zustimmung der Stimmberechtigten. Nach einer komplizierten Vorgeschichte wurde letztlich der Stararchitekt als Marketing-Argument eingesetzt, um die nötige Überzeugungsarbeit in der Öffentlichkeit zu leisten. Nur durch ein einzigartiges und bis heute unerreichtes strategisches Vermittlungskonzept des projektverantwortlichen Managers konnte diesem Bau zum Sieg verholfen werden.

Es bleibt zum Schluß das Wiener MuseumsQuartier der Architekten Ortner+Ortner mit dem Denkmalschutzexperten Manfred Wehdorn. Bedrängt von einer einzigartigen Medienmacht, gesegnet mit schwankenden und wechselnden Politikern, ist die Realisierung letztlich durch das Durchhaltevermögen der Architekten gelungen.

Mit dieser Publikation galt es, die zeitgenössische Architekturproduktion unter kulturindustriellen Bedingungen, verbunden mit dem politischen Auftrag und dem öffentlichen Diskurs, in ihren Wirkungsmächten darzustellen. Dies wird in der Folge anhand der Baugeschichten der ausgewählten Projekte verdeutlicht. Die Auswahl der vorliegenden Projekte konzentrierte sich insbesondere auf die verschiedenartigen Rollen, die die Akteure der einzelnen Projekte innehatten.

Es gibt schlichtweg kein allgemein gültiges Muster der Entstehung: Jeder Beteiligte, ob Politiker, Architekt, Projektmanager oder Medienzar, kann seine Rolle mit einer spezifischen Bedeutung und Kraft versehen.

In den folgenden Geschichten gibt es immer eine zentrale Figur, sei es der „verjagte Architekt" bei dem Sydney Opera House, sei es der Architekt in der Rolle des „einzigen Überlebenden" beim MuseumsQuartier. Für das Louvre-Projekt präsentiert sich der „mächtige Politiker" als entscheidender Faktor, wogegen das Museum Mönchengladbach vor allem dem „weitsichtigen Direktor" zu verdanken ist. Ein Kulturzentrum Luzern von Jean Nouvel gäbe es nicht ohne den „erfolgreichen Manager" und ein Museum in Groningen nicht ohne den „großzügigen Sponsor".

Allen diesen Geschichten ist das Kräftedreieck von Architektur, Politik, Öffentlichkeit gemein. Die Erkenntnis daraus geht in zwei Richtungen: Erstens sollten Architekten lernen, daß bei derartigen Aufgaben die erste Vision nie die Realisierung garantiert. Der demokratische Prozeß der Entscheidungsfindung bringt immer neue Argumente ein. Und andererseits muß die Politik lernen, die angefragten Visionen auch zeitgerecht mit den entsprechenden Vermittlungsstrategien zu verbinden. Unberechenbar bleibt dabei immer die öffentliche, medial gesteuerte Reaktion. Hier kommen stets Interessen ins Spiel, die nicht absehbar und oftmals nur vorgeschoben sind, um andere Ziele zu verfolgen.

Alle diese Bauten sind als „Monumente" unserer Zeit zu verstehen. Aber niemand thematisierte bisher die wirklichen „Bedingungen" dieser unserer Zeit. Die Interpretation schwankte bisher zwischen zwei extremen Positionen: Der Architekt als Künstler hat seine Vision, und

ing argument in the public relations work necessary to win approval. It was only through the project manager's unique and to this day unmatched strategic concept of arbitration on the part of the manager responsible for the project that this building could ultimately be built.

And last but not least we present the Vienna Museum Quarter designed by the architects Ortner & Ortner in cooperation with the monument protection expert Manfred Wehdorn. Harassed by an unparalleled media power, enjoying only the tenuous blessings of indecisive and changing politicians, its realization must ultimately be attributed to the stamina of the architects.

With this publication our objective was to show the production of contemporary architecture in the context of the conditions in the cultural sector, and in connection with the need to meet political interests and public discourse. These interactions are illustrated in the following pages by presenting the detailed building history of the selected projects. The selection focuses in particular on the different kinds of roles that were played by the main protagonists in each individual project.

There is, simply put, no universal pattern of genesis: every participant, whether politician, architect, project manager or media czar, can lend his or her role specific meaning and power.

In the following studies there is always a central figure, whether it is the "banished architect", in the case of the Sydney Opera House, or the architect as the "sole survivor", in the case of the Museum Quarter. In the Louvre project it is the "powerful politician" who emerges as the crucial figure, whereas in the Mönchengladbach Museum it is the "visionary director". The Culture Centre Lucerne by Jean Nouvel would never have been built if it were not for the "successful manager", nor would a museum in Groningen exist today if not for the "generous sponsor".

What all these stories have in common is the power triad of architecture, politics, and public sphere. The understanding gleaned from this is twofold: first, architects should learn that in these kinds of tasks there is no guarantee that the first vision will ever be realized. The democratic process of arriving at a decision always introduces new arguments. And on the other hand, politicians must learn how to coordinate the visions in question with the corresponding arbitration strategies and do so in a timely way. What always remains an unpredictable factor is the public, media-controlled reaction, where unforeseen interests come into play, which are often merely a front for pursuing other goals.

All these buildings can be regarded as "monuments" of our time. But to this day no one has addressed the real "conditions" of our time. The interpretation has always vacillated between two extremes: the position of the architect as artist, who has a vision which society at large – deemed incompetent in this regard – is expected to simply and duly accept, and the other position that holds that the representative buildings of a democratic society should ultimately reflect the majority decision of the public. Our stories are intended to give only

die darin inkompetente allgemeine Gesellschaft hat diese pflichtschuldigst zu akzeptieren. Und die andere extreme Position behauptet, daß repräsentative Bauten einer demokratischen Gesellschaft letztlich Mehrheitsbeschlüssen der Bevölkerung zu entsprechen haben. Unsere Geschichten sollen nur faktisch belegen, daß beide Positionen falsch sind. Daß sich vielmehr die Monumente der zeitgenössischen Architektur in einem Kraftfeld der unterschiedlichen Interessen befinden und damit in ihrem jeweiligen Ergebnis ganz wesentliche und grundlegende kulturhistorische Auskünfte geben können. Diese bieten immer mehr als das gebaute Resultat allein.

„Größere Gegner gesucht!" verkündet keine neue architektonische Ideologie, bietet keine Revue der Highlights und ist eben deshalb vermutlich neu. Ein starker Begriff, gewiß, aber er reflektiert die Situation, daß heute derartige kulturelle Projekte überwiegend protegiert, nicht aber diskutiert und ihre Entstehungsgeschichten damit nicht mehr thematisiert werden.

Die vorliegende Publikation versucht, Architektur neu zu erzählen. Nachdem die internationale Architekturkritik nach dem Eintritt der Architektur in die Kulturindustrie ihrer alten ideologischen Kriterien der moralischen Verpflichtung zur Modernität verlustig ging und zum PR-Agenten des Star-Systems mutierte, muß eine neue Beschreibungsform gefunden werden. Das vorliegende Buch will mit seinen Geschichten eine neue Methodik der Beschreibung und Erklärung von Architektur eröffnen. Es wäre als Fortschritt zu bezeichnen, wenn die hier vorliegenden Geschichten zu den ausgewählten Bauten bei anderen Beispielen als Fragen formuliert werden.

Ich darf zum Schluß noch einmal auf das Guggenheim-Phänomen und Gehrys Bilbao-Projekt zurückkommen. Tatsächlich markierte dieses Projekt eine neue Dimension der kulturindustriellen Bedingungen. Die Sensation des Gebäudes eines Star-Architekten ist eingebettet in eine weltweite Unternehmensstrategie. Lokale politische Einflüsse sind angesichts des Investments nur mehr lästige Störgeräusche. Es könnte sein, daß in Zukunft der „Spektakelbau" mit integrierter Vermarktung und garantiertem Publikumserfolg nicht mehr als kulturelles, sondern als touristisch-geschäftliches Investment gesehen wird. Architektonisches „branding", die Popularisierung einer „Architektenmarke", wird dann unter rein wirtschaftlichen und nicht mehr unter politischen Gesichtspunkten verhandelt. Das wäre aber eine andere Geschichte, und vielleicht haben wir ihre Frühzeit gerade noch rechtzeitig recherchiert.

„Größere Gegner gesucht!" ist den unermüdlichen Recherchen von Sasha Pirker und Katharina Ritter zu verdanken, die schon die Ausstellung im Architektur Zentrum Wien kuratierten und für diese Publikation die einzelnen Geschichten zum Teil vor Ort verifizierten.

Besonderen Dank gilt unseren Gesprächspartnern: Rolf Brönnimann (Verwaltungspräsident KKL AG), Johannes Cladders (ehemaliger Direktor Museum Mönchengladbach), Rosie Bitterli-Mucha (Stadt Luzern, Leitung Kultur), Hannelore Kersting (stellvertretende Direktorin Museum Mönchengladbach), Franz Kurzmeyer (Stadtpräsident a.D.), Manfred Ortner, Direktor Kees van Twist (Groninger Museum), Henk Weulink

factual proof that both positions are false, that what is the case is that the monuments of contemporary architecture are caught in a force field of different interests, and that they are thus in the position to provide us with very essential and fundamental cultural-historical information. What they offer is always more than just the built product alone.

"Stronger Opponents Wanted" is not a declaration of new architectonic ideology, nor is it a review of the highlights, and is unique precisely for this reason. A strong concept, to be sure, but it considers the situation that while the majority of these kinds of cultural projects receive sponsoring today, they are not discussed, and their stories of genesis are thus no longer being addressed.

This publication attempts to find a new approach to telling the story of architecture. Since international architecture criticism — following the entry of architecture into the culture industry — has shed its ideology of being the moral arbiter of modernity and mutated into the PR agent of the system of superstars, a new form of description needs to be found. This book seeks to establish a new methodology of the description and explanation of architecture. We would be making headway if these stories about the selected buildings were to give rise to questions being asked in future cases.

In closing, let me return to the Guggenheim phenomenon and Gehry's Bilbao project. This project indeed marked a new dimension of the conditions of the cultural industry. The sensational effect of a building designed by a star architect is embedded in a worldwide corporate strategy. Local political influences are mere bothersome disturbances in terms of investment. Perhaps in the future the "spectacular building" with integrated marketing and guaranteed audience satisfaction will no longer be regarded as a cultural but as a tourist-commercial investment. Architectonic "branding", the popularization of an "architecture brand name" will then be negotiated under purely economic and no longer under political considerations. That, however, is another (hi)story altogether, and perhaps we have investigated its beginnings at precisely the right moment in time.

"Stronger Opponents Wanted!" was made possible by the tireless, unremitting research work of Sasha Pirker and Katharina Ritter, who also curated the aforementioned exhibition at the Architektur Zentrum Wien and who verified the individual stories for this publication, in some cases on location.

Special acknowledgements are also in order for our contacts: Rolf Brönnimann (administrative president KKL AG), Johannes Cladders (former director of the Mönchengladbach Museum), Rosie Bitterli-Mucha (city of Lucerne, cultural director), Hannelore Kersting (deputy director of the Mönchengladbach Museum), Franz Kurzmeyer (retired city manager of Luzern), Manfred Ortner, Kees van Twist (director of the Groningen Museum), Henk Weulink (project manager of the Groningen Museum).

We gratefully acknowledge the following people and institutions for providing information and material:

Museum Quarter: MuseumsQuartier Errichtungs- und Betriebsgesellschaft, Architects Ortner + Ortner, Elisabeth Schweiger, Manuela

(Projektmanager Groninger Museum).

Dank auch an die Informanten und Leihgeber:

MuseumsQuartier: MuseumsQuartier-Errichtungs- und Betriebs-gesellschaft; Architekten Ortner & Ortner; Elisabeth Schweiger, Manuela Hötzl (Büro Ortner & Ortner); Architekt Manfred Wehdorn.

Sydney Opera House: Daryl Dellora; Françoise Fromonot; Margot Riley (State Library of New South Wales); Eric Sierins (Archiv Max Dupain).

Le Grand Louvre: Elisabeth Laurent (Musée du Louvre), Jean-Claude Dumont, Fabienne Chaudagne (E.P.M.O.T.C - Cité Administrative).

Kultur- und Kongreßzentrum Luzern: Thomas Held (Trägerstiftung Luzern); Andreas Zumbach (Trägerstiftung Luzern), Rolf Brönnimann (Verwaltungspräsident KKL AG), Bettina Müller (Kultur- und Kongreßzentrum Luzern AG), Rosie Bitterli-Mucha (Stadt Luzern, Leitung Kultur), Franz Kurzmeyer (Stadtpräsident a. D.), Architkt Jean Nouvel; Architekt Rudolphe Luscher.

Museum Mönchengladbach: Museum Mönchengladbach, Hannelore Kersting (Museum Mönchengladbach/stellvertretende Direktorin), Johannes Cladders (ehemaliger Direktor Museum Mönchengladbach), Architekt Hans Hollein, Madeleine Jenewein (Atelier Hans Hollein).

Groninger Museum: José Selbach/PR, Direktor Kees van Twist (Groninger Museum), Henk Weulink (Projektmanager Groninger Museum), Architekt Alessandro Mendini; Architekten Coop Himmelb(l)au.

Unser Dank gilt ferner Melanie van der Hoorn, die mit ihrem Essay zum Wiener MuseumsQuartier einen objektiven Blick „von außen" auf die Geschichte geworfen hat. Über diesen Beitrag hinaus hat sie eine umfangreiche ethnologische Arbeit zu diesem Thema geschrieben.

Und zum Schluß danken wir allen an den vorgestellten Projekten Beteiligten: den Architekten, Politikern, Managern, Direktoren und Sponsoren. Ohne sie alle hätten unsere Geschichten nicht geschrieben werden können.

Dietmar M. Steiner

Hötzl (Büro Ortner + Ortner), Architekt Manfred Wehdorn;

Sydney Opera House: Daryl Dellora, Françoise Fromonot, Margot Riley (State Library of New South Wales), Eric Sierins (Archive Max Dupain);

Le Grand Louvre: Elisabeth Laurent (Musée du Louvre), Jean-Claude Dumont, Fabienne Chaudagne (E.P.M.O.T.C - Cité Administrative);

Culture and Convention Centre Lucerne: Thomas Held and Andreas Zumbach (Trägerstiftung Luzern), Rolf Brönnimann (Verwaltungspräsident KKL AG), Bettina Müller (KKL AG), Rosie Bitterli-Mucha (Stadt Luzern, Leitung Kultur), Franz Kurzmeyer (Stadtpräsident a.D.), Architect Jean Nouvel, Architekt Rudolphe Luscher;

Mönchengladbach Museum: Museum Mönchengladbach, Hannelore Kersting (Mönchengladbach Museum deputy director), Johannes Cladders (former director of the Mönchengladbach Museum), Architect Hans Hollein, Madeleine Jenewein (Atelier Hans Hollein).

Groningen Museum: José Selbach/PR (Groningen Museum), Kees van Twist (Director Groningen Museum), Henk Weulink (Projectmanager Groningen Museum), Architect Alessandro Mendini, Architects Coop Himmelb(l)au;

We'd also like to thank Melanie van der Hoorn, whose essay on the Vienna Museum Quarter provided us with an objective view of the story, an approach "from the outside". She has also written a comprehensive ethnological work on this subject, which goes beyond the scope of this essay.

And in conclusion we thank everyone who participated in the projects presented here: the architects, politicians, managers, directors, and sponsors. Without them these stories could never have been told.

Dietmar M. Steiner

MuseumsQuartier Wien

Der einzige Überlebende/The Sole Survivor

Der amputierte Architekt

So mancher Passant mag seinen Augen nicht getraut haben, als er sah, was am 1. April 1998 in den vormaligen kaiserlichen Stallungen zu Wien vor sich ging. Scharen von Menschen gingen mit alten Stühlen, Leuchtern, Spiegeln, Türen und Marmorfliesen aus und ein. Es war offizieller „Plünderungstag" in dem architektonischen Ensemble, das nach dem letzten Mieter, der Wiener Messe, allgemein als „Messepalast" bezeichnet wurde. Damals war der Gebäudekomplex längst renovierungsbedürftig. Einige Gebäudeteile wurden zwar noch benutzt, aber von den meisten waren nur noch graffitiverschmierte Mauern und das Dach übrig. Wie sollte ein Passant sich damals vorstellen können, daß einen Tag später die Revitalisierung beginnen und innerhalb dieser Mauern ein so ehrgeiziges Projekt wie das Wiener Museumsquartier in Angriff genommen werden würde? Wie sollte er wissen können, daß die Initiatoren dieser Revitalisierung sich jahrelang einer breiten Front von Gegnern gegenübersahen, die in den vormaligen barocken Stallungen ein wertvolles Juwel und im neuen Projekt des Museumsquartiers einen brutalen architektonischen Anschlag sahen?

Ein paar Monate zuvor, im Dezember 1997, erschien in der Tageszeitung Die Presse eine Karikatur von Ironimus[1] mit dem Titel „Der amputierte Architekt". Sie zeigt Laurids Ortner, den Architekten des Museumsquartiers: Ihm fehlt zwar ein Arm und ein Bein, doch zeigt er immer noch ein verhältnismäßig ungerührtes Gesicht – nicht zufrieden, nicht enttäuscht, höchstens verunsichert. Ein Plan auf einer Schautafel hinter ihm läßt die Veränderungen an dem historischen architektonischen Komplex erkennen, die er zusammen mit Manfred Wehdorn, einem auf Revitalisierung historischer Bauten spezialisierten Architekten, ausgearbeitet hat. Die Namen beider Architekten verschmelzend, betitelte Ironimus das gemeinsame Werk: „O Weh!" – eine Anspielung auf die endlosen Diskussionen, die das Projekt ausgelöst hatte.

1990 gewinnen Laurids und Manfred Ortner den Architekturwettbewerb für das Museumsquartier. Acht Jahre später wird der Beginn der Realisierung offiziell gefeiert. Nach all den Kämpfen um dieses Projekt könnte man glauben, daß Laurids Ortner der einzige Überlebende ist. Die Karikatur von Ironimus lädt zu einer genaueren Betrachtung jener Umstände ein, die an der Wiege eines der wichtigsten Kulturvorhaben der Zweiten Republik geradezu zu einer Katastrophenstimmung führten.

Internationale Ambitionen und lokale Ideale

Seit Beginn der achtziger Jahre, als die Revitalisierung der barocken Hofstallungen, die im 20. Jahrhundert von der Wiener Messe genutzt, verändert und ergänzt worden waren, von der Wiener Stadtverwaltung und dem österreichischen Staat ernsthaft in Betracht gezogen

20

On April Fool's Day in 1998 more than a few passers-by must surely
have been perplexed by what they were seeing at the former imperial
stables in Vienna. Throngs of people came and went, carrying old chairs,
chandeliers, mirrors, doors and marble tiles. It was the official "Day
of Looting" on the entire premises of the architectonic ensemble, which
had come to be known as "Messepalast" after its last tenant, the
Wiener Messe (Vienna Trade Fair). At the time, the building complex
had long been in a state of disrepair. A few wings were in use, but
for the most part all that existed of the buildings was walls covered
with graffiti and the roof. How was a passer-by to imagine that the
revitalization of this complex would start the very next day, and that
within these walls such an ambitious undertaking as the Vienna
Museum Quarter was about to be launched? How could a
passer-by know that the initiators of this revitalization had for years
battled against a vast army of opposition that viewed the Baroque
stables as a precious jewel and the new Museum Quarter project as
a brutal architectonic attack?

A few months earlier, in December 1997, the Austrian daily Die
Presse had published a cartoon by Ironismus[1] entitled: "The Amputated" Architect. It depicted Laurids Ortner, the architect who had
drawn up the plans for the Museum Quarter, and although an arm
and a leg had been cut off, he still wore a relatively calm expression
on his face – not content, not disillusioned, perhaps only unsure of
himself. Behind him a diagram shows the changes to the historically
important architectural complex, which he had conceived together
with Manfred Wehdorn, an architect who specializes in the revitalization of historical buildings. The caption — "O Weh" — is an allu-
sion to the names of both architects and also a German interjection
of lamentation, a sigh of resignation at the endless bickering the project had brought.

Laurids and Manfred Ortner won the architecture competition for
the Museum Quarter in 1990, but it would take eight years before the
official ground breaking marked the start of the realization of the project. At the end of the day, after all the battles have been waged, one
might think that Laurids Ornter is the only survivor to come out of this
project. Ironimus' cartoon, however, invites a closer inspection of the
circumstances which — at the birth of one of the major cultural projects of the Second Republic — have produced an atmosphere of sheer
catastrophe.

International Ambitions and Local Ideals

Since the beginning of the 1980s, when the City of Vienna and the
Republic of Austria began serious consideration of revitalizing the imperial Baroque stables, which in the twentieth century had been used,

wird, hatten die Initiatoren den Ehrgeiz, eine repräsentative Kultur-institution zu schaffen.

Nach dem Zweiten Weltkrieg wurden die Wiener Staatsoper und viele Theater renoviert. Die Institutionen der bildenden Kunst aber, die Museen, blieben verlottert und in ihrer Substanz vergessen: ein Muse-um Moderner Kunst, untergebracht in mehreren Provisorien – im trans-lozierten Österreich-Pavillon der Weltausstellung 1958 in Brüssel und im barocken Palais Liechtenstein. Dem monarchischen Erbe wurde kein bedeutender Kulturbau mehr hinzugefügt.

Nun soll ein Zeichen gesetzt werden. Österreichische Medien und Politiker beginnen, Vergleiche mit anderen repräsentativen Kultur-bauwerken herzustellen. Bereits 1982 stellt sich der damalige Wiener Kulturstadtrat Helmut Zilk einen künftig revitalisierten Messepalast als das österreichische Centre Georges Pompidou vor: Ein großstädtischer Treffpunkt, an dem sich Kultur mit Unterhaltung verbindet. Kein Ver-gleich scheint stark genug, als Wissenschaftsminister Erhard Busek das Vorhaben ankündigt. Journalisten spekulieren über die Wirkung des Museumsquartiers auf die Stadt insgesamt. Thomas Trenkler vergleicht es im Standard (15.1.1994) mit ähnlich konzentrierten Kulturkomple-xen wie dem Grand Louvre, dem Grand Palais und Petit Palais in Paris oder mit den großen Museen zwischen Capitol und Weißem Haus in Washington. Auch Wien brauche solch ein Quartier nahe dem Stadt-zentrum. Ansonsten könne es von den im Aufschwung begriffenen Städten Osteuropas wie Budapest oder Prag überflügelt werden.

Doch sobald das Projekt Museumsquartier ernsthaft Gestalt an-nimmt, scheint die Republik in eine Ansammlung widerstreitender Konfliktparteien zu zerfallen, die alle ihr eigenes Konzept eines Museumsquartiers realisiert sehen wollen. Die Unvereinbarkeit dieser Ebenen – internationale Ambitionen einerseits und konfliktträchtige lokale Unstimmigkeiten andererseits – führten zu einer permanenten Diskussion des aus dem Wettbewerb hervorgegangenen Projekts.

Ein lokales Kräftemessen

Der Wettbewerbsentwurf der Brüder Ortner von 1990 sieht vor, die Barockfassade und die neobarocke Winterreithalle aus dem 19. Jahr-hundert intakt zu lassen und eine urbane Revitalisierung des gesam-

altered and expanded by the Vienna Trade Fair, the initiators had had ambitious plans to create a representative cultural institution.

After WWII the Vienna Opera House and many theatres were renovated. The fine arts institutions, however, the museums, were left rundown and their core structures neglected: a Museum of Modern Art housed in separate provisional structures – in the Austrian pavilion salvaged from the 1958 World Fair in Brussels and in the Baroque Liechtenstein Palace. The imperial heritage has not been augmented by any major cultural buildings since.

Now it's time for a change. Austrian media and politicians are starting to draw comparisons with other representative cultural edifices. As early as 1982, Helmut Zilk, the municipal representative for cultural affairs in Vienna, has a vision of revitalizing the Messepalast grounds into an Austrian version of the Centre Georges Pompidou: a meeting-place in the metropolis where culture and entertainment converge. And when the Minister of Science announces his plan, there doesn't seem to be a comparison strong enough. Journalists speculate about the effect of the Museum Quarter on the city as a whole. In the Austrian daily Der Standard (15 January 1994) Thomas Trenkler compares it with similarly compact cultural complexes like the Grand Louvre, the Grand Palais and Petit Palais in Paris, or with the great museums along the Mall between the Capitol and the White House in Washington D.C. He claims that Vienna too needs a museum quarter near the centre of town. Otherwise it runs the risk of being outdone by fast-changing Eastern European cities like Budapest or Prague.

But as soon as the Museum Quarter project starts to take serious shape, the Republic appears to collapse into a heap of conflicting parties, each with its own vision of a museum quarter. The incompatibility of these two levels – international ambitions on the one hand, and local discord, on the other – has led to a perpetual debate surrounding the original project.

Museumsquartier um 1990; offizieller „Plünderungstag" am 1. April 1998

Museum Quarter around 1990; official "Day of Looting" on 1 April 1998

A Local Power Struggle

The competition design submitted in 1990 by the Ortner brothers calls for the preservation of the Baroque façades and the nineteenth-century neo-Baroque winter riding hall, and for an urban revitalization

ten Gebietes mittels Neubauten in den Innenhöfen zu erreichen. Die barocken Bauteile werden für kleinere Einrichtungen wie Wohnungen, Büros und Galerien genutzt. Die Winterreithalle wird zu einer Mehrzweckhalle mit Foyer umgebaut, die den Neubau des Museums Moderner Kunst mit dem der Kunsthalle der Stadt Wien verbindet.

Zudem sind Neubauten für die Kunsthalle, ein Medienforum und ein Museum Österreichischer Moderne sowie ein den Komplex überragender Turm – der Informations- und Leseturm – als Bibliothek für Gegenwartskultur und Medien im Haupthof und schließlich ein Film- und Photographiemuseum auf dem Vorplatz des Museumsquartiers geplant.

Das Aufsehen, das das Projekt in Verbindung mit der EXPO '95 machen würde, die damals noch als gemeinsames Projekt von Wien und Budapest stattfinden sollte, ist bereits Tagesgespräch. Aber sofort nach dem Wettbewerb und der Etablierung einer Museumsquartier-Errichtungsgesellschaft entsteht durch die Gründung einer Bürgerinitiative eine heftige Protestbewegung. Der Widerstand wächst – verschiedene Institutionen wenden sich gegen das Projekt und unterstützen einander teilweise: Die Bürgerinitiative „Messepalast-Hofstall-Ensemble", die Neue Kronen Zeitung (ein Boulevardblatt von großem politischen Einfluß), die rechtspopulistische FPÖ sowie das Bundesdenkmalamt. Eine heftige Debatte bricht aus, sowohl über die Ausprägung der kulturellen Manifestation der Zweiten Republik, als auch darüber, wer die Verantwortung, das Recht und die Macht hat, um über eine solche nationale kulturelle Selbstdarstellung zu entscheiden.

Wiens equestrische Wurzeln

Historische Aufnahme der
Hofstallungen um 1900

Historical picture of the imperial
stables around 1900

Die bereits im Juli 1990 gegründete Bürgerinitiative ist die erste Gruppierung, die offen gegen das Museumsquartier Stellung bezieht. Sie plädiert für eine schlichte Renovierung der Hofstallungen. Der beklagenswerte Zustand des über Jahrhunderte unkoordiniert gewachsenen Ensembles ist für sie kein Hindernis, es zum nationalen „Juwel" zu erklären. Ihr erster Alternativvorschlag sieht die Wiederherstellung der kaiserlichen Stallungen in ihrer ehemaligen Funktion vor: Pferde und Wagen sollen als Dependance der Spanischen Hofreitschule und der Wagenburg übersiedelt werden, Pferdeausstellungen sollen stattfinden und eine Pferdetramway soll durch die nahegelegene Mariahilferstraße führen. Mitglieder der Bürgerinitiative verstehen nationale Identität als Erbe der Vergangenheit, das als solches geschützt werden müsse. Ihrer Ansicht nach begann die Verschandelung der Hofstallungen schon mit der infamen Umbenennung in „Messepalast".

Die Gegner des Museumsquartiers fordern eine Veranschaulichung des Projektes. Die Neubauten werden als „Transistorenfabrik"[2] und „Tumor"[3] beschimpft. Zur Unterstützung ihrer Argumente stellen sie Fotomontagen her und versuchen, mit Netzen und Ballons ein Modell des geplanten Museumsquartiers im Maßstab 1:1 nachzubauen. In ihren Flugblättern rufen sie die Wiener Bürger auf, im Namen von Kultur, Geschichte und Demokratie für „unser" Wien zu unterschreiben.

of the entire area through the construction of new buildings in the inner courtyards. The Baroque sections are to be used for smaller facilities like apartments, offices and galleries. The winter riding hall is to be converted into a lobby and multipurpose hall that will connect the new Museum of Modern Art building with the Kunsthalle Wien.

Also planned are new buildings for the Kunsthalle Wien, a media forum, and a Museum of Austrian Modernism, as well as a tower in the main courtyard, overlooking the whole complex – the Info and Reading Tower – which will function as a library for contemporary art and media, and finally a Film and Photography Museum in the entrance area of the Museum Quarter.

The attention the project attracts in connection with EXPO '95 – planned as a joint project between Vienna and Budapest – soon becomes the topic of the day. But it isn't long after the competition has come to a close and the Museum Quarter Development and Operation Co. Ltd been established, before a mighty protest movement emerges in the form of a newly founded citizens' action committee. Opposition grows – various institutions turn against the project and partially support each other: the "Messepalast-Hofstall-Ensemble" citizens' action committee, the Neue Kronen Zeitung (or Kronenzeitung), an Austrian tabloid with strong political influence), the right-wing populist Austrian Freedom Party, and the Federal Chancellery. An intense debate ensues, over both the form and expression of the cultural manifestation of the Second Republic, and who should have the responsibility, the authority and the power to determine the nation's cultural self-image.

Vienna's Equestrian Roots

The citizens' action committee, which was founded back in July 1990, is the first group openly to take a stand against the Museum Quarter. It calls for a simple, unpretentious renovation of the imperial stables. The deplorable state of the ensemble, which has grown haphazardly over centuries, does not prevent them from declaring it a national "jewel". The committee's first alternative proposal suggests that the imperial stables should be restored to serve their original function: horses and carriages are to be moved there and it is to become a second home of the Spanish Riding School and the carriage house; there are to be horse shows and a horse-drawn tram that would run along Mariahilferstrasse, a nearby street. Members of the citizens' action committee interpret national identity as the heritage of the past, which must be protected. In their opinion, the debasement of the imperial stables began when they were given the disgraceful new name "Messepalast". The opponents of the Museum Quarter call for a visualization of the project. The new buildings are referred to disparagingly as "Transistor Factory"[2] and "Tumour"[3]. To support their arguments they assemble photomontages and try to construct a 1:1 scale model of the planned Museum Quarter using nets and balloons. In their fliers they appeal to the Viennese people to give their signatures for "our" Vienna in the name of culture, history, and democracy.

Auf grünen Pfaden

Eine Gruppe, die einen der Bürgerinitiative „Messepalast-Hofstall-Ensemble" entgegengesetzten Standpunkt vertritt, ist die Bürgerversammlung Messepalast. Der Bezirksvorstand des 7. Bezirks veröffentlicht eine Informationsbroschüre, die sämtliche Vorzüge des Museumsquartiers für seine direkte Umgebung auflistet. Der Hauptakzent liegt dabei auf dem Quartier als erholsames Freizeitgebiet mit neuen Grünflächen und der städtebaulichen Öffnung eines bislang abgeschlossenen Bereichs.

Schutz der Skyline

Die Kronenzeitung, die ebenfalls für eine sanfte Renovierung der Hofstallungen eintritt, ist der am stärksten präsente Akteur in der Debatte. Ihre Vorgehensweise besteht anfangs in der Betonung auf dem herausragenden historischen Wert des Gebäudes für Wiens Geschichte und Identität.

Die Auflage des Boulevardblattes macht 40 Prozent aller täglich in Österreich verkauften Tageszeitungen aus. Dazu trägt eine effiziente Kombination von Faktoren bei: Aggressives Marketing, eine beispiellos große Reichweite, regelmäßige Empörungskampagnen und eine wirksame patriarchalische innere Struktur.

Die Kampagne gegen Ortner setzt im September 1992 ein, als die Zeitung zunehmend verfemende Schlagzeilen wie „Museumsquartier ist ein Tumor" (8.9.1992), „Gegen Skandalbau im Wiener Messepalast!" (26.9.1992) und „Weg mit den Monstren!" (28.9.1992) verwendet. Begleitet wird diese Kampagne mit der suggestiven Verwendung von Statistiken, die eine Zunahme der Projekt-Gegner zu vermitteln sucht. Auch die scharfe Kritik der Kosten soll die Empörung der Leserschaft schüren.

Höhepunkt der Medienkampagne ist der Versuch der Kronenzeitung, den 67 Meter hohen Leseturm, geplant als Bibliothek für zeitgenössische Kultur und Medien, zu eliminieren. Jede Reduktion der Höhe wird als ein Etappensieg gefeiert, und die Kronenzeitung versucht, den „Architekturskandal" durch gefälschte Bilder anschaulich zu machen. Der Widerstand wird solange verschärft, bis Ortner beginnt, sein Projekt „auf gesunde Dimensionen zu schrumpfen"[4]. Die Zeitung verlegt sich darauf, systematisch Bauteile aus dem ursprünglichen Projekt auszustreichen – als Siegesserie in einem Konflikt, der zu einem veritablen „Krieg" um Wien geworden ist.

In dem von der Kronenzeitung als wünschenswert proklamierten Stadtbild werden neue Elemente als Bedrohung gesehen, weil sie die historischen Teile „erdrücken".

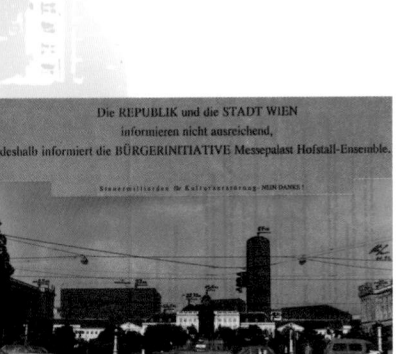

Die REPUBLIK und die STADT WIEN
informieren nicht ausreichend,
deshalb informiert die BÜRGERINITIATIVE Messepalast Hofstall-Ensemble.

Blick vom Ring auf das Bauvorhaben "Museumsquartier"

Teile und herrsche

Die politischen Parteien können auch innerparteilich keine gemeinsame Linie finden. Aussagen einzelner Funktionäre widersprechen sich nicht selten, und die Kronenzeitung versäumt es nicht, sowohl innerparteiliche wie auch Meinungsverschiedenheiten zwischen den einzelnen Parteien zu kommentieren.

Ein Wendepunkt wird im September 1992 erreicht, als Bernhard Görg, neugewählter Landesparteiobmann der Wiener ÖVP, sich uner-

One group opposed to the "Messepalast-Hofstall-Ensemble" citizens' action committee is another citizens' group called "Bürgerversammlung Messepalast". The district head of the 7th district publishes an information brochure that lists all the advantages the Museum Quarter would bring to the immediately surrounding area. The main focus here is on the Quarter serving as an area for leisure and relaxation, which would add new grass-covered spaces and whose urban plan would open up a formerly closed-off area.

Green Paths

The Kronenzeitung, which also supports a moderate renovation of the imperial stables, is the most prominent actor in the debate. Its initial approach emphasizes the building's exceptional historical importance in Vienna's history and identity. The circulation of the tabloid makes up 40% of all daily newspapers sold in Austria. Moreover, an efficient combination of factors also contribute to its influence: aggressive marketing, a range second to none, regular smear campaigns, and an effective internal patriarchal structure.

Protection of the Skyline

The campaign against Ortner begins in September 1992, when the expressions used by the newspaper become more and more aggressive, e.g. "The Museum Quarter is a Tumour" (8 September 1992), "Stop Scandalous Building on the Messepalast Grounds!" (26 September 1992) and "Away with the Monstrosities!" (28 September 1992). The campaign is accompanied by statistics that indicate a growing number of people is opposed to the project. Moreover, harsh criticism of the expenditure is also intended to rouse the anger of the readers.

The climax of the media campaign is the Kronenzeitung's attempt to eliminate the 67-metre-high Reading Tower, which is intended to serve as a library for contemporary culture and media. Each reduction in height is celebrated as a nail in the project's coffin, and the Kronenzeitung tries to illustrate the "architectural scandal" using forged pictures, announcing that opposition will be intensified until Ortner "reduces [his project] to healthy dimensions"[4]. The newspaper makes it its goal to eliminate building sections from the original project – as a series of victories in a conflict that has become a veritable "war" to win Vienna. In the ideal picture of the city, as proclaimed in the Kronenzeitung, new elements are seen as a threat because they "smother" the historical parts.

Divide and Conquer

Even within their own ranks the political parties can't seem to find a common line. It is not uncommon for utterances by individual officials to be contradictory and the Kronenzeitung doesn't fail to comment on differences in opinion both within the parties themselves and from one party to the next.

A turning point is reached in September 1992 when Bernhard Görg, newly elected leader of the Vienna state section of the Austrian Peoples' Party, unexpectedly takes a stand against the Ortner project. He contends that the right moment for a Museum Quarter has not yet come, that there is not a definite concept, the politicians can't agree,

Von links nach rechts: „Unter uns gesagt", in: Die Neue Kronenzeitung, 12.3.1995; Anzeige der FPÖ, in: Die Neue Kronenzeitung, 4.10.1992; Anzeige der Grünen, in: Der Standard, 29.9.1992; In: Die Neue Kronenzeitung, 24.8.1993; In: Wiener Journal, November 1992; In: Die Neue Kronenzeitung, 7.9.1992

From left to right: "Unter uns gesagt", in: Die Neue Kronenzeitung, 12.3.1995; FPÖ advertisement , in: Die Neue Kronenzeitung, 4.10.1992; Green Party advertisement, in: Der Standard, 29.9.1992; In: Die Neue Kronenzeitung, 24.8.1993; In: Wiener Journal, November 1992; In: Die Neue Kronenzeitung, 7.9.1992

wartet gegen das Ortner-Projekt stellt. Der richtige Zeitpunkt für ein Museumsquartier sei noch nicht gekommen, es gäbe kein schlüssiges Konzept, die Politiker könnten sich nicht einigen und das Denkmalamt stimme nicht zu. Und schließlich sei die Erhaltung historischer Architektur wichtiger als künstlerische Freiheit.[5]

Viele Tageszeitungen stellen nach diesem politischen Vorstoß den Einfluß politischer Interessen auf Kunst und Kultur in Frage und werfen Görg vor, sich nach dem Willen der FPÖ zu richten. Eine Karikatur von Dieter Zehentmayr im Kurier (30.9.1992) sieht die damaligen Machtverhältnisse kritisch: Görg wird als Spielzeug in den Händen der FPÖ dargestellt, das sich ferngesteuert anschickt, den Leseturm zu zerstören.[6]

Als einziges Blatt gratuliert die Kronenzeitung Görg offen zu seinem „erstaunlichen Mut".[7]

Infolge des Kurswechsels von Bernhard Görg – und mit ihm der ÖVP – bleibt die SPÖ als einzige große Partei übrig, die für Ortners Museumsquartier eintritt. Hannes Swoboda, als Planungsstadtrat direkt involviert und plötzlich isoliert, wagt es nicht mehr, das Projekt offen zu unterstützen. Die Grünen kritisieren, er habe sich dem Willen der FPÖ und der Kronenzeitung gebeugt, stehen aber selbst nicht geschlossen genug hinter dem Projekt, um für die SPÖ einen verläßlichen Verbündeten abzugeben.

Die FPÖ kann von den inneren und äußeren Zerwürfnissen der anderen Parteien ebenso profitieren wie von der fast durchgehenden und wertvollen Unterstützung der Kronenzeitung. Sie greift die angeblichen Anliegen der Bevölkerung auf und fordert in enger Zusammenarbeit mit der Bürgerinitiative „Messepalast-Hofstall-Ensemble" eine Volksbefragung über das Museumsquartier.

Moderne Einrichtungen in alten Mauern

Natürlich bleiben auch die Kunsthistoriker der Diskussion nicht fern. 1993 tritt ein internationales Komitee zusammen und bezieht offen Stellung gegen das Ortner-Projekt, das ihrer Meinung nach respektlos mit historischen Denkmälern umgeht. Das Museumsquartier wird einen

and the Bureau for the Protection of Monuments doesn't approve. After all, he adds, the preservation of historical architecture is more important than artistic freedom.[5]

Following this political sally a number of daily newspapers call into question the influence of political interests in art and cultural affairs, and accuse Görg of complying with the will of the Austrian Freedom Party. A cartoon by Dieter Zehentmayr in the daily Kurier (30 September 1992) sheds critical light on the power politics of the time: Görg is shown as a remote-controlled toy in the hands of the Freedom Party, being guided to destroy the Reading Tower.[6] The Kronenzeitung is the only daily to congratulate Görg openly for his "remarkable courage."[7]

As a result of Bernhard Görg's change of course – and with him that of the Peoples' Party as a whole – the only large party left to stand up for Ortner's Museum Quarter is the Austrian Socialist Party. Hannes Swoboda, who as the municipal representative for urban planning is directly involved and who suddenly finds himself all alone, no longer has the nerve to support the project publicly. The Greens criticize him for bending to the will of the Freedom Party and the Kronenzeitung, but they too are unable to reach sufficient consensus in their ranks to support the project and are thus not a reliable ally of the Socialist Party.

The Freedom Party is able to take advantage of the internal discord within the other parties and the external bickering among parties as well as the indispensable and virtually constant support of the Kronenzeitung. It takes up the purported concerns of the people, and working in close co-operation with the "Messepalast-Hofstall-Ensemble" citizens' action committee, it calls for a plebiscite on the Museum Quarter.

Modern Facilities within Old Walls

Of course the art historians get involved in the debate too. In 1993, an international committee convenes and takes a public stand against the Ortner project, claiming that it doesn't show the proper respect when handling historical monuments. The Museum Quarter will set a precedent for similar interventions in the future and it therefore poses a

Präzedenzfall für weitere derartige Eingriffe schaffen und stellt daher eine Gefahr für das Image Wiens und den Ruf Österreichs als Kulturnation und „Schützer historischen Erbes" dar. Eine einfache Renovierung der Hofstallungen sei für die notwendigen kulturellen Einrichtungen – wie der Sammlung Moderner Kunst, einer Ausstellungshalle und einer Erweiterung des Kunsthistorischen Museums – vollkommen ausreichend. Die Kronenzeitung unterstützt die Anliegen des Komitees und nennt dieses in ihren Artikeln häufig „Gruppe international anerkannter Experten". Darauf reagiert 1994 eine andere Aktionsgruppe von Kunsthistorikern für das Museumsquartier und fordert die rasche Verwirklichung der ursprünglichen Pläne. Die Gruppe unterstreicht die Notwendigkeit von zeitgemäßen Kultureinrichtungen mit entsprechender Architektur und Infrastruktur. Trotz der großen Zahl an Mitstreitern kann diese Gruppierung die Realisierung des Museumsquartiers nicht wirksam unterstützen.

Vergleiche mit großen Kulturprojekten im Ausland sind nun nicht mehr Ansporn, sondern Anlaß für neue Vorwürfe. FPÖ-Politiker unternehmen eine Reise nach Madrid (Museo Thyssen-Bornemisza und Centro de Arte Reina Sofia) und nach Paris (Musée d'Orsay und Grand Louvre) und kommen zu dem Schluß, daß für die Schaffung einer großen Attraktion Innenumbauten völlig ausreichen. Gerhard Sailer, damals Direktor des Bundesdenkmalamts, konstatiert, er hätte den Bau des Pariser Centre Georges Pompidou niemals bewilligt. Moderne Architektur habe ihren Platz an der Peripherie, erläutert er – außerhalb der Stadtzentren oder in Städten wie Bilbao. Zur Untermauerung der Ansicht, „so etwas wie das Museumsquartier" wäre in anderen Hauptstädten „undenkbar", und um weiter Empörung zu schüren, veröffentlicht die Kronenzeitung Montagen des Ortner-Projekts auf dem Markusplatz in Venedig oder im Pariser Louvre.[8]

Laut Auskunft des Denkmalamts müssen Gebäude von historischer, künstlerischer oder kultureller Bedeutung und ihre Erhaltung im öffentlichen Interesse sein. Im Falle des Museumsquartiers fordert Gerhard Sailer einen Gegenbeweis: Das Interesse an der Erhaltung sei gegeben – die Befürworter des Projekts haben nun den Beweis zu führen, daß das öffentliche Interesse an einem neuen Museumsquartier überwiege.

Schließlich kann das Denkmalamt seinen Einfluß direkt geltend machen – über die Person Manfred Wehdorns, eines auf Rekonstruktion und Renovierung spezialisierten Architekten. Unter dem Druck wachsenden Widerstandes gegen das ursprüngliche Projekt und unter Berücksichtigung der neuen funktionalen Anforderungen entwickeln die Architekten Ortner und Wehdorn ein neues Projekt, das 1995, fünf Jahre nach dem Wettbewerbsentwurf, vorliegt.

Ich sage „Nein", weil ich ein

Ein historisiertes Museumsquartier

1994 ergibt sich durch den Ankauf der Sammlung Leopold durch den österreichischen Staat eine wichtige Änderung des funktionalen und museologischen Konzepts. Diese private Sammlung von Kunstwerken aus der Zeit der Jahrhundertwende sollte ursprünglich Teil eines

threat to Vienna's image and Austria's reputation as a cultural nation and "guardian of historical heritage". A simple, unpretentious renovation of the imperial stables would be perfectly sufficient for the necessary cultural facilities – for example the collection of modern art, an exhibition hall, and an expansion of the Art History Museum. The Kronenzeitung supports the interests and concerns of this committee and quotes it frequently in its articles, referring to it as a "group of internationally recognized experts". In response to this, another action committee of art historians speaks up for the Museum Quarter, demanding the swift realization of the original plans. This group emphasizes the need for modern cultural facilities with the adequate architecture and infrastructure. Despite the large number of people fighting for this cause, the group is unable to support the realization of the Museum Quarter effectively.

Comparisons with large-scale cultural projects in other countries are no longer a stimulus, but the basis for new accusations. Freedom Party politicians travel to Madrid (Museo Thyssen-Bornemisza and Centro de Arte Reina Sofia) and to Paris (Musée d'Orsay and Grand Louvre) and come to the conclusion that major attractions can be created by focusing on interior modifications. Gerhard Sailer, at the time director of the Federal Bureau for the Protection of Monuments, states that he would never have approved construction of the Centre Georges Pompidou in Paris. Modern architecture belongs in the periphery, he adds, outside the urban centres or in cities like Bilbao. To illustrate the viewpoint that "a thing like the Museum Quarter" would be "unthinkable" in other capitals, and in order to stir up more indignation, the Kronenzeitung publishes montages of the Ortner project at the Piazza San Marco in Venice or in the Paris Louvre.[8] According to the Bureau for the Protection of Monuments, buildings of historical, artistic or cultural significance, and their preservation must be in the public interest. In the case of the Museum Quarter Gerhard Sailer demands proof of the opposite: the interest in the preservation of the complex, he says, is a fact, and it is up to the project's supporters to prove that the public interest in a new Museum Quarter is stronger.

In the end, the Bureau for the Protection of Monuments manages to assert its influence directly – in the person of one Manfred Wehdorn, an architect specializing in reconstruction and renovation. Under the new functional demands the pressure of growing opposition to the original project and taking into consideration, Ortner and Wehdorn develop a new project that is submitted in 1995, five years after the selection of the original plan.

In 1994 an important change takes place in the prevailing functional and museum concept, with the acquisition of the Leopold Collection by the Republic of Austria. This private collection of art from the turn of the twentieth century was originally intended to become part of a

Anzeige der FPÖ, in: Die Neue
Kronenzeitung, 4.10.1992

FPÖ advertisement , in:
Die Neue Kronenzeitung, 4.10.1992

A Museum Quarter with an Accent on History

Museums Österreichischer Moderne werden – eines Museums zur Wiener Kulturgeschichte um 1900. Die Gegner des ursprünglichen Plans für das Museumsquartier wollten diesem Museum mehr Gewicht verleihen und damit versuchen, historische Werte zu sichern. Dies gelingt mit dem Ankauf der Sammlung durch die Republik Österreich und der Etablierung eines unabhängigen Leopold-Museums mit Rudolf Leopold als Direktor auf Lebenszeit.

Als Folge dieser Entwicklungen ändern Ortner und Wehdorn die Pläne drastisch ab: Die Kunsthalle wird hinter die renovierte Winterreithalle verlegt und das Museum Leopold im großen Haupthof angesiedelt, gegenüber dem Museum Moderner Kunst. Jene Obergeschosse, die aus dem Entwurf gestrichen wurden, weil sie die Fischer-von-Erlach-Fassade überragten, werden durch unterirdische Geschosse ersetzt. Kleinere Institutionen wie das Medienzentrum und das Film- und Photographiemuseum fallen zur Gänze. Dem Denkmalamt wird die letzte Entscheidung zugesprochen. Nach einigen weiteren Änderungen und einer 1:1-Visualisierung der Gebäudehöhen (mittels Kränen und Metallträgern) bewilligt das Denkmalamt Anfang 1997 die Pläne – mit der Realisierung des neuen Museumsquartiers kann begonnen werden.

Widerstand gegen dieses neue, historisierte Konzept des Museumsquartiers bleibt erfolglos.

Schon vor diesem neuen Projekt, im November 1992, prangerte eine Gruppe von Architekten, Künstlern, Architekturkritikern, Schriftstellern und einigen Politikern die zusehends subjektiven Agitationsweisen der Kronenzeitung an. Die Gruppe veröffentlichte eine Artikelreihe im Wiener Journal und persiflierte darin die Illustrationen, wie sie die Kronenzeitung verwendete. Man forderte ein modernes Kunst- und Kulturzentrum und eine zeitgemäße Selbstdarstellung der Zweiten Republik. Allerdings herrscht unter den einzelnen Befürwortern zu wenig Zusammenhalt, um längerfristig geschlossen für ein neues Museumsquartier einzutreten.

Visualisierung der Gebäudehöhen, Anfang 1997

Visualization of the building heights in early 1997

Museum of Austrian Modernism – a museum dedicated to the cultural history of Vienna around 1900. The opponents of the original plan for the Museum Quarter wanted to increase the profile of this particular museum in the hope of securing historical significance for the entire project. These ambitions are realized through the acquisition of the collection by the Republic of Austria and the establishment of an independent Leopold Museum, with Rudolf Leopold as its director for life.

As a result of these developments Ortner and Wehdorn make drastic changes to the plans: the Kunsthalle is moved behind the renovated winter riding hall, and the Leopold Museum is brought into the large main courtyard across from the Museum of Modern Art. The upper floors, cut from the plan because they would have towered above the Fischer von Erlach façade, are to be replaced by underground levels. Smaller institutions like the Media Centre and the Film and Photography Museum are eliminated altogether. The Bureau for the Protection of Monuments has the last word. After several further changes and a 1:1 visualization of the building heights (using cranes and scaffolding) the Bureau for the Protection of Monuments approves the plan in early 1997 – the realization of the Museum Quarter can finally get underway.

Resistance to this new, more historical plan for the Museum Quarter meets with no success. In November 1992, long before the new project is proposed, a group of architects, artists, architecture critics, writers and politicians denounced the increasingly subjective agitation methods used by the Kronenzeitung. The group publicized a series of articles in the Wiener Journal in which they satirized illustrations used by the Kronenzeitung. They called for a modern art and cultural centre and an image of the Second Republic that corresponded with current times. However, there was not enough cohesion among the individual supporters to ensure long-term united support for a new Museum Quarter.

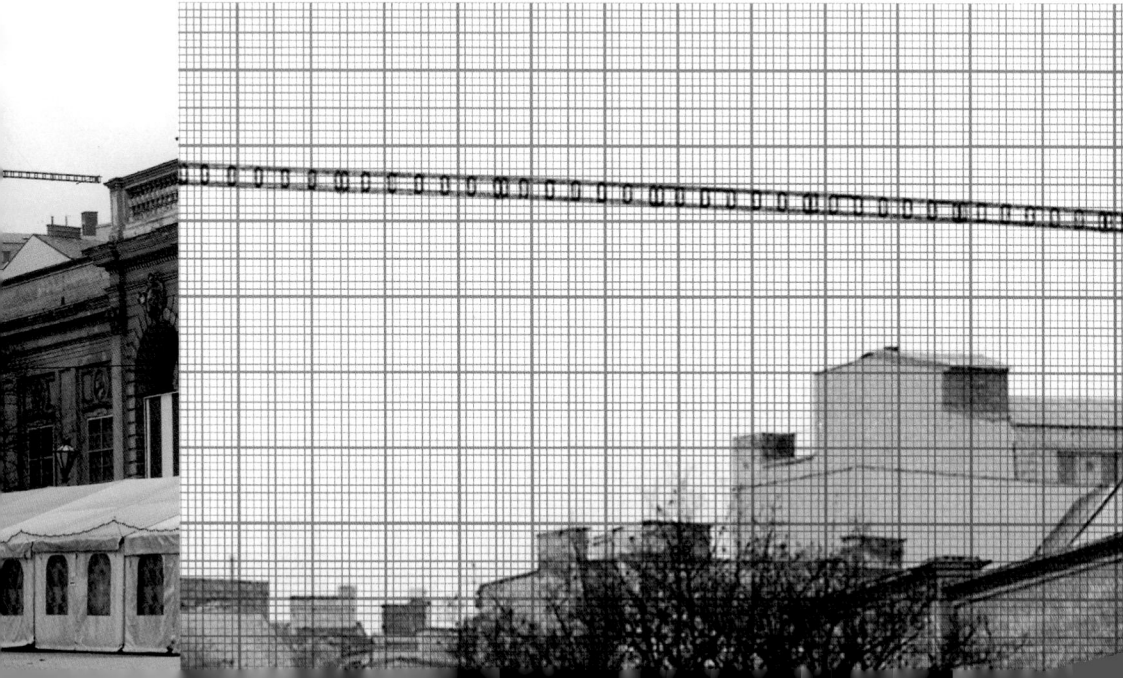

Die wortmächtige Nation

Die Geschichte des Wiener Museumsquartiers ließe sich auch als „Die Geschichte einer wortmächtigen Nation" übertiteln. Nicht nur Architekten, Stadtplaner und offizielle Entscheidungsträger, sondern auch Journalisten, Künstler, politische Parteien, Aktionsgruppen und Anrainer – sie alle brachten ihre Meinung zum Ausdruck, die weit über das rein Architektonische hinausging: Was ist die gebotene Einstellung gegenüber Wiens historischer Bausubstanz? Wie können und sollen alte und neue kulturelle Ausdrucksformen nebeneinander bestehen? Wer hat die offizielle Macht oder den inoffiziellen Einfluß, um über Veränderungen der baulichen Umwelt zu entscheiden, und wer sollte sie haben? Informationstreffen werden abgehalten und Aktionsgruppen gegründet, Hunderte Leserbriefe geschrieben, und die Zeitungen berichten fast täglich.

Der Begriff der wortmächtigen Nation ist auch ein wiederkehrendes Thema in der Argumentation sowohl der Befürworter als auch der Gegner des ursprünglichen Projekts. Einige fordern das Recht der Bevölkerung ein, über große öffentliche Ausgaben wie die Milliarden für das Museumsquartier mitzuentscheiden. Andere stellen die Frage, ob ein solches Projekt unter demokratischen Umständen überhaupt je zu realisieren sei. Das Kräftemessen, in dem die öffentliche Debatte letztlich steckenbleibt, hat nicht mehr viel mit den internationalen Ambitionen der Initiatoren des Museumsquartiers gemein.

Erfolgsdruck

Das Museumsquartier, das als Folge dieser Debatte als typisch „österreichischer Kompromiß" gilt, wird sich erst beweisen müssen – sowohl international gegenüber Scharen verwöhnter Touristen als auch lokal gegenüber einer Reihe nur teilweise zufriedengestellter Zyniker.

Die langwierigen Konflikte auf lokaler Ebene machen das Museumsquartier als nationales Symbol wenig überzeugend. Die Wiener werden einige Zeit brauchen, ehe sie die mühselige Entstehungsgeschichte vergessen und anfangen können, sich mit dieser kulturellen Selbstdarstellung „ihrer" Republik zu identifizieren.

Da das inhaltliche Konzept für das Museumsquartier nicht von Anfang an klar definiert war und sich mehrmals änderte, muß sein Charakter als große Kulturinstitution erst noch Gestalt annehmen. Auf einem Plakat für „Printed Matter"[9] listet Christian Philip Müller sämtliche Institutionen auf, die im Museumsquartier angesiedelt wurden. Er stellt die Frage, ob das Museumsquartier tatsächlich als größeres Ganzes aus der Summe seiner Teile hervorgehen wird oder „worin genau der Mehrwert einer Konzentration so vieler Kulturinstitutionen im Zentrums Wiens bestehen soll".

Seit Baubeginn haben Journalisten, Architekturkritiker und auch Laurids Ortner selbst wiederholt die Frage nach der Repräsentanz gestellt. Der Zeithistoriker Wolfgang Kos äußerte im Standard (22.12.1998) seine Sorge über die (Un-)Sichtbarkeit des Museumsquartiers. Er meint, die langen Konflikte um den Bau hätten mehrere Generationen kreativer Köpfe zum Stillschweigen gebracht, aus

„Der amputierte Architekt", Karikatur, in: Die Presse, 10.12.1997 (unten); „Wehe, wenn sie loslassen", Karikatur, in: Der Kurier, 10.10.1992 (rechts)

"The Amputated Architect", cartoon in: Die Presse, 10.12.1997 (below) "Woe, if they let go", cartoon in: der Kurier, 10.10.1992 (right)

A Verbose Nation

The history of the Vienna Museum Quarter could also be entitled "The History of a Verbose Nation". And it wasn't just architects, urban planners and official decision makers, but also journalists, artists, political parties, action groups and the inhabitants of nearby buildings – all these people were only too ready to add their own two cents' worth, and their opinions were not restricted to architectonic considerations. Which view of Vienna's historical architectonic core is called for here? Can old and new forms of cultural expression coexist, and if so, how? Who actually has the official power or the unofficial influence to decide changes in the architectural environment, and who ought to have them? Information meetings are held and action committees founded, hundreds of letters are written to editors, and it has become regular, almost everyday fare in the local newspapers.

The idea of the verbose nation is a recurring theme in the arguments of both the supporters and the opponents of the original project. Some demand the right of the people to have a say in big public expenditures like the billions of schillings earmarked for the Museum Quarter. Others pose the question of whether or not a project of this kind could ever be realized in a democratic process. The power struggle in which the public debate has eventually become locked no longer has anything to do with the international ambitions of the initiators of the Museum Quarter.

Pressure to Succeed

The Museum Quarter, which has emerged from this debate as a typical "Austrian compromise", will now have to prove itself worthy – both internationally, to crowds of spoiled tourists, and locally, to all the only partially satisfied cynics.

The long-drawn-out conflicts on a local level detract from the Museum Quarter's status as a national symbol and diminish its credibility. The Viennese people will need some time before they can forget the tiresome and laborious start and begin to identify with this cultural image of "their" republic.

Since the concept for the content of the Museum Quarter was initially unclear and since even this has undergone repeated changes, the character of the complex as a large-scale cultural institution has yet to unfold and take shape. On a poster for "Printed Matter"[9] Christian Philip Müller lists all the institutions located on the Museum Quarter grounds. He poses the question of whether or not the Museum Quarter will indeed "emerge as a larger whole from the sum of its parts" or "exactly what the added value of concentrating so many cultural institutions in the centre of Vienna will be".

From the time construction began, journalists, architecture critics, and even Laurids Ortner himself have repeatedly considered the question of representation. The contemporary historian, Wolfgang Kos, expressed his concerns about the (in)visibility of the Museum Quarter in Der Standard (22 December 1998). He maintains that the long conflicts about construction have silenced generations of creative minds, for fear of causing a moratorium on construction. Sections of the initial

Angst vor einem Baustopp. Teile des anfänglichen Projekts wie der Leseturm und das Film- und Photographiemuseum, die den relativ geschlossenen Komplex der Hofstallungen hätten öffnen können, wurden nach Jahren des Widerstands gestrichen. Da das ursprüngliche inhaltliche Konzept 1995 offenkundig historisiert wurde, würden zusätzliche Anstrengungen nötig sein, um daraus eine zeitgenössische Attraktion zu machen. Andernfalls könne der Wettbewerb mit dem KIASMA in Helsinki oder dem Guggenheim Museum in Bilbao ziemlich schwer werden, befürchtet Kos.

Der einzige Überlebende?

Abschließend mag man sich die Frage stellen, ob dieses repräsentative Kulturprojekt immer noch als Erfolgsgeschichte für den Architekten gelten kann. Viele läßt der Bau unbefriedigt; sie halten den endgültigen Kompromiß für ein jämmerliches Gerangel um den kleinsten gemeinsamen Nenner, mit der Betonung auf „kleinsten". Dieser Kompromiß muß nicht notwendigerweise architektonischer Natur sein, war doch der siegreiche Entwurf des Wettbewerbs vielleicht gar nicht als endgültige Version zu sehen, sondern eher als Vorschlag oder Auslotung der Möglichkeiten. Jedenfalls änderte sich das funktionale Konzept. Es ist seinerseits ein Kompromiß – nicht zuletzt weil der Leopold-Kollektion mehr Wichtigkeit beigemessen und dafür mehrere zeitgenössische Institutionen gestrichen wurden. Ortner mußte in Zusammenarbeit mit Wehdorn seinen ursprünglichen Plan inhaltlich diesem historisierenden Konzept anpassen.

Ihm wurde von einer Reihe von Kollegen und anderen am Projekt Beteiligten vorgeworfen, er habe seine Seele dem Teufel verkauft. Man bezichtigte ihn des Opportunismus und Verrats der künstlerischen Ziele. Aus dieser Sicht erscheint es recht fragwürdig, ihn als Überlebenden dieses Unternehmens zu bezeichnen; ein Überlebender vielleicht, aber um welchen Preis? Andererseits mag man sich fragen, ob es ohne Ortners Flexibilität und Bereitschaft, mit wechselnden und oft ungünstigen Bedingungen umzugehen und daraus ein neues Projekt zu entwickeln, das Museumsquartier heute überhaupt gäbe. In diesem Sinne verkörpert Ortner das Überleben des österreichischen Museumsquartiers.

Melanie van der Hoorn

Von links nach rechts:
Museum Moderner Kunst –
Stiftung Ludwig Wien;
Gesamtansicht MuseumsQuartier;
Leopold Museum

From left to right:
Museum of Modern Art –
Ludwig Foundation Vienna;
Overall view of the Museum Quarter;
Leopold Museum

36

project, like the Reading Tower and the Film and Photography Museum, which might have opened up the relatively closed-off complex of the imperial stables, were scratched after years and years of protests. Since the original concept openly acknowledged its dedication to historical considerations in 1995, additional efforts would be required to make a contemporary attraction out of it. Otherwise, fears Kos, it will be difficult to compete with the KIASMA in Helsinki or with the Guggenheim Museum in Bilbao.

The Only Survivor?

In the end one might ask oneself if this representative cultural project can still be considered a success story for the architect. The complex leaves many dissatisfied; there is a feeling that the final compromise is a miserable wrangling over the smallest common denominator, with an emphasis on "smallest". This compromise does not necessarily have to be of an architectural nature, after all, the design that won the competition might not have been meant to be the final version in the first place but more of a proposal or exploration of the various possibilities. In any case the functional concept changed. It has itself become a compromise – not least because the Leopold Collection has been given more importance, and as a consequence several contemporary institutions have been eliminated. Ortner, in cooperation with Wehdorn, was forced to adapt the content of his original plan to fit this new concept with its emphasis on historical considerations.

He was attacked by several of his colleagues and other persons involved in the project who claimed he had sold his soul to the devil. They accused him of opportunism and of betraying the artistic objectives. From this point of view it seems a dubious claim to call him a survivor of this undertaking; a survivor perhaps, but at what cost? On the other hand, one might ask whether there would even be a Museum Quarter today if it weren't for Ortner's flexibility and willingness to deal with and develop a new project out of the constantly changing and often unfavourable circumstances. In this sense Ortner indeed embodies the survival of the Austrian Museum Quarter.

Melanie van der Hoorn

**Im Uhrzeigersinn: Leopold Museum;
Kunsthalle Wien; Museum Moderner Kunst –
Stiftung Ludwig Wien;
Veranstaltungshalle E+G**

Clockwise: Leopold Museum;
Kunsthalle Wien; Museum of Modern
Art – Ludwig Foundation Vienna;
Multipurpose hall E+G

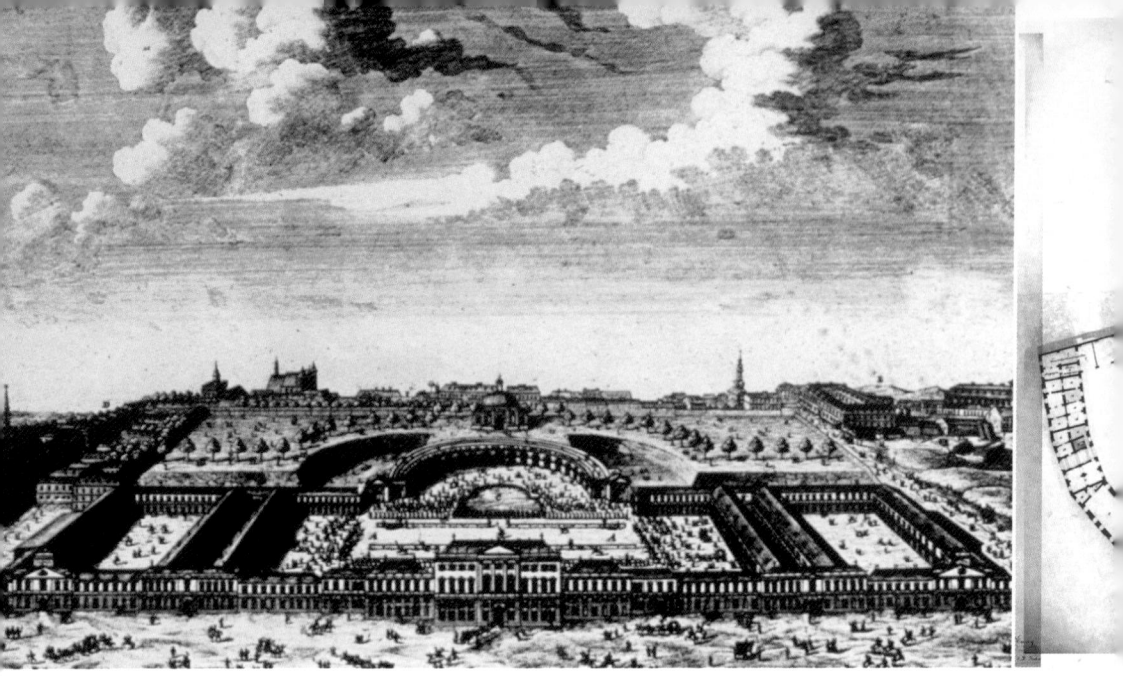

Die Baugeschichte

Niemals mehr wird es einen Aufbruch zur Neugliederung der Wiener Museumslandschaft geben, wie dies in der ersten Hälfte der achtziger Jahre der Fall war.

Als Ende der siebziger Jahre erstmals die Idee aufkam, die vormaligen Hofstallungen im Zentrum Wiens, die jahrzehntelang von der Wiener Messe AG genutzt wurden und als Messepalast bekannt waren, einer kulturellen Nutzung zuzuführen, brachte dies enorme Bewegung in die Wiener Kulturpolitik. Unzählige Arbeitsgruppen wurden gebildet, die neue Ideen hervorbrachten und zugleich die gesamte Strukturierung der Museen in Frage stellten. Könnte nicht das Museum des 20. Jahrhunderts auch wirklich alle Bestände dieses Jahrhunderts aufnehmen, wie zum Beispiel die „Sammlung Stallburg" oder die Sammlung der österreichischen Galerie etc.?

Sollte es eine neue Organisation für ein Museum der Jahrhundertwende oder für ein neues Museum des 19. und 20. Jahrhunderts geben?

Doch es kam zu keiner einheitlichen Lösung dieser Problemansätze. Vielmehr erfolgte nach zahlreichen öffentlichen Debatten eine klassische Ausschreibung eines zweistufigen Architektenwettbewerbs für den Umbau und die Erweiterung des Messepalastes.

Das Programm hierfür versuchte sehr genau und detailliert alle bekannten Raumbedürfnisse für eine Restrukturierung der Wiener Museumsordnung abzudecken und war verbunden mit der Frage an die teilnehmenden Architekten, wieviel davon tatsächlich auf dem Gelände unterzubringen sei. Sieben Projekte der Architekten Georg Friedler, Hans Hollein, Ernst Hiesmayr/Rudolf Prohazka, Stefan Hübner, Werner Krakora, (alle Wien), Ortner + Ortner (Düsseldorf, Linz) und Oswald Matthias Ungers (Köln) werden für die Bearbeitung in der

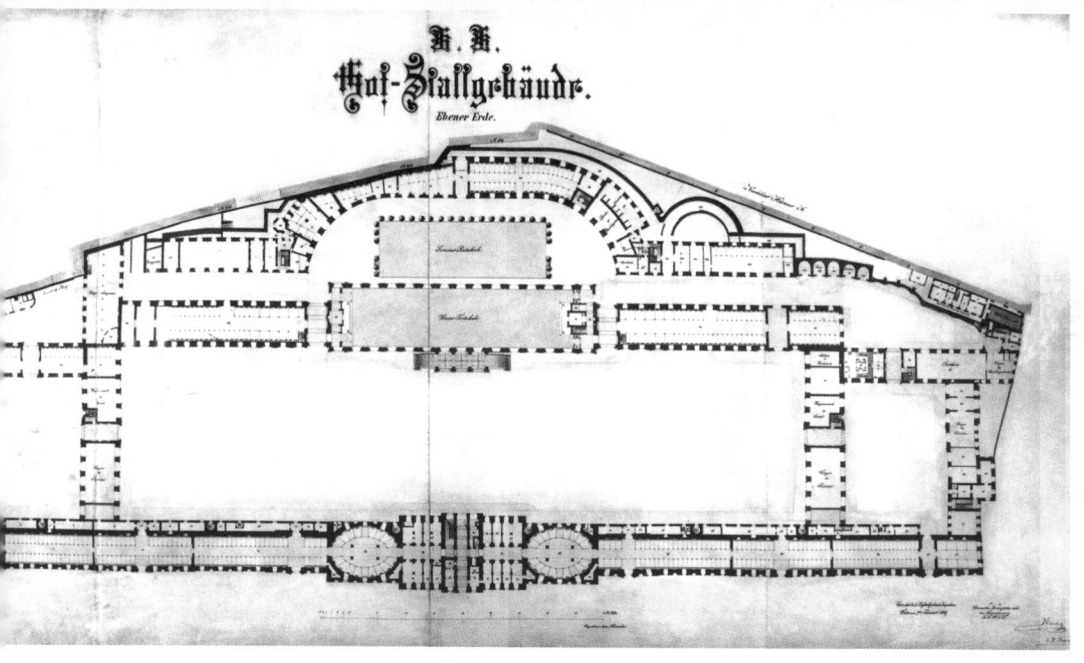

K. K.
Hof-Stallgebäude.
Ebener Erde.

History of Construction

Never again will there be another new beginning in the reorganization of the Vienna museum landscape like the one that took place in the first half of the eighties.

In the late seventies, when the idea of allowing cultural utilization of the former imperial stables — located in the centre of Vienna and then known as "Messepalast" after having been used by the Wiener Messe AG (Vienna Trade Fair) for decades — first arose, this sparked a complex dynamic in Vienna's cultural politics. Countless working committees were formed, introducing new ideas and at the same time questioning the overall structure of the museums. Wouldn't the Museum of the Twentieth Century be able to house all the contemporary collections, the "Stallburg Collection", for instance, or the collection of the Austrian Gallery etc? Should there be a new organization for a museum of the turn of the century or for a new museum of the nineteenth and twentieth centuries?

But these problems were not to be resolved in a unified manner. Rather, after many public debates what followed was a classical two-stage architecture competition for the reconstruction and the expansion of the Messepalast.

In an attempt to consider all known spatial requirements for restructuring the museum organization in Vienna as precisely and in the greatest detail possible, the programme was tied to a question directed at all participating architects: How much would it really be possible to house on the grounds? Seven projects by the architects Georg Friedler, Hans Hollein, Ernst Hiesmayr and Rudolf Prohazka, Stefan Hübner, Werner Krakora (all Vienna), Ortner + Ortner (Düsseldorf, Linz) and Oswald Matthias Ungers (Cologne) are selected by the jury in October 1987 for further elaboration in the second round of competition.

Kaiserlicher Marstall –
Gesamtkonzept (links);
Hofstallgebäude – Grundriß 1869
(rechts)

Imperial stables –
general concept (left)
Imperial stables – site plan
in 1869 (right)

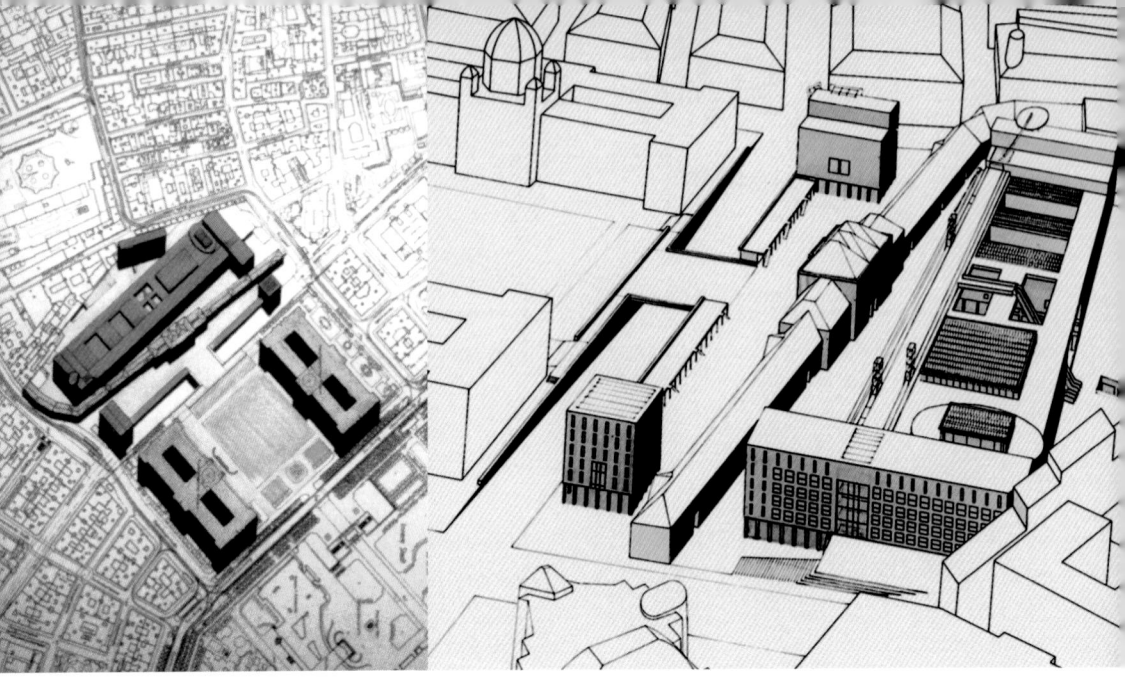

zweiten Stufe des Wettbewerbs von der Jury im Oktober 1987 ausgewählt. Ungeachtet dieser Ergebnisse tauchen in der Folge wieder neue Vorschläge für die kulturelle Nutzung des Messepalastes auf. Ein Vorschlag will ein „Museum der Völker und Kulturen" etablieren, ein weiterer sollte bloß der Erweiterung des Kunsthistorischen Museums dienen.

Ein Neubeginn erfolgt 1989 mit der Ernennung von Erhard Busek zum Wissenschaftsminister. Ungeachtet der Tatsache, daß zwischenzeitlich ein Vorschlag des Architekten Wilhelm Holzbauer für die Adaptierung eines Teilbereichs des Messepalastes für eine Kunsthalle unaufgefordert auf den Tischen der verantwortlichen Politiker gelandet ist, schreibt Busek die noch offene zweite Stufe des Wettbewerbs aus. Das neue Programm erweist sich sowohl detaillierter als auch reduzierter. Auf Grundlage eines städtebaulichen Gesamtkonzepts soll in einer ersten Phase bis 1995 – dem Jahr der geplanten Weltausstellung in Wien und Budapest – vor allem das neue Museum Moderner Kunst, aber auch eine gemeinsame Kunst- und Veranstaltungshalle der Gemeinde Wien und des Bundes verwirklicht werden. In einer zweiten Phase sollen unter anderem ein Medienforum mit Film- und Photografiemuseum, ein Museum der Ideengeschichte der Moderne mit der Sammlung Leopold und ergänzende kulturelle Einrichtungen, wie eine aktuelle Kunstbibliothek, realisiert werden. Das Kunsthistorische und das Naturhistorische Museum werden angewiesen, ihre Raumbedürfnisse innerhalb ihrer eigenen Häuser zu realisieren.

Im April 1990 fällt dieselbe Jury einstimmig die Entscheidung für das Projekt der Architekten Ortner + Ortner. Noch im Juni desselben Jahres wird eine eigene Errichtungs- und Betriebsgesellschaft für das Museumsquartier gegründet, an der der Bund mit 75 und die Stadt Wien mit 25 Prozent beteiligt sind. Geschäftsführer werden der Kunsthistoriker

1. Wettbewerbsentwurf von 1987 (links);
2. Wettbewerbsentwurf von 1990 (rechts)

1. Competition design in 1987 (left)
2. Competition design in 1990 (right)

Nevertheless, new proposals for the cultural utilization of the Messe-palast continue to appear later. One proposal seeks to establish a "Museum of Nations and Cultures", another suggests just expanding the Art History Museum.

A new beginning comes in 1989 when Erhard Busek is appointed Minister of Science. Although a proposal by the architect Wilhelm Holz-bauer for the adaptation of a section of the Messepalast for an art hall had in the meantime landed unsolicited on the desks of the politicians responsible, Busek calls for submissions for the second round of the competition still to be conducted. The new programme turns out to be both more detailed and reduced. Based on an overall urban plan, the first construction phase to be realized by 1995 – the year of the planned world exposition in Vienna and Budapest – was primarily to entail completion of the new Museum of Modern Art and a combined art hall and Hall of Events funded by both the City of Vienna and the Republic of Austria. In a second phase a Media Forum with a Film and Photography Museum, a museum of the history of the idea of Modernism with the Leopold Collection, and supplementary cultural facilities, like a contemporary art library, were to be realized. The Art History and Natural History Museums are left to meet their growing space requirements within their own walls.

In April 1990, the jury unanimously chooses the architects Ortner + Ortner for the project. In June of the same year a special Museum Quarter Development and Operation Co. Ltd is founded, in which the Republic of Austria has a 75% share and the city of Vienna 25%. Managers are the art historian Dieter Bogner and the lawyer and real estate manager Günther Bischof.

The project by the architects Ortner + Ortner comprises the inter-national Kunsthalle Wien, the Museum of Modern Art, and a multi-

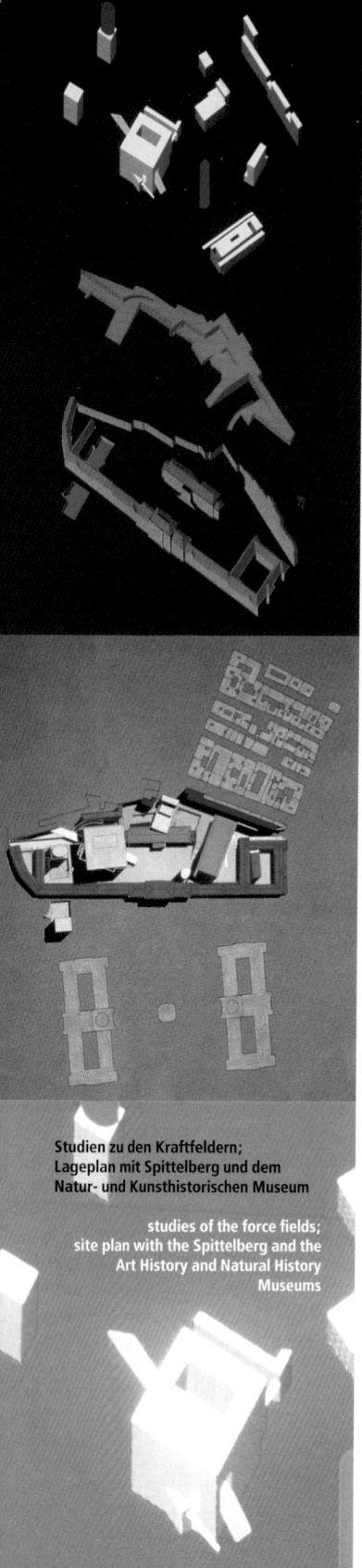

Studien zu den Kraftfeldern;
Lageplan mit Spittelberg und dem
Natur- und Kunsthistorischen Museum

studies of the force fields;
site plan with the Spittelberg and the
Art History and Natural History
Museums

Dieter Bogner und der Jurist und Immobilienmanager Günther Bischof.

Das Projekt der Architekten Ortner + Ortner umfaßt die internationale Kunsthalle Wien, das Museum Moderner Kunst und eine multifunktionelle Veranstaltungshalle hinter der Winterreithalle. Als signalhaftes Objekt ist ein 67m hoher „Leseturm" im Haupthof geplant. Im westlich gelegenen Seitenhof soll ein Museum österreichischer Moderne mit der Sammlung Leopold errichtet werden und im östlich gelegenen Seitenhof ein Medienzentrum.

Noch während der Gründung der Museumsquartier-Errichtungsgesellschaft etabliert sich eine Bürgerinitiative gegen das Projekt. Sie bekämpft von Beginn an jede geplante zeitgenössische Architektur im Zentrum Wiens – egal welchen Inhalts – und fordert zunächst ein Pferdemuseum in den ehemaligen Hofstallungen. Die zweifellos obskuren Ziele der Bürgerinitiative werden vorerst nicht ernst genommen, da sich Politik und Medien voll auf das Zukunftsprojekt „Weltausstellung Wien-Budapest" konzentrieren. Der Medienzar Hans Dichand eröffnet mit seiner einflußreichen Kronen Zeitung eine Kampagne an zwei Fronten: gegen die Weltausstellung und gegen das Museumsquartier. Im Mai 1991 wird bei einer Volksabstimmung in Wien der Weltausstellung eine Absage erteilt. Für das dafür vorgesehene Gelände an der Donau wird nun intensiv nach einem neuen Nutzungsprogramm gesucht. Ein neuer Stadtteil soll entstehen und unter anderem auch kulturelle Nutzungen enthalten. Die Auslagerung gewisser zeitgenössischer Einrichtungen aus dem Programm des Museumsquartiers – wie zum Beispiel des Medienforums – scheinen sich anzubieten.

Dennoch wird das gesamte Nutzungsprogramm für das Museumsquartier geplant. Die Flächenwidmung wird jedoch erst 1993 mit den Stimmen der SPÖ und der Grünen beschlossen. Im Herbst 1991 beginnt eine mediale Debatte über die Größe und die Nutzungen des Museumsquartiers mit heftigen Kontroversen für und wider das Projekt. Mit Bernhard Görg bekommt die Wiener ÖVP – die Partei, der auch Minister Busek angehört – einen neuen Parteiobmann. In einer seiner ersten Amtshandlungen hebt Bernhard Görg alle Beschlüsse seiner Partei auf und wendet sich somit gegen das Projekt.

Eine wesentliche und neue Wendung ergibt sich 1993 durch den politisch beschlossenen Ankauf der Sammlung Leopold durch den Bund. Damit rückt auch das Projekt eines zweiten Museums im Museumsquartier in greifbare Nähe. Bis zum Sommer 1994 wird dieses Museum hinter der Winterreithalle anstelle der ursprünglichen Veranstaltungshalle geplant. Im medialen und politischen Vordergrund steht aber der sogenannte „Leseturm". Die Idee, den Leseturm als zeitgenössisches Kunst-Informationszentrum zu etablieren, kann sich nicht durchsetzen.

Nachdem klar ersichtlich wird, daß die Sammlung Leopold nun einen bedeutenden Anteil des neuen Museumsquartiers einnehmen wird und die Vorschläge für zeitgenössische Initiativen nicht berücksichtigt werden, verabschiedet sich Dieter Bogner 1994 aus der Geschäftsführung der Errichtungs- und Betriebsgesellschaft des Museumsquartiers.

Der öffentliche und politische Druck für ein selbständiges Museum

purpose Hall of Events behind the winter riding hall. As a landmark a 67-m-high Reading Tower is planned in the main courtyard. To the left and right of the main courtyard are two adjoining courtyards, the one to the west intended for the Leopold Collection, and the one to the east for a Media Centre.

And while the Museum Quarter Development and Operation Co. Ltd was being established, a citizens' action committee against the project was also forming. From the start, this action committee is opposed to any contemporary architectural building planned in the centre of Vienna – no matter what the content – and its initial proposal calls for a horse museum in the former imperial stables. At first the obscure objectives of the citizens' action committee are not taken seriously because politics and the media are all so focused on the future project "World Expo Vienna-Budapest". Using his influential Kronenzeitung as a vehicle, media czar Hans Dichand launches a campaign on two fronts: against both the world expo and the Museum Quarter. Then in May 1991, the world expo is rejected in a plebiscite in Vienna. The grounds along the Danube earmarked for that project suddenly become available and an intensive search for a new utilization programme begins. The site is to be developed into a new urban district, partially dedicated to cultural projects. This almost seems to be an invitation for the outsourcing of certain contemporary facilities – for example the Media Forum – from the core of the Museum Quarter.

Nevertheless, the utilization programme for the Museum Quarter is still planned out in its entirety. The zoning, however, isn't settled until 1993 with the Socialist Party and Green votes. In the autumn of 1991, a media debate over the size and use of the Museum Quarter begins, and there is intense discussion of the pros and cons of the project. Bernhard Görg becomes the new leader of the Vienna section of the Austrian People's Party – the party Minister Busek also belongs to. In one of his first official acts Bernhard Görg reverses all the decisions of his party and in doing so revokes his support for the project.

A significant and new turn of events comes in 1993 with the political decision of the Republic of Austria to acquire the Leopold Collection. With this, a second museum project in the Museum Quarter comes within reach. Until the summer of 1994 the plan is to build this museum behind the winter riding hall in place of the original Hall of Events. But the Reading Tower is in the media and political spotlight. In the end the idea of the Reading Tower as an information centre for contemporary art fails to assert itself. Then in 1994, after it has become clear that the Leopold Collection will take up a significant part of the new Museum Quarter, and that the proposals for contemporary initiatives will not be taken into consideration, Dieter Bogner resigns as manager of the new Museum Quarter Development and Operation Co. Ltd.

Public and political pressure for a separate Leopold Museum grows following the acquisition. During the course of 1995, a new project arises. The Museum of Modern Art – Ludwig Collection remains an

Präsentation des 1:100-Modells des überarbeiteten Wettbewerbsprojekts im Büro Ortner + Ortner (von links oben bis rechts unten: Markus Spiegelfeld, Dietmar Steiner, Helmut Zilk, Franz Vranitzky, Erhard Busek)

Presentation of the 1:100 model of the reworked competition project at the office of Ortner + Ortner (from left above to right below: Markus Spiegelfeld, Dietmar Steiner, Helmut Zilk, Franz Vranitzky, Erhard Busek)

Leopold nimmt nach dem Ankauf der Sammlung zu. Im Laufe des Jahres 1995 entsteht nun ein neues Projekt. Unbestritten bleibt das Museum Moderner Kunst – Sammlung Ludwig. Die Kubatur der beiden Museen soll annähernd gleichwertig sein.

Während der Bund die beiden Museen betreiben wird, übernimmt die Stadt Wien die alleinige wirtschaftliche Verantwortung für die Kunsthalle und die Veranstaltungshalle der Wiener Festwochen. Mit dem Architektur Zentrum Wien und dem Kindermuseum ZOOM, die bereits seit 1993 im Museumsquartier Programm machen, kommen zwei weitere Nutzungen hinzu, die im Raumprogramm des Wettbewerbs keine Berücksichtigung fanden.

Die kulturellen Gewichte und Intentionen des Projektes Museumsquartier verschieben sich also erneut, erstmals sind die künftigen Nutzungen definitiv beschlossen. Diesem neuen Programm folgend, erstellen Ortner + Ortner mit dem im Mai 1995 hinzugezogenen Architekten und Experten für Denkmalschutz Manfred Wehdorn einen vollkommenen überarbeiteten Projektentwurf, der auch den immer präziser formulierten Anforderungen des Denkmalschutzes und den Vorstellungen der Kronenzeitung entspricht. Die beiden Neubauten der Museen folgen dem ursprünglichen städtebaulichen Konzept von Ortner + Ortner, werden aber als massive, ortsbildende und dauerhafte Manifeste architektonisch neu formuliert. Deren Kubatur wird tief in den Boden gerammt, damit die inzwischen „heilig" gesprochene „Firstlinie" der barocken Stallungen nicht überschritten wird. Die ebenfalls neue Kunsthalle wird nun hinter der historistischen Reithalle aus dem 19. Jahrhundert geplant, und die Reithalle selbst wird ausgehöhlt und für zwei Veranstaltungshallen adaptiert.

Das Kindermuseum ZOOM und das Architektur Zentrum Wien werden ohne neue architektonische Signale in die Altbausubstanz der beiden seitlichen Höfe integriert. Immer noch wird um den „Leseturm" gestritten. Das Zeichen des Neuen wird gefordert, aber es findet sich kein politisch Verantwortlicher, der dieses auch vertreten würde.

In all diesen Jahren kämpft der Geschäftsführer Günther Bischof der Errichtungs- und Betriebsgesellschaft Museumsquartier für das Projekt, ohne aber von der Architektur wirklich überzeugt zu sein. So versucht er noch 1996 Ortner + Ortner davon zu überzeugen, daß Archi-

uncontested certainty. The weight of these two museums is to be of comparable importance.

While the Republic of Austria will be operating both museums, the City of Vienna will take over sole economic responsibility for the Kunsthalle and the Vienna Festival's Hall of Events. Two further projects that had not been considered in the spatial programme of the competition, the Architektur Zentrum Wien and the ZOOM Children's Museum, part of the Museum Quarter since 1993, are integrated into it.

The cultural focus and intentions of the Museum Quarter project have shifted anew, and for the first time the future utilities are settled definitively. In accordance with this new programme, Ortner + Ortner together with the architect and monument protection expert Manfred Wehdorn, who joined the project in May 1995, draw up a completely revised project plan that meets the ever more precisely formulated demands of monument protection and the expectations of the Kronenzeitung. The two new museum buildings follow Ortner + Ortner's original urban planning concept, but are architecturally reformulated into massive, visually site-defining, and permanent manifestos. Their magnitude has been rammed deep into the ground to keep from crossing the "sacred" line of the Baroque stables. The Kunsthalle – also new – is planned to be erected behind the historical nineteenth-century riding hall, and the riding hall itself will be excavated and converted into two event halls.

The ZOOM Children's Museum and the Architektur Zentrum Wien are to be integrated into the old building's core structures of the two adjoining courtyards without any additional architectonic signals. The battle of the Reading Tower is still being waged. There is a call for the new, but no political representative has stepped forward to take on the responsibility.

In all these years Günther Bischof, the manager of the Museum Quarter Development and Operation Co. Ltd, has been fighting for the project without believing in it fully himself. In 1996, he tries to convince Ortner + Ortner that architects like Wilhelm Holzbauer or Rüdiger Lainer should help contribute to a new project design.

During the course of 1997 the new plan by Ortner + Ortner in

Fotomontage des Projekts, Stand September 1992; Fotomontage mit reduzierten Kubaturen, Stand Dezember 1992; Variation Leseturm, Stand 1993

Photomontage of the project, phase September 1992
Photomontage with reduced building cubatures, phase December 1992
Variation of the "Reading Tower", phase 1993

WITHDRAWN-UNL

**Museum Moderner Kunst –
Stiftung Ludwig Wien, Stand 1994
(links) und 1999 (rechts)**

Museum of Modern Art –
Ludwig Foundation Vienna,
phase 1994 (left) and 1999 (right)

**Leopold Museum, Stand 1994
(links) und 1999 (rechts)**

Leopold Museum, phase 1994
(left) and 1999 (right)

**Kunsthalle, Stand 1999
mit Winterreithalle (links)
und 1994 (rechts)**

Kunsthalle, phase 1999
with the historical winter riding hall
(left) and 1994 (right)

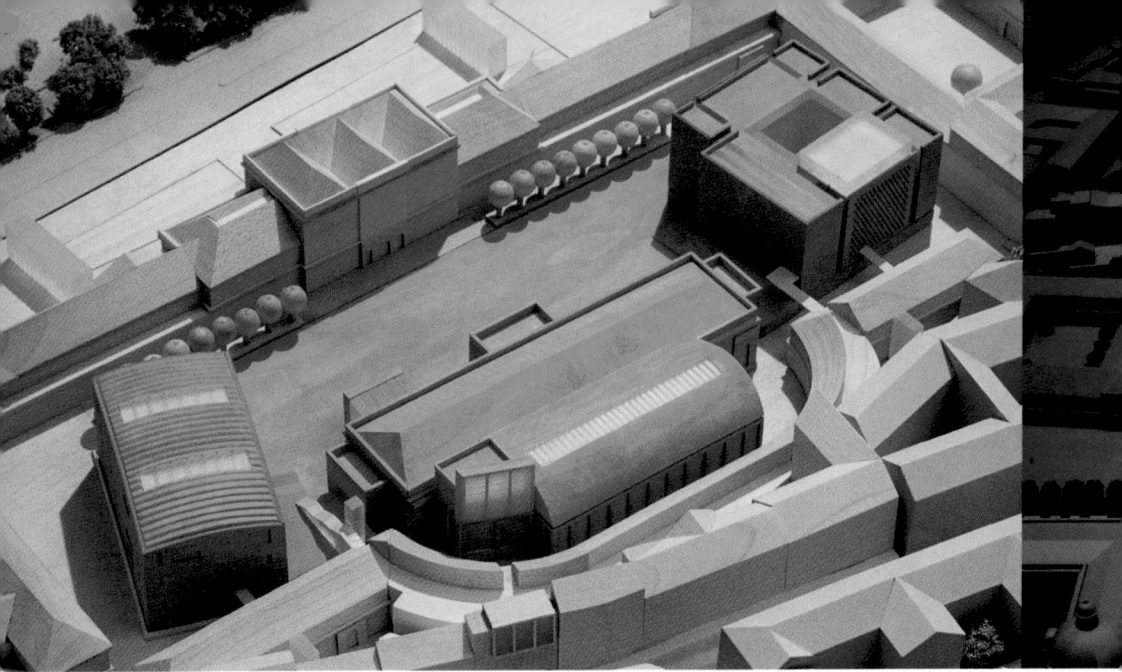

tekten wie Wilhelm Holzbauer oder Rüdiger Lainer an einem neuen Projektentwurf mitwirken sollten.

Im Laufe des Jahres 1997 wird schließlich der neue Entwurf der Arbeitsgemeinschaft Ortner + Ortner mit Manfred Wehdorn fertiggestellt, eingereicht und bewilligt. Anfang April 1998 erfolgt der Baubeginn, und bereits im Jahr 2001 wird das MuseumsQuartier, als einer der weltgrößten neuen Kulturbezirke eröffnet werden.

Auch in dem neuen Projekt bleibt die im barocken Idealplan enthaltene Struktur nachvollziehbar, wird aber von den neuen Bauten überlagert. Das Quartier, das bislang in sich abgeschlossen im Stadtzentrum lag, soll mit Hilfe von zehn Eingängen (sechs davon sind neu) eine weitreichende Öffnung zur städtischen Umgebung erfahren, und auch der Vorplatz vis á vis des historischen Zentrums soll neu gestaltet werden.

Im zentralen Haupthof des MuseumsQuartiers finden sich nun zwei erratische, geheimnisvolle Blöcke: das mit weißem Sandstein bekleidete Museum Leopold und gegenüber das mit anthrazitfarbenem Basalt verkleidete Museum Moderner Kunst – Stiftung Ludwig. Ihre Anordnung markiert die städtebauliche Struktur der Umgebung, die auf das Quartier Einfluß nimmt. Die Linie der Hofmuseen wird vom „ewigen weißen Wert" des Museums Leopold aufgenommen, die Linie des an das Areal anschließenden bürgerlichen „Spittelbergs" wird vom „dynamisch dunklen Wert" des Museum Moderner Kunst – Stiftung Ludwig fortgesetzt.

Architektonisch verbunden sind diese beiden Museen mit der historischen „Winterreithalle", die mit großem technischen Aufwand ausgehöhlt und untergraben wurde. Sie beherbergt nun zwei multifunktionale Veranstaltungshallen für die Wiener Festwochen, das neue Tanzquartier und bietet Raum für andere Veranstaltungen. Als dritter

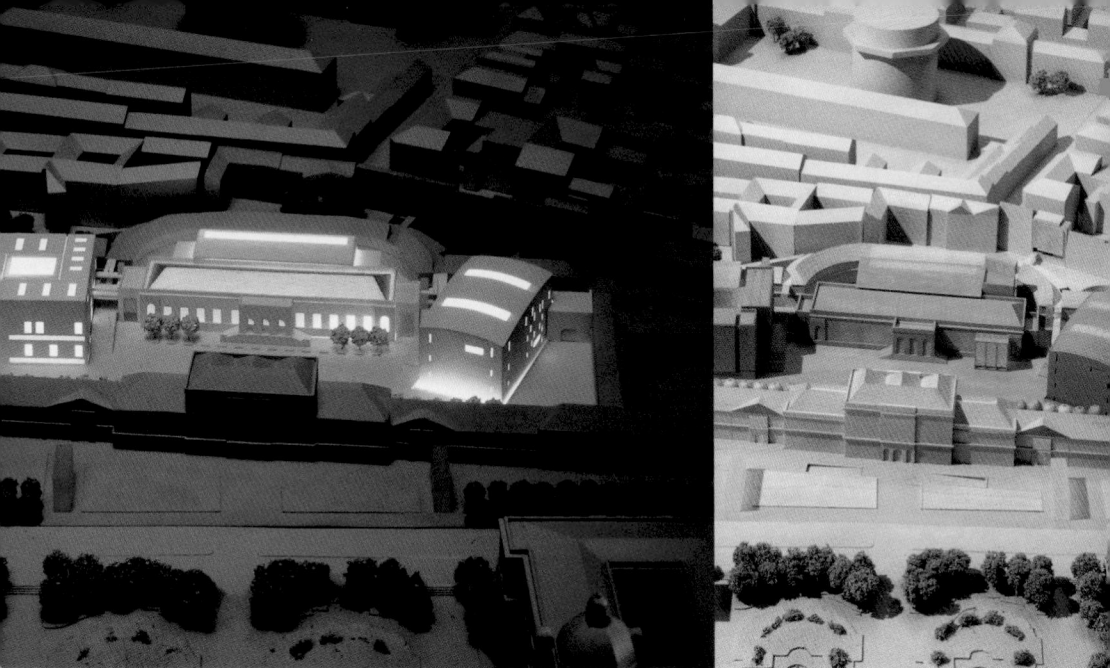

Entwurf der Arbeitsgemeinschaft Ortner +
Ortner mit Manfred Wehdorn, Stand 1995
(links);
Nachtansicht des Gesamtmodells,
Stand 1999 (rechts)

Design by Ortner + Ortner with Manfred
Wehdorn, phase 1995 (left)
Overall model by night,
phase 1999 (right)

co-operation with Manfred Wehdorn is finally completed, submitted and approved. Construction starts in the beginning of April 1998, and by the year 2001 the Museum Quarter project — as one of the biggest new cultural quarters worldwide — is to be inaugurated.

The new project, too, preserves the structure contained in the Baroque ideal plan, although the new buildings are superimposed upon it. The Quarter — until now closed off and encapsulated in the middle of the city — will be radically opened to its urban surroundings via ten entranceways (six of which are new), and the entrance area plaza across from the historical centre will also undergo remodelling.

In the central, main courtyard of the Museum Quarter, visitors will find new erratic, mysterious blocks. The Leopold Museum with its exterior of white sandstone, and across from it the anthracite-coloured Museum of Modern Art — Ludwig Foundation made of basalt. Its arrangement is marked by the urban planning structure of the surroundings, which impose their influence on the Quarter. The line of the imperial museums absorbs the "endless white value" of the Leopold Museum; the line of "Spittelberg", the bourgeois residential district adjacent to the grounds, is extended in the "dynamic dark value" of the Museum of Modern Art — Ludwig Foundation.

These two museums are linked architecturally by the historical "winter riding hall", which was excavated and extended below ground level using expensive technology. It now houses two multipurpose event halls for the Vienna Festival and the new Tanzquartier, and provides space for other events. The third erratic block — enclosed entirely in a sheath of red brick — is the newly erected Kunsthalle, located behind and attached to the winter riding hall.

The architectonic message of the Vienna Museum Quarter deals with the theme of interaction between historical and new building

erratischer Block – gänzlich in roten Ziegel gehüllt – ist die dahinterliegende neuerrichtete Kunsthalle an die Winterreithalle angebunden.

Die architektonische Botschaft des MuseumsQuartiers Wien thematisiert das Zusammenspiel von historischer und neuer Bausubstanz. Nahezu surrealistisch schweigsame Objekte treten einzig über ihre körperliche Prägnanz und die Struktur ihrer Haut mit der historischen Umgebung in einen Dialog. Eine Haut, die sich jeweils homogen über die ganzen Gebäude zieht. Die Haut (rot, schwarz, weiß) ist die jeweils primäre Botschaft des Objekts.

Erst im Inneren der Gebäude entfaltet sich die gesamte räumliche und architektonische Dimension. Beim Betreten der beiden Museen realisiert man, daß von außen nur die oberirdische Hälfte des gesamten Volumens sichtbar ist. Durchdringende Innenhöfe und Durchblicke eröffnen eindrucksvoll die innere Komplexität der Gebäude.

Wie ein kraftspendendes Implantat strahlen die neuen Bauten auf die Struktur und Substanz der erhaltenen alten Bauteile aus. Der Altbestand wird technisch und infrastrukturell unter denkmalpflegerischen Aspekten sorgfältig und mit hohem Aufwand neu organisiert. Neue kulturelle Nutzungen ziehen in die alten Hofstallungen, die jahrelang als Lagerhallen und Garagen zweckentfremdet wurden.

Das neue Architekturzentrum Wien wird den westlich gelegenen historischen Hof mit seinen Räumen ganz umschließen. Im östlichen Hof sind das neue ZOOM-Kindermuseum, ein Kindertheaterzentrum und ein Tanzquartier angesiedelt. Weitere kulturelle und kommerzielle Nutzungen, Studios, Geschäfte, Büros und Wohnungen, sorgen für die notwendige Vielfalt und Durchmischung, die ein völlig neues und bislang einzigartiges Kulturquartier des 21. Jahrhunderts auszeichnet.

Dietmar M. Steiner

substance. The almost surrealistically mute objects communicate with their historical surroundings through their physical weight and the structure of their skin alone, a skin that is stretched homogeneously over the entire building. The skin (red, black and white) is in each case the primary message of the object.

The full spatial and architectonic dimension unfolds to visitors only once they are inside the buildings. Upon entering the two museums, they realize that only part of the entire volume – the half that is above ground – is visible from the outside. Penetrating interior courtyards and views reveal the internal complexity of the buildings in an awe-inspiring way.

Like an energy-giving injection, the new buildings shed a new light on the structure and substance of the restored sections of the old buildings. Carefully, and at no mean cost, the old remnants are technically and infrastructurally reorganized, taking monument preservation aspects into consideration. The old imperial stables, which for years had served as a depot and garage, are transformed into cultural spaces for new uses.

The rooms of the new Architekturzentrum Wien will completely enclose the historical courtyard to the west. The east courtyard will house the ZOOM Children's Museum, a children's theatre centre, and the Tanzquartier. Further cultural and commercial utilizations, studios, stores, offices and apartments will ensure the necessary diversity and mix that make for this completely new and to date unique cultural district of the twenty-first century.

Dietmar M. Steiner

Leopold Museum (links);
Museum Moderner Kunst –
Stiftung Ludwig Wien (rechts)

Leopold Museum (left)
Museum of Modern Art –
Ludwig Foundation Vienna (right)

Flächennutzung

Nutzfläche gesamt	60.000 m^2
davon kulturelle Nutzungen	53.000 m^2
Leopold Museum	12.600 m^2
Museum Moderner Kunst – Stiftung Ludwig Wien	14.000 m^2
Kunsthalle Wien und Halle E + G/ Wiener Festwochen	10.600 m^2
ZOOM Kindermuseum	1.500 m^2
Architekturzentrum Wien	1.900 m^2
Theaterhaus für Kinder	1.000 m^2
Tanzquartier Wien	1.000 m^2
Kulturnahe Einrichtungen	5.900 m^2
Reserveflächen	4.500 m^2
Wohnungen	7.000 m^2

Baukosten (in ATS)

Gesamt (netto)	2,0 Milliarden
Anteil des Bundes	1,6 Milliarden
Anteil der Stadt Wien	400 Millionen

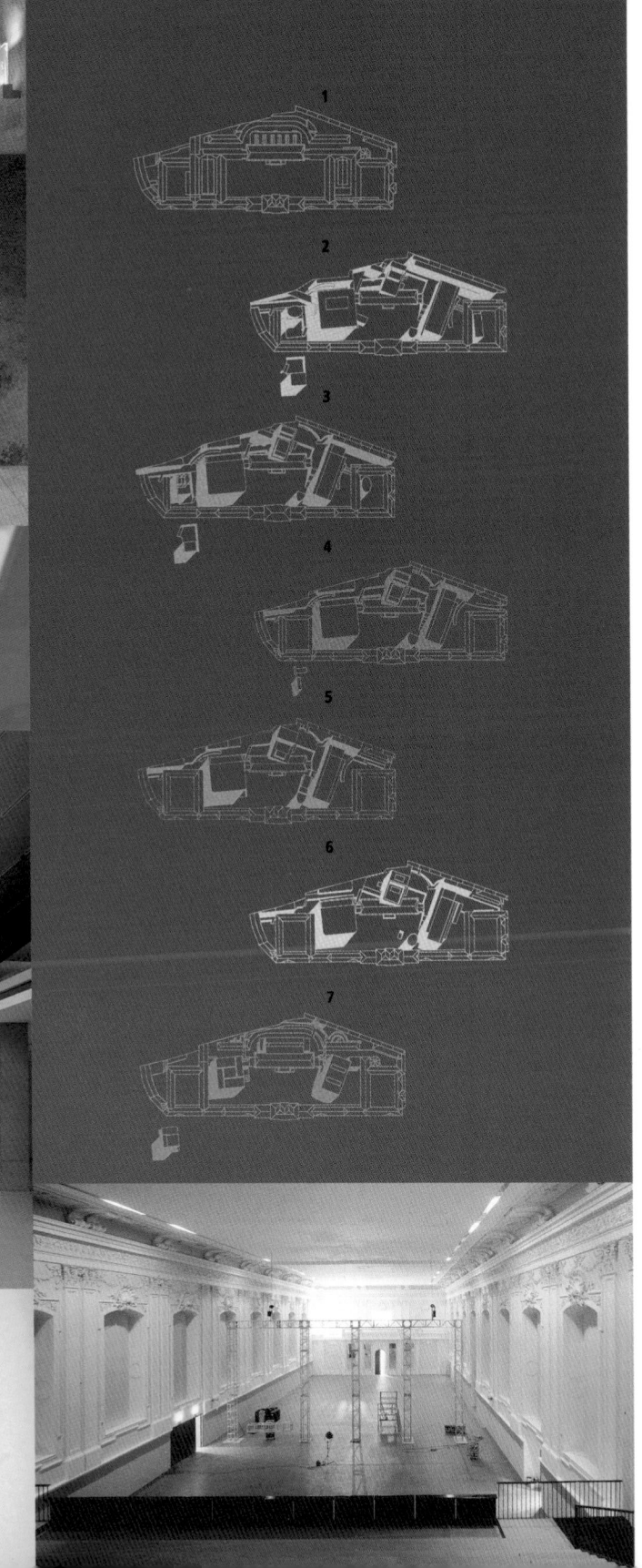

Leopold Museum,
Museum Moderner Kunst, Halle E+G (links);
Lagepläne:
Vor dem Wettbewerb 1990 (1); um 1990 (2);
Mai 1991 (3); September 1992 (4);
Dezember 1992 (5); Oktober 1994 (6);
Januar 1999 (7) (rechts)

Leopold Museum, Museum of Modern Art –
Ludwig Foundation Vienna,
Halls E+G (left)
Site plans:
before the competition in 1990 (1); 1990 (2);
May 1991 (3); September 1992 (4);
December 1992 (5); October 1994 (6);
January 1999 (7) (right)

Area use:

Total usable area	60,000 m^2
Area dedicated to cultural use	53,000 m^2
Leopold Museum	12,600 m^2
Museum of Modern Art – Ludwig Foundation Vienna	14,000 m^2
KUNSTHALLE Wien and Halls E + G/Vienna Festival	10,600 m^2
ZOOM Children's Museum	1,500 m^2
Architekturzentrum Wien	1,900 m^2
Children's Theatre	1,000 m^2
Tanzquartier Wien	1,000 m^2
Culture-related facilities	5,900 m^2
Expansion area	4,500 m^2
Apartments	7,000 m^2

Building costs:

Total (net)	ATS 2.0 billion
Federal share	ATS 1.6 billion
City of Vienna's share	ATS 400 million

Sydney Opera House

Der verjagte Architekt/The Pursued Architect

Sydney 2000

Sydney 2000: Die ganze Welt blickt nach Sydney, dem Ort der Olympischen Sommerspiele.

Sydney Opera House 2000: Jørn Utzon arbeitet wieder an der Sydney Oper. 32 Jahre, nachdem er Australien verlassen und die Sydney Oper unfertig zurücklassen mußte, unterzeichnet Jørn Utzon 1999 wieder einen Vertrag mit der Regierung von New South Wales.

Eine einzigartige Situation in der Architekturgeschichte des 20. Jahrhunderts und für ein Projekt, das trotz seines tragischen Scheiterns zu einem internationalen Symbol neuer Architektur geworden ist.

Utzon wird als Konsulent ein „Statement of Design Principles" erstellen, das als Referenz für zukünftige Renovierungsarbeiten der Sydney Oper dienen soll. Technologische Entwicklungen heutigen Standards, verbunden mit seiner ursprünglichen Vision dieses Opernhauses, sollen dem australischen Architekturbüro DCM als Grundlage für die Ausarbeitung eines 25jährigen Masterplanes dienen. Die Kosten dieses Masterplans für Renovierungsarbeiten im Gebäudeinneren belaufen sich laut Schätzungen auf über 66 Millionen Australische Dollar.

Als Partner und Sohn wird Jan Utzon in Sydney die Ausführung überwachen.

2001 soll mit den Arbeiten begonnen werden, die vor allem eine Akustikoptimierung der großen und kleinen Halle, eine Vergrößerung der Orchestergraben im Opernsaal, Behindertenzugänge sowie mobile Außenbühnen mit Sitzen und Service für Freiluftevents umfassen.

Erwogen wird auch eine Serienproduktion einzelner Möblierungsvorschläge Utzons aus den siebziger Jahren sowie eine Neugestaltung der Glasfassaden nach Originalplänen.

Drei Männer sind für Utzons späte Rückkehr verantwortlich: Premierminister Bob Carr, Joseph Skrzynski, Vorsitzender des Opera House Trusts, und Richard Johnson, Vorstand von DCM, Denton Corker Marshall Architekten. Am 23.10.1998 richtet Premierminister Carr eine briefliche Anfrage an Utzon, die von Richard Johnson persönlich überbracht wird: „Meine Regierung teilt die Meinung der Bevölkerung von Sydney, die rückblickend auf die Umstände Ihres Abgangs vor 32 Jahren ein tiefes Gefühl des Verlusts und des Bedauerns empfindet. Vor allem bedauern wir, daß der Architekt, der dieses großartige Projekt entwickelt hatte, nicht hier war, um es fertigzustellen. Obwohl das Opernhaus über Jahrhunderte hinweg Bestand haben wird, so wird es zweifellos notwendig sein, das Innere von Zeit zu Zeit aus technischen und funktionellen Gründen zu erneuern oder zu verändern. Für diese Aufgaben, in Verbindung mit allen Arbeiten, die von zukünftigen Regierungen unternommen werden, wäre die Erfassung einer umfangreichen und dauerhaften Darstellung der Entwurfsprinzipien sehr hilfreich. Es ist uns ein großes Anliegen, daß ein solches ‚Statement of Design Principles' Ihrer Vision gerecht wird und Ihren Zuspruch findet."[1]

Sydney 2000

Sydney 2000: the whole world is looking to Sydney, the host for the Olympic Summer Games.

Sydney Opera House 2000: once again, Jørn Utzon is working on this building. Thirty-two years after leaving Australia and having to turn his back on the unfinished Sydney Opera House, Jørn Utzon signed another contract with the government of New South Wales in 1999.

A unique situation in the history of twentieth-century architecture especially for a project that has become an international symbol of new architecture despite its tragic failure.

In the role of consultant, Utzon will draft a "Statement of Design Principles" as a guide for future renovations to the Sydney Opera House. Current technology in combination with Utzon's original vision for this opera house will provide the basis for Australian architects DCM to develop a twenty-five-year master plan. The costs for this master plan for renovations to the building's interior are estimated at over 66 million Australian dollars.

The architect's son, Jan Utzon, will supervise the execution in Sydney as a partner. The work is scheduled to begin in 2001, comprising optimizations to the acoustics in the large and small halls, expanding the orchestra pit in the opera hall, installing wheelchair access as well as mobile external stages with seating and service installations for open-air events.

A series production of Utzon's customized furniture designs from the 1970s is under consideration, as is a redesign of the glass façades according to the original plans.

Three men are responsible for Utzon's return after so many years: Prime Minister Bob Carr, Joseph Skrzynski, the chair of the Opera House Trust, and Richard Johnson, chair of DCM, Denton Corker Marshall Architects.

On 23 October 1998, Prime Minister Carr issued a statement to Utzon, which was personally delivered by Richard Johnson. In it, Carr stated: "My Government shares in the view of the people of Sydney, who feel a sense of profound loss and regret when recalling the circumstances of your departure 32 years ago. We regret, especially, that the architect who conceived this great project was not here to complete it. It is clear that, while the Opera House will stand for centuries to come, its interiors will from time to time need renewal or modification for technical and functional reasons. These tasks, together with any other work undertaken by future governments, will be greatly assisted by the development of a comprehensive and enduring statement of design principles. It is our fervent wish that such a statement of principle should faithfully reflect your vision and meet with your approval." [1]

Der große Plan

Bald nach dem Zweitem Weltkrieg entstand der Plan, in Sydney ein „Haus der Kultur" zu schaffen, das allen Einwohnern Sydneys offenstehen sollte. Großer Befürworter dieser Idee war Eugene Goossens, britischer Dirigent des Sydney Symphony Orchestras, der seine beliebten Aufführungen nur im Rathaus zeigen konnte. Starkes Interesse kam auch von Charles Moses, General Manager der Fernsehkommission des australischen Fernsehsenders ABC. Trotz der Rezession und der hohen Arbeitslosigkeit greift John Joseph Cahill, Premierminister von New South Wales 1955 schließlich die Anliegen auf und gründet das „Opera House Committee" (OHC)[2], das Standort und Inhalt des Hauses festlegen soll. Noch im September desselben Jahres schreibt das OHC einen internationalen Wettbewerb für ein „National Opera House" aus, das neben Opern auch Theater, Konzerte und Kongresse beherbergen sollte. Der Standort: Bennelong Point, eine kleine Landzunge mitten im Hafen Sydneys, Ort einer aufgelassenen Remise.

Die Architekten-Jury verkündet am 29. Januar 1957 aus 234 Einreichungen und 30 verschiedenen Ländern das Siegerprojekt. In der Jury sind zwei internationale Granden vertreten: John Leslie Martin, Professor für Architektur in Cambridge, und Eero Saarinen, finnischer Architekt, tätig in Michigan/USA. Der Legende folgend, stößt Saarinen erst Tage später zur Jury und zieht aus den bereits ausgeschiedenen Projekten den Entwurf von Jørn Utzon mit den Worten hervor: „Meine Herren, hier haben Sie Ihr Opernhaus!"[3]. Und so sollte es auch kommen[4]: Der erst 38jährige dänische Architekt Jørn Utzon gewinnt den Wettbewerb. Sein Projekt überzeugt die Jury, obwohl er in wichtigen Punkten die Wettbewerbsauflagen mißachtet. In einem Report der Jury heißt es: „Seiner Originalität wegen ist es sicherlich ein umstrittener Entwurf. Allerdings sind wir von seinen Vorzügen vollkommen überzeugt."[5] Einzigartig an seinem Entwurf ist die Platzierung der beiden Säle. Er stellt sie nebeneinander, wodurch beide von der Stadt aus sichtbar sind und sich ihrerseits zum Wasser hin öffnen. Die Plattform sieht Utzon als eigenes architektonisches Element und greift dabei die Idee der Aztekenbauten auf, bei denen die Plattform des Tempels zugleich auch das Fundament darstellt. Die Präsentation seines außergewöhnlichen Entwurfs löst bei der internationalen und nationalen Presse sowohl Euphorie wie scharfe Kritik aus.

Sydney 1956 mit Bauplatz
Bennelong Point (links)
Wettbewerbsentwurf 1957:
Auditorien und Skizze (rechts)
Zeitungsartikel aus "Woman's Day with Woman" vom 18.2.1957

Sydney, 1956 - building site
Bennelong Point (left page)
competition entry 1957:
plans and sketch (right page)
newspaper article from "Woman's Day with Woman", 18.2.1957

60

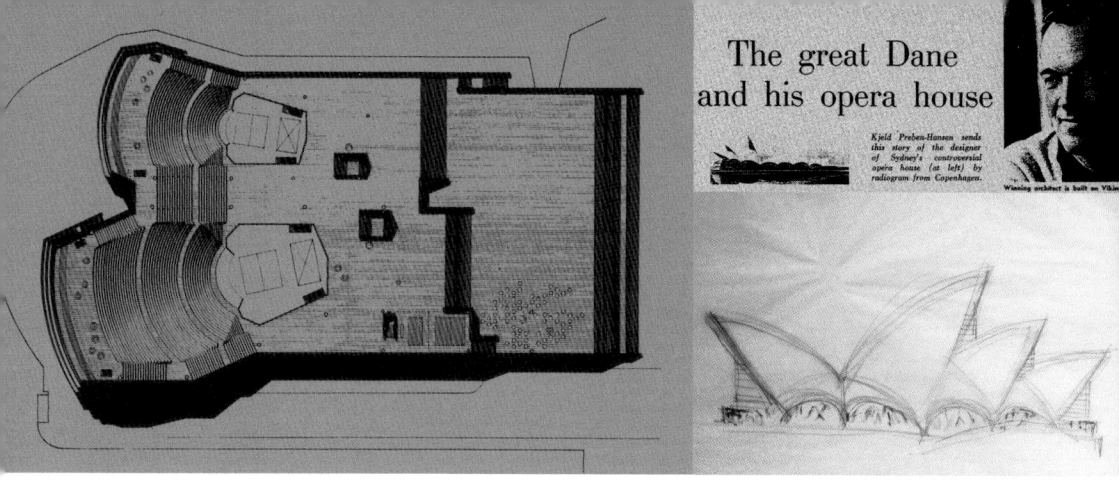

The great Dane
and his opera house

Kjeld Preben-Hansen sends
this story of the designer
of Sydney's controversial
opera house (at left) by
radiogram from Copenhagen.

Winning architect is built on Viking-

The Great Plan

Soon after the Second World War, the plan for a "House of Culture" open to all inhabitants of Sydney was born. Eugene Goossens, the British conductor of the Sydney Symphony Orchestra, whose only venue for his popular performances was the town hall, was one of the main supporters of this idea. Strong interest was also expressed by Charles Moses, directing manager of the television commission of the Australian broadcasting station ABC. Despite recession and high unemployment rates, Joseph Cahill, Prime Minister of New South Wales, responded to these ideas in 1955 by founding the "Opera House Committee" (OHC)[2], whose mandate it was to determine the site and programme of the house.

In September of the same year the OHC tenders an international competition for a "National Opera House" to be a venue for theatre, concerts and conventions, in addition to opera. The chosen site: Bennelong Point, a small peninsula in the middle of Sydney's harbour, the site of a disused shed.

On 29 January 1957, the jury of architects announced the winning project chosen from 234 competition entries from 30 different countries. The jury includes two international stars in the field: John Leslie Martin, professor of architecture at Cambridge and Eero Saarinen, Finnish architect, active in Michigan, USA. Legend has it that Saarinen joined the jury days late and pulled Jørn Utzon's design from the stack of projects that had already been rejected with the words: "Gentlemen, here is your opera house!"[3] Prophetic words as it turned out[4]: the young Danish architect Jørn Utzon, just thirty-eight years old, won the competition.

His project convinces the jury although he ignores important points in the competition specifications. A report by the jury states: "Because of its originality, it is clearly a controversial design. We are, however, absolutely convinced about its merits."[5] His plan for the placement of the two halls is unique. He sets them side by side, making them both visible from the city and open to the water. Utzon interprets the platform as an autonomous architectural element, an idea he borrowed from Aztec buildings in which the temple platform doubled as foundation. The presentation of his unconventional design unleashes euphoria as well as sharp criticism in the national and international press.

„Das ist reine Sensationsgier, sonst nichts. Dieses Projekt hat für Australien keine Relevanz. Das ist kein Opernhaus, sondern nur eine Muschel."
(Frank Lloyd Wright, in: Françoise Fromonot, Jørn Utzon, The Sydney Opera House)

"It's sensationalism and nothing else. This project has no significance for Australia, it isn't an opera house, it's only a shell."
(Frank Lloyd Wright, in: Françoise Fromonot, Jørn Utzon, The Sydney Opera House)

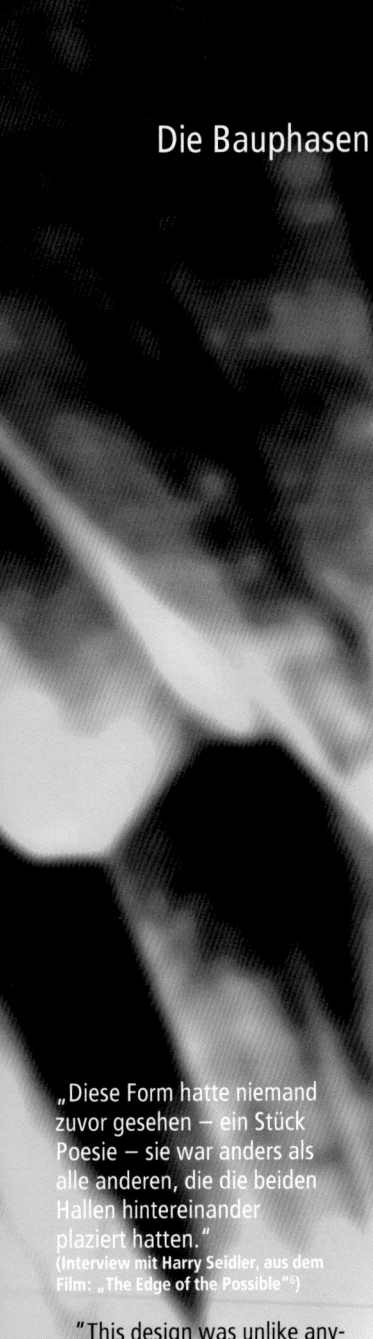

Die Bauphasen

„Diese Form hatte niemand zuvor gesehen – ein Stück Poesie – sie war anders als alle anderen, die die beiden Hallen hintereinander plaziert hatten."
(Interview mit Harry Seidler, aus dem Film: „The Edge of the Possible"[6])

"This design was unlike anything else – a piece of poetry – it was different from all the others, which had placed the halls one behind the other."
(Interview with Harry Seidler in the documentary "The Edge of the Possible"[6])

Schon im Vorfeld zeichnet sich eine starke Opposition gegen das Vorhaben ab, da dringendst Mittel für Wohn- und Schulbau benötigt werden und man sich gegen die Schaffung einer Oper für eine „kulturelle Elite" ausspricht. Eine erste Kostenschätzung von sieben Millionen Australischen Dollar wird veröffentlicht und scheint das Projekt ernsthaft zu gefährden. Diese Schätzung wird von einem – von der Regierung beauftragten – Baukostenkalkulator auf Basis des Wettbewerbsentwurfs erstellt und war schon damals eine rein fiktive politische Zahl, die einzig die Fragen der Finanzierbarkeit beantworten sollte. J.J. Cahill vermag nur knapp eine Zustimmung der Staatsregierung zu erreichen. Er versichert, keinerlei zusätzliche staatliche Mittel zu verwenden. Die Finanzierung soll sich wie folgt zusammensetzen: Neben einem einmaligen Zuschuß des Staates sowie Zuschüssen der Stadt Sydney und der ABC soll eine eigens für diesen Zweck ins Leben gerufene staatliche Lotterie die Baukosten abdecken.

Das Opera House Committee beschließt, den Bau in drei Abschnitte zu unterteilen: Phase I: Bauplatz und Plattform; Phase II: Gebäude und Dachkonstruktion; Phase III: Ausbauarbeiten (Glasfassaden, Innengestaltung, Auditorien etc). Als Eröffnungstermin wird der 26. Januar 1963 festgelegt.

Laut Vertrag soll Utzon sämtliche Konsulenten selbst wählen. Bei der Wahl des Statikers wird ihm jedoch von mehreren Seiten nahegelegt, mit einer Firma von internationalem Rang wie Ove Arup & Partners, London, oder Christiani & Nielsen, Kopenhagen, zusammenzuarbeiten. Utzon fährt nach London und findet in Ove Arup einen Bewunderer seines Projekts und einen Freund – zumindest für die folgenden Jahre.

Ove Arup & Partners sind wie Utzon selbst direkt der Regierung von New South Wales unterstellt. Da in den Phasen I und II der Schwerpunkt auf der statischen Konstruktion liegt, erhalten Ove Arup & Partners die Verantwortung für Vertragserfüllung und Arbeitspläne. Erst für Phase III – die hauptsächlich „architektonisch" ist – sollen die Statiker die übliche Rolle als Konsulenten des Architekten einnehmen. Diese Vorgehensweise ist auch in Australien völlig unüblich und ergibt eine unklar definierte Kompetenzaufteilung, die später auch einer der Hauptgründe sein wird, an dem die Zusammenarbeit scheitern wird.

Phase I

J.J.Cahill setzt, entgegen den Warnungen des Statikers und des Architekten, einen frühen Baubeginn durch. Eine politische Entscheidung, die später noch viel Geld kosten wird, da einerseits die geologischen Gutachten unzureichend sind und andererseits noch keine statische Lösung für die Umsetzung von Utzons Entwurf der Dachkonstruktion vorliegt.

Am 2. März 1959 findet die Grundsteinlegung statt. Sieben Monate später stirbt Cahill.

Erst 1961 kann die statische Frage der Dachkonstruktion gelöst werden – mit dem Ergebnis, daß das Fundament verstärkt werden muß. Phase I wird 1963 abgeschlossen.

Even during the preliminary phase there is strong opposition to the project, as money is desperately needed for social housing and schools, and the creation of an opera is denounced as serving a "cultural elite". A preliminary estimate of 7 million Australian dollars is published and the entire project seems at risk. The estimate is drawn up by a government-appointed assessor of construction costs. Even at the time of its publication, this is a purely fictional figure, politically motivated with the sole purpose of answering to questions of financial feasibility. Cahill manages to gain a narrow majority in the national government. He promises not to use additional public money. The financing plan is as follows: in addition to a one-time state subsidy as well as subsidies from the city of Sydney and ABC, the national broadcaster, a state lottery, founded specifically for this project, is to cover the construction costs.

The Opera House Committee decides to divide the construction into three phases: Phase I – site and platform; Phase II – building and roof construction; Phase III – finishing work (glass façades, interior, auditoriums etc.). 26 January 1963, is chosen as the inauguration date.

The contract authorizes Utzon to select all the necessary consultants. But when it comes to choosing a structural engineer, several parties advise him to collaborate with a firm of international stature, such as Ove Arup & Partners, London, or Christiani & Nielsen, Copenhagen. Utzon travels to London and discovers an admirer and friend in Ove Arup – at least for the coming years.

Like Utzon, Ove Arup & Partners answer directly to the government of New South Wales. Since the focus during phases I and II is on the structural construction, Ove Arup & Partners are given the responsibility of fulfilling the contract and producing the work plans. Only for Phase III – when the focus is "architectural" – will the structural engineers take on the usual role of consultants to the architect. This approach is completely unknown even in Australia and leads to a poorly defined division of responsibilities, which will later become one of the main causes for the collapse of the collaboration.

Phase I

Against the advice of the structural engineer and the architect, J. J. Cahill insists upon an early construction start. A political decision that will cost dearly in the future, for the geological expert reports are insufficient and there is no static solution on the table for how to implement Utzon's design of the roof structure.

The foundation stone was laid on 2 March 1959 and Cahill died seven months later.

A structural solution for the roof was not found until 1961, with the result that the foundation had to be reinforced. Phase I was finally completed in 1963.

Phase II

For four years, from 1957 to 1961, Ove Arup & Partners worked on the structural implementation of what was then a completely new form of roof for the two halls.

Utzon's proposal, a type of shell, creates problems because – based

The Building Phases

Baustellenbesichtigung: Jørn Utzon und H. Ingham Ashworth,
Südansicht aus dem „Roten Buch" –
ein 1958 entstandenes, Cahill gewidmetes Portfolio des Projektes mit Skizzen, Plänen und begleitenden Texten.[7]

Site visit: Jørn Utzon and H. Ingham Ashworth
South elevation from the 1958 "Red book"–
a portfolio of the project with sketches, plans and accompanying text, which was dedicated to Cahill.[7]

Phase II

Vier Jahre, von 1957 bis 1961, arbeiten Ove Arup & Partners an der statischen Umsetzung der damals neuartigen Dachformen der beiden Hallen. Utzons Vorschlag, eine Art Muschelform, stößt auf Probleme, da man – ausgehend von seinen Skizzen – rechnerisch nicht auf eine regelmäßige Geometrie (regular geometry) kommt. Peter Rice, damals im Büro von Ove Arup tätig, entwickelt die ersten Computerprogramme für die geometrischen Berechnungen. Aber keiner der Vorschläge, die zwar technisch machbar, aber finanziell noch völlig ungelöst sind, genügt Utzons Ansprüchen.

Im Herbst 1961 ist es Utzon selbst, der auf die sphärische Lösung stößt: Sämtliche Oberflächen der Muschelform werden aus einer einzigen Kugel kalkuliert. Die Kalotten lassen sich wie bei einer geviertelten Orange herausnehmen, sind somit geometrisch identisch und können problemlos berechnet und vorfabriziert werden.

Utzon: „Über lange Zeit hinweg fuhren wir zweispurig, (aber im Laufe) der letzten sechs Monate wurde eine wirklich ideale Lösung für alle technischen und ästhetischen Fragen entwickelt, und darüber hinaus war es sogar die billigste Art der Realisierung, die man sich erträumen könnte."[8]

Arups Büro investierte 375.000 Arbeitsstunden in die Entwicklung der mathematischen Lösung.

Mogens Prip-Buus, ein Mitarbeiter Utzons meinte: „Die Erfindung der sphärischen Bögen war für uns vergleichbar mit der Erkenntnis, daß die Erde rund statt flach ist."[9]

Anfang 1963 wird mit der Produktion der Rippenelemente begonnen, und im Herbst wird der erste Bogen errichtet. Die Regierung bewilligt in einem Zusatz zum „Sydney Opera House Act"[10] von 1960 die Budgeterhöhung auf 25 Millionen Australische Dollar.

Für die Verkleidung der Muscheln wählt Utzon einen Kontrast zum Blau des Meeres. Utzon: „Ein Dach aus weißen Fließen unterstreicht den plastischen Charakter des Gebäudes."[11] Die schwedische Firma Höganäs entwickelt nach 3jähriger Forschung eine Keramik, die dem geforderten Oberflächeneffekt entspricht: glänzend, jedoch ohne Spiegeleffekt.

Jørn Utzon erstellt das „Gelbe Buch" für seinen Bauherrn. Es dokumentiert die Suche nach der statischen Umsetzung der Muschelform und erklärt eingehend die sphärische Lösung.

Jørn Utzon issues the "Yellow Book" for his client. It documents the search for a structural implementation of the shell form and explains the spherical solution in detail.

64

on the sketches – it is impossible to calculate a regular geometry. Peter Rice, then at Ove Arup's firm, develops the first computer programs for geometrical calculations. But none of the suggestions, which are technically feasible but financially still unsolved, satisfy Utzon's demands.

In the autumn of 1961, Utzon himself hit on the spherical solution: calculating all surfaces of the shell from a single sphere. The spherical vaults were extruded in the manner of a quartered orange, and were geometrically identical, easily calculable and simple to prefabricate.

Utzon: "We were riding two horses for a long time (but over) the last six months the real ideal solution for everything was developed technically and aesthetically and it was even the cheapest way of making it you could dream of."[8]

Arup's firm invested 375,000 man-hours in the development of the mathematical solution.

Mogens Prip-Buus, a member of Utzon's team, commented: "The invention of the spherical vaults was, for us, rather like the transition from thinking of the earth as flat to thinking of it as round."[9]

Production of the rib elements began in early 1963 and in the autumn of the same year the first vault was erected. In an amendment to the "Sydney Opera House Act"[10] from 1960, the government approved a budget increase of 25 million Australian dollars.

For the cladding of the shells Utzon selects a colour that will contrast with the blue of the sea. Utzon: "A roof of white tiles would emphasize the sculptural character of the building."[11] After three years of research, the Swedish firm Höganäs develops a ceramic tile that delivers the required surface effect: glossy, yet non-reflective.

Phase III

For the façade, Utzon develops a system of overlapping glass panels, supported by a jointed plywood structure that is stretched between the roof structure and the foundations like a light-weight membrane. In collaboration with the Australian firm Ralph Symonds Ltd, Utzon develops a method of using plywood in this manner for the glass façade and also for the interior panelling of the hallways and auditoriums.

Von links nach rechts:
Baustelle 1964 (links) und 1966 (Mitte),
Präsentationsmodell für die sphärische Lösung der Muschelform,
Untersicht – Große Halle

From left to right:
Construction site, 1964 (left) and 1966 (middle)
Presentation model for the spherical forms of the vaults,
Superstructure of the Major Hall

Baukalender

Construction Schedule

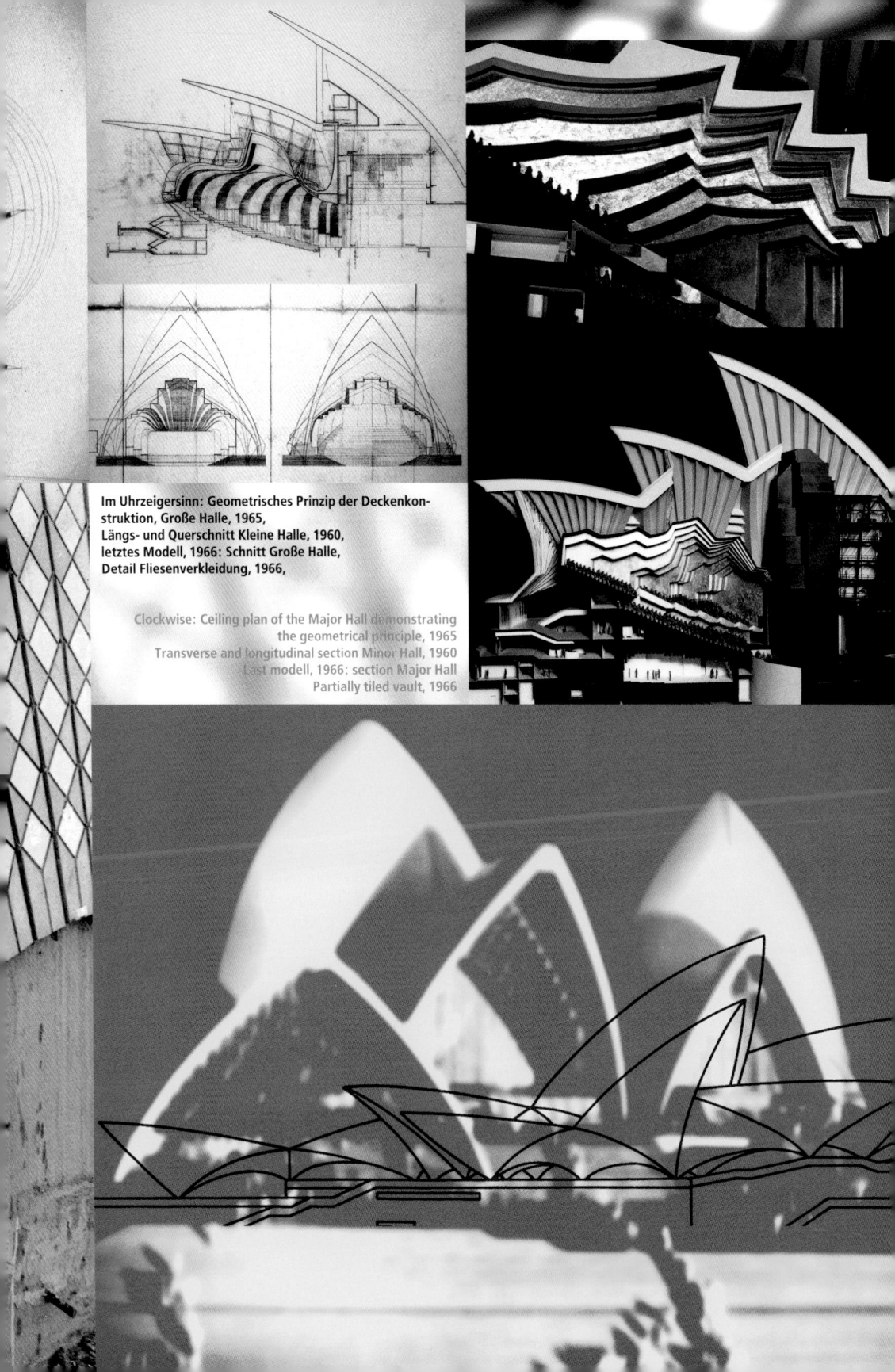

Im Uhrzeigersinn: Geometrisches Prinzip der Deckenkonstruktion, Große Halle, 1965,
Längs- und Querschnitt Kleine Halle, 1960,
letztes Modell, 1966: Schnitt Große Halle,
Detail Fliesenverkleidung, 1966,

Clockwise: Ceiling plan of the Major Hall demonstrating
the geometrical principle, 1965
Transverse and longitudinal section Minor Hall, 1960
Last modell, 1966: section Major Hall
Partially tiled vault, 1966

Alle gegen einen

Phase III

Für die Fassade des Gebäudes entwickelt Utzon ein System von einander überlappenden Glaspaneelen, die durch eine gelenkige Sperrholzkonstruktion getragen werden, die wie eine leichte Membran zwischen Dachkonstruktion und Sockel eingespannt ist. Gemeinsam mit der australischen Firma Ralph Symonds Ltd. arbeitet Utzon an dieser Anwendung von Sperrholz sowohl für die Glasfassade als auch für die Innenverkleidung der Korridore und Auditorien.

Aus Gründen der Symbolik sowie des Lärmschutzes will Utzon das Bühnengeschehen von der Außenwelt abkoppeln und hängt beide Säle (Oper und Konzert) von der Dachkonstruktion ab. Für die Akustik der beiden Säle verläßt sich Utzon wieder auf den Vorteil von Geometrie und Vorfertigung. Er entwickelt ein System aus großen aneinandergereihten Sperrholzträgern, die die Hülle strukturieren und den Innenraum in Abstimmung mit der optimalen Akustik modellieren. Die Balken sollen unter die Kalotten gebracht und vor Ort „wie ein überdimensionales Puzzle" zusammengesetzt werden. Akustische Tests der Modelle weisen außergewöhnliche Ergebnisse auf.

Als Dekorationen der Balkensegmente sind für die große Halle konzentrische und für die kleine Halle strahlenförmige Motive vorgesehen. Das letzte Modell von Anfang 1966 dokumentiert, daß Utzon farbige, lebhafte Auditorien plante, die einen scharfen Kontrast zum Sichtbeton der Kalotten darstellen: rote und goldene für die große Halle; blaue und silberfarbige für die kleine.

Sämtliche Originalpläne zu Phase III befinden sich heute im Mitchell-Library-Archiv in Sydney.

Es sind viele Bücher, Artikel und Statements über die Sydney Oper und Jørn Utzons Scheitern geschrieben und gleich viele Theorien über Ursache, Wirkung und Schuldzuweisungen entwickelt worden. Wir können heute nur die Kernpunkte jenes Konfliktes aufzeigen, der Jørn Utzon schließlich dazu veranlaßt hat, sein bis heute architektonisch bedeutendstes Projekt zu verlassen:

Utzon übersiedelt 1963 mit seiner ganzen Familie nach Sydney, wo er die längste Zeit als Celebrity gefeiert wird. Doch nach und nach wenden sich Architekten, Bauunternehmer, Presse, die (neue) Regierung von New South Wales und das Statikerteam von Ove Arup gegen ihn. Zunächst verursacht Phase I aufgrund der falschen geologischen Gutachten und des verfrühten Baubeginns einen finanziellen Mehraufwand von 12 Millionen Australischen Dollar. Obwohl für sämtliche Kostenschätzungen ein von der Regierung beauftragter Baukostenkalkulator verantwortlich ist und die Projektverantwortung für die beiden ersten Phasen beim Büro Ove Arup liegt, gibt man Utzon im nachhinein die Schuld für die mißliche Lage. Die Vorwürfe kommen schleichend und für Jørn Utzon völlig überraschend. Während er sich stets auf der fieberhaften und kompromißlosen Suche nach der Ideallösung befindet — immer nur das erhabene Ziel des architektonischen Meisterwerks vor Augen —, wird er zum Sündenbock für die Kosten-

Utzon's aim is to isolate the auditoriums from the external skin for symbolic reasons and to create a sound barrier, and he suspends both halls (opera and concert) from the roof structure. For the acoustics of both halls, Utzon once again relies on the advantages of geometry and prefabrication. He develops a system of large, aligned plywood girders that structure the hall and mould the interior into an optimum shape for acoustics. The girders are to be placed beneath the spherical vaults and assembled on site "like an oversized puzzle". Acoustic tests deliver extraordinary results.

The girder sections will be decorated with concentric patterns in the large hall and with star-shaped motifs in the small hall. The final model from 1966 documents that Utzon envisioned the halls in bright and lively colours, in striking contrast to the exposed concrete of the spherical vaults: red and gold for the large hall; blue and silver for the small hall.

All original plans for Phase III are now housed in the Mitchell Library Archive in Sydney.

Many books, articles and statements have been written about the Sydney Opera and Jørn Utzon's failure and just as many theories have been developed about cause, effect and blame. Today, all we can do is to lay bare the key factors of the conflict that ultimately led Jørn Utzon to abandon the most important architectural project of his career.

Utzon moved to Sydney with his entire family in 1963 and was fêted for a long time as a celebrity.

One by one, however, architects, developers, the press, the (new) government of New South Wales and Ove Arup's team of structural engineers began to turn against him.

To begin with, Phase I comes at the price of an additional 12 million Australian dollars because of incorrect geological reports and the precipitous start of construction. Although a government-appointed cost assessor is responsible for all cost estimates, and although project responsibility lies with the firm of Ove Arup for the first two construction phases, Utzon is later blamed for this unfortunate situation. The accusations are voiced surreptitiously, taking Jørn Utzon completely by surprise. While committed to a feverish and uncompromising quest for the ideal solution – completely focused on the lofty goal of his architectural masterpiece – the architect doesn't realize that he is being made the scapegoat for the cost explosion and the stagnation of the project and is unprepared to defend himself.

In hindsight, there has been much speculation whether the countless changes to the plans were indeed caused by Utzon's perfectionism or, rather, by the frequent changes in the OHC's specifications for the spatial programme. Regardless of the truth, not a single design for Phase III was ever realized.

In the preceding years, the opposition had increased gradually in numbers and strength. During the preparations for Phase III, things deteriorated into an open conflict. As a result of the change of power

All Against One

Kostenschätzungen (in AUD):

Juni 1957	7.200.000
April 1958	9.625.000
Januar 1959	9.760.000
Oktober 1961	17.940.000
August 1962	27.500.000
April 1964	34.809.000
Juli 1965	48.400.000

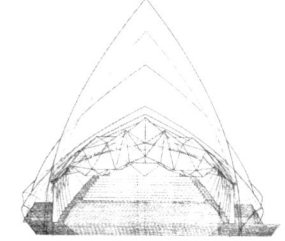

Cost estimates (in AUD):

June 1957	7,200,000
April 1958	9,625,000
January 1959	9,760,000
October 1961	17,940,000
August 1962	27,500,000
April 1964	34,809,000
July 1965	48,400,000

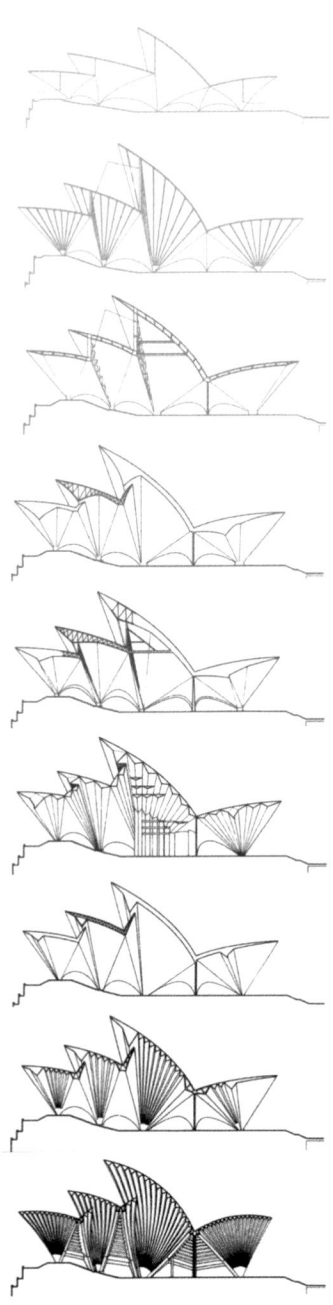

explosion und die Stagnation des Projektes gestempelt, ohne dies selbst rechtzeitig zu bemerken und Gegenmaßnahmen ergreifen zu können.

Hinterher wurde auch viel darüber spekuliert, ob die ständigen Änderungen der Pläne eher Utzons Streben nach Perfektion oder den oft wechselnden Vorgaben der OHC an das Raumprogramm zuzuschreiben waren. Tatsache ist, daß kein einziger Entwurf von Phase III umgesetzt wurde.

Während sich in den Jahren zuvor nur langsam eine stärker werdende Opposition gebildet hatte, bricht der Streit während der Vorbereitung zu Phase III offen aus. Durch den Regierungswechsel verliert Utzon seinen politischen Rückhalt, und das australische Statikerteam von Ove Arup schien nicht gewillt zu sein, mit Utzon unterzugehen.

Utzon verläßt 1967 das Land – mit vielen Vorwürfen beladen. Die einen meinten, ihm sei sein Projekt brutal entzogen worden, während andere davon sprachen, Utzon hätte aufgegeben.

Utzons Streben nach der perfekten Lösung

Utzons Arbeitsmethode wurzelte in der europäischen Tradition, mit ausgewählten Firmen neue Produkte und Produktionsweisen zu entwickeln, und nicht über vorab detaillierte Studien, einer abgeschlossenen Planung und anschließende Ausschreibungen zu einem Produkt zu gelangen.

Diese Vorgehensweise entspricht aber nicht den australischen Ausschreibungs- und Baubedingungen und bescherte ihm immer wieder Probleme. So bleibt die schwedische Firma Höganäs für die eigens entwickelten Fliesen trotz Ausschreibung Bestbieter, worauf australische Firmen Gerüchte über unlauteren Wettbewerb in Umlauf bringen. Für die Verkleidung der Plattform sucht Utzon zuerst vergeblich nach einem Naturstein. Schließlich entwickelt die australische Firma Concrete Industries nach 30 verschiedenen Mustern einen passenden Kunststein. Die ebenfalls australische Firma Ralph Symonds Ltd. war weltweit der einzige Produzent, der die gewünschten Sperrholzbalken in einer Länge von 15-22 Metern herstellen konnte. In beiden Fällen wird der Wahl des Architekten vom Bauherrn nicht mehr stattgegeben.

Noch 1996 schrieb Utzon in einem Brief an Ralph Symonds Sohn, Ken: „Kein anderer Sperrholzproduzent der Welt konnte diese schwierigen Elemente in der Qualität herstellen, die ich wollte. Es war ein Wunder! Wenn man bedenkt, daß wir bis nach Schweden gehen mußten, um die richtige Qualität für eine Million Keramikfliesen für die Verkleidung der Kalotten zu bekommen. Oder daß wir für eine geeignete Bühnentechnik erst in Österreich fündig wurden."[12]

Der Bruch mit der Regierung

Bereits 1962 startet die Oppositionspartei unter Robert Askin (Liberal Party) ihre Kampagne gegen die Oper. Sie verlangt die Einsetzung einer Kontrollinstanz, um die steigenden Kosten und die Projektorganisation zu überwachen. Dabei kann sie vermehrt auf die Unterstützung der Presse zählen. Bereits am 15.Oktober 1962 titelt zum Beispiel der Mirror „Opernhaus Monstrosität", „Werft sie in den Hafen". Die Labour

Verschiedene Lösungsansätze für die Dachform von 1957 – 1963 (Ove Arup & Partners)

Different roof solutions from 1957–1963 (Ove Arup & Partners)

in government, Utzon lost his political support and the Australian team of engineers at Ove Arup seemed determined not to sink with him.

Utzon left the country in 1967 – under a heavy cloud of many accusations. Some felt that his project had been ruthlessly wrenched from his control, others commented that Utzon had simply thrown in the towel.

Utzon's Quest for the Perfect Solution

Utzon's working method was rooted in the European tradition of developing new products and production methods in collaboration with selected firms, instead of embarking on a project with detailed studies, a complete plan and subsequent commissions.

But this approach doesn't correspond to Australian conditions of competition and construction and several conflicts arise. The Swedish firm Höganäs, for example, tables the best bid for the custom-made tiles, despite an open call for tenders. Australian manufacturers respond by starting a rumour mill about unfair competition. Another example is Utzon's search for a natural stone suited for the platform covering. After thirty different trial attempts, the Australian firm Concrete Industries finally develops a suitable artificial stone. And then there is Ralph Symonds Ltd, another Australian firm, the only manufacturer in the world capable of producing the required plywood girders ranging in length from 15 to 22 metres.

In both cases, the client no longer agreed to the architect's choice. Many years later, in 1996, Utzon still maintained in a letter to Ralph Symonds' son, Ken: "No other plywood factory in the world was able to produce these difficult elements with the quality I desired. It was a miracle! Considering the fact that we had to turn all the way to Sweden to obtain the right quality of the one million ceramic tiles covering the shells. Also that we had to go to Austria for the production of the stag towers and the stage machinery..."[12]

A Parting of Ways with the Government

The opposition led by Robert Askin (Liberal Party) began its campaign against the opera as early as 1962. Voices were raised, demanding that an independent body should monitor the rising costs and the overall project organization. The opposition found increasing support in the press. One need only look at some headlines of the time: "Opera House Monstrosity", "Kick them into the harbour" (Mirror: 15 October 1962). The Labour Party refuted the accusations with the argument that the costs were covered by the successful lottery. "The money is there (...) It should enable us to get the best, no matter what the cost, and it would be disastrous to start chivying the Opera House executive into pinchpenny policies."[13]

In 1965, the power shifted from the Labour Party to a Liberal-Conservative coalition (Liberal-Country Party). Robert Askin, Liberal Party leader, entered the election campaign with the slogan "[a] policy of fixing up the Opera House" and won.[14] Robert Askin appointed Davis Hughes as Minister of Public Works. Hughes gradually seized control of the Sydney Opera from the Opera House Committee (OHC). All payments and the overall control were henceforth handled directly through

Detail Unteransicht Große Rampe
(links),
Studie für die Glasfassade aus dem
„Gelben Buch" (rechts)

Detail under the superstructure (left page)
study of the glas façade from the
"Yellow Book" (right page)

Party hält den Vorwürfen entgegen, daß die Kosten durch die gutgehende Lotterie gedeckt seien. „Geld ist vorhanden, (...). Es sollte uns ermöglichen, dafür das Beste zu bekommen, egal was es kostet, und es wäre nun wirklich ein Verhängnis, den Vorstand des OHC auf einen pfennigfuchserischen Kurs zu drängen."[13]

1965 kommt es jedoch zum Machtwechsel von der Labour-Partei zu einer Koalition liberal-konservativer Parteien (Liberal-Country Party). Robert Askin, Parteichef der Liberalen, geht mit dem Slogan „policy of fixing up the Opera House" in den Wahlkampf und gewinnt.[14]

Robert Askin ernennt Davis Hughes zum Minister für öffentliche Bauten (public works). Dieser zieht schrittweise die Kontrolle über die Sydney Oper von dem Opera House Committee (OHC) an sich. Zahlungen und Gesamtkontrolle erfolgen fortan direkt über den Minister.

Während mit der Fliesenverkleidung des Daches begonnen wird, arbeitet Utzon an der Verwendung von Sperrholz für die Fassade und die Auditorien. Er beantragt die Produktion von Prototypen für die beiden Auditorien, um anschließend die Detailplanung fertigstellen zu können. Kosten: 60.000 Australische Dollar. Es kommt zu einer Pattstellung zwischen Utzon und Hughes. Davis Hughes verlangt detaillierte Pläne der Innenausstattung und Glaswände und sieht keine Notwendigkeit für eine derartig hohe Investition. Utzon verweigert die Herausgabe von Plänen ohne vorherige Tests an Prototypen. Hughes wiederum sieht in der Nichtabgabe der Pläne einen Beweis der ineffizienten Organisation.

Im Januar 1966 übergibt das Team von Ove Arup in Sydney, allen voran Mick Lewis, der Regierung einen Report, indem es Utzons Vorschlag für die Deckenkonstruktion als unrealisierbar, unpraktikabel und zu teuer beurteilt. Sie unterbreiten einen Gegenvorschlag: Eine Stahlskelettkonstruktion mit Sperrholzverkleidung.

Gegen Ende 1965 ist die Situation zwischen Architekt und Regierung bereits so gespannt, daß die monatliche Honorarzahlung ausgesetzt wird. Nach einem Streitgespräch mit Davis Hughes entschließt sich Utzon zu jenem legendären Brief vom 28.2.1966:

„In der heutigen Sitzung (...) haben Sie erklärt, daß Sie mein Honorar für (...) die Bühnentechnik, welches ich von Ihnen während der vergangenen Monate erbeten habe und welches vollkommen gerechtfertigt ist, nicht akzeptieren können. (...) Wie ich Ihnen erklärt habe, und wie Sie auch aus Besprechungen und Diskussionen wohl wissen, fehlte es während der letzten Monate völlig an der Zusammenarbeit von Seiten Ihrer Abteilung in bezug auf die notwendigsten Dinge für diese Arbeit. Ich sehe mich somit gezwungen, die Arbeit aufzugeben, da ich klar erkenne, daß Sie mich als Architekt (des Projektes) nicht respektieren. (...)."[15] Davis Hughes reagiert noch am selben Tag: „Ich habe Ihr Rücktrittsschreiben mit tiefem Bedauern erhalten."[16] Dieser Wortlaut ergeht auch sofort an die Presse.

Am 7. März unterbreitet die Regierung Utzon noch das Angebot, eingebunden in eine straffe Hierarchie und ohne Projektverantwortung, die künstlerische Oberleitung für Phase III zu übernehmen. Utzon macht im Gegenzug das Angebot, auf die Änderungswünsche des Bauherren einzugehen, unter der Bedingung, weiterhin projektverantwortlich zu

the Minister. As work begins on the tile covering of the roof, Utzon turns his attention to the use of plywood on the façade and in the halls. He requests prototypes for both halls, to complete his detail plans. The cost: 60,000 Australian dollars. A stalemate ensues between Utzon and Hughes. Davis Hughes demands detailed plans for the interior and the glass walls and refuses to approve such a high investment. Utzon refuses to release plans without prior tests on prototypes. Hughes, in turn, interprets the failure to produce plans as proof of poor organization.

In January 1966 Ove Arup's team in Sydney, led by Mick Lewis, presented the government with a report in which Utzon's proposal for the roof structure is assessed as unrealizable, impractical and too expensive. The team made a counter-proposal: a steelframe structure with plywood cladding.

By the end of 1965, the situation between architect and government had deteriorated so severely that payment of the monthly fee was withheld. After a heated debate with Davis Hughes, Utzon decided to write the now legendary letter dated 28 February 1966:

"In the meeting (...) today, you stated that you could not accept my fee claim for (...) Stage Technique which I have requested from you for the past several months and which is completely justified. (...) As I explained to you and as you know also from meetings and discussions, there has been no collaboration on the most vital items on the job in the last many months from your Department's side, and this also forces me to leave the job as I see clearly that you do not respect me as the architect. (...)"[15] Davis Hughes responds on the same day: "I have received your letter of resignation which I deeply regret."[16]

This exchange is immediately passed on to the press.

On 7 March, the government makes Utzon the offer of accepting artistic control for phase III, albeit subject to a rigid hierarchical management structure and without any project responsibility. Utzon replies with an offer to consider the client's requests for change, but only on the condition that he continues to be responsible for the project. He receives no answer.

On 8 March, Utzon writes one last letter to the Minister:

"In my letter of February 28th, 1966, and contrary to statements made in the Press, I did not resign as architect of the Sydney Opera House. I stated that, in view of the fact that payments due to me were being withheld and that my client has withheld decisions and collaboration which are, normally, the duty of any client, I will be forced to leave the job. Your interpretation in your answer dated February 28th, 1966, to my letter is incorrect."[17]

A Media Campaign

After praising the architectonic genius of the project in the beginning, the media begin to focus on the annual rise in cost estimates and the constant delays of the completion date. Jørn Utzon is singled out as being responsible. The media contribute to his bad image and increasingly accuse him of chaotic working methods, stubbornness and a lack of organization. The election campaign of the Conservative Party in 1965 adds the final drop to the brew. With the crisis already on a

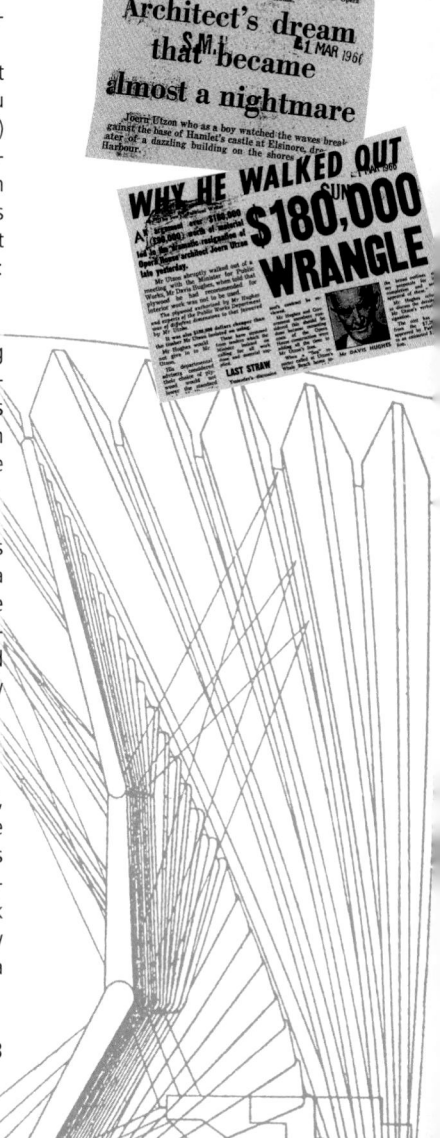

73

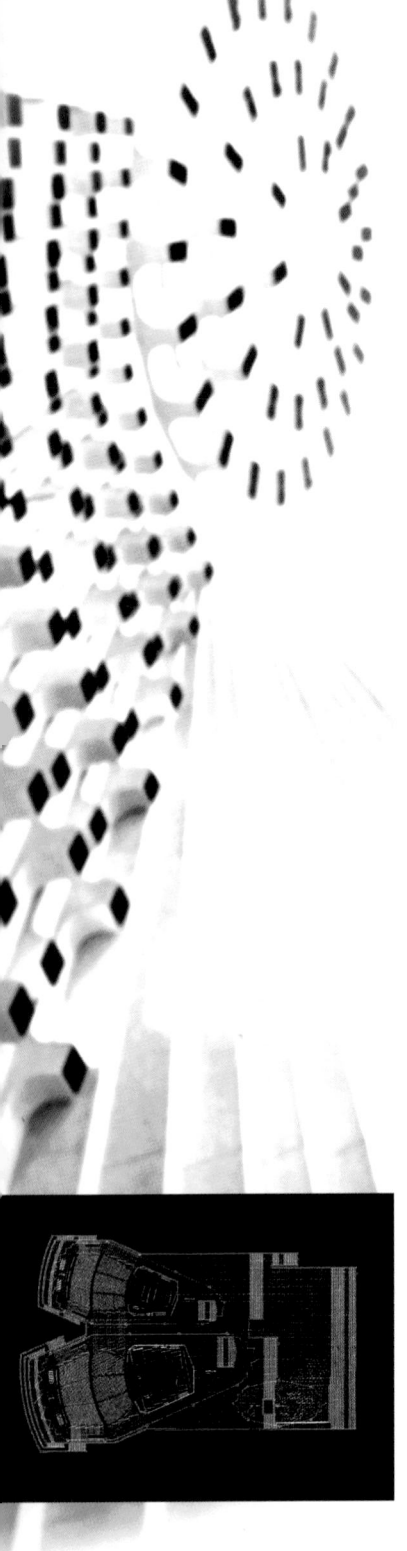

sein. Er erhält keine Antwort mehr.

Utzon schreibt dem Minister am 8.3.1966 nochmals:

„Mein Brief vom 18. Februar 1966 war – im Gegensatz zu Erklärungen in der Presse – keine Rücktrittserklärung als Architekt des Opernhauses von Sydney. Ich erklärte, daß ich mich dazu gezwungen sah, die Arbeit niederzulegen. Dies in Anbetracht der Tatsache, daß mir ausstehende Zahlungen vorenthalten wurden und daß mein Bauherr mir Entscheidungen und die Zusammenarbeit, die im Normalfall die Pflicht jedes Bauherren sind, entzog. Ihre Interpretation in Ihrer Antwort vom 28. Februar 1966 auf meinen Brief ist nicht korrekt."[17]

Medienkampagne

Nachdem die Medien anfangs die architektonische Genialität des Projektes loben, verlagern sie ihr Interesse später auf die jährlich nach oben revidierten Kostenschätzungen und den permanent nach hinten verschobenen Fertigstellungstermin. Die Hauptschuld dafür wird Jørn Utzon angelastet. Die Medien schüren sein schlechtes Image, werfen ihm zunehmend chaotische Arbeitsmethoden, Starrsinn und fehlendes Organisationstalent vor. Der Wahlkampf der konservativen Partei 1965 trägt das Seinige dazu bei. Als sich die Krise schon zuspitzt, veröffentlicht die Sunday Morning Herald Zahlen bezüglich bezahlter und noch ausstehender Honorare und Aufwendungen an Utzon, die für einen Laien exorbitant anmuten, in Wirklichkeit aber auf den üblichen Architektenhonoraren beruhen.[18] Robert Askin, Parteichef der Liberalen, bestätigt zusätzlich Pressegerüchte, wonach die endgültigen Kosten des Gebäudes 50 Millionen Australische Dollar erreichen würden.

Die Sunday Morning Herald titelt dann auch am 1. März 1966: „Why he walked out – $180.000 wrangle" („Warum er ging – ein 180.000-Dollar-Streit"). Utzon hätte gekündigt, da Davis Hughes sich weigere, die ausstehenden Honorare zu bezahlen. Im gleichen Artikel wird die große Ranch der Utzons samt Swimming Pool und Fuhrpark detailliert beschrieben.[19]

Die große Unbekannte: Ove Arup & Partners

Auch wenn das Statikerteam über die Jahre einen engen und direkten Kontakt zum Bauherrn aufgebaut hatte, bereitete diese unübliche Verteilung der Verantwortlichkeiten lange kein Problem. Ove Arup und Jørn Utzon kämpfen gemeinsam für ihre Vision – oft im Widerspruch zu den Ansichten der Partner von Ove Arup, wie beispielsweise während der Suche nach der sphärischen Lösung. Erst nach dem Umzug Utzons nach Sydney 1963 bricht der enge Kontakt mit den Ingenieuren in London ab.

Fortan entwickelt Utzon seine Ideen selber und schickt sie erst zur Ausarbeitung an das Ove-Arup-Team. Die enge Kooperation der beiden Persönlichkeiten ist damit vorbei, und Utzon beginnt zunehmend, sich mit den in Sydney ansässigen Partnern von Ove Arup auseinanderzusetzen.

Die direkte Verantwortlichkeit der Statiker gegenüber der Regierung und das gegenseitig entstandene Vertrauen stellt nun ein großes

downward spiral, the Sunday Morning Herald publishes figures that represent outstanding fees and expenses payable to Utzon. These sums seem exorbitant to the lay person, but are in fact simply based on standard architect fees.[18] Robert Askin, Liberal Party leader, confirms other rumours in the press stating that the final costs for the building are expected to reach 50 million Australian dollars.

On 1 March 1966, the Sunday Morning Herald headline reads: "Why he walked out – $180,000 wrangle" – Utzon, the article proclaims, had resigned because Davis Hughes had refused to pay outstanding fees. The same article gives a detailed account of the Utzon family ranch, complete with swimming pool and a fleet of cars.[19]

The Great Unknown: Ove Arup & Partners

Although the team of structural engineers had built a close and direct contact to the client, this unusual distribution of responsibilities posed no problems for a long time. Ove Arup and Jørn Utzon were united in their struggle for their vision – often in conflict with the view of Ove Arup's partners, as in the quest for the spherical solution. The close contact to the engineers in London ended only with Utzon's move to Sydney in 1963.

From that point forward, Utzon develops his ideas on his own, sending them to the Ove Arup team only for completion. The close collaboration between the two personalities has thus come to an end and Utzon deals increasingly with Ove Arup's partners in Sydney.

The direct line of accountability between the structural engineers and the government and the mutual trust that resulted from it, now creates a great barrier for Utzon. They (Ove Arup & Partners) pursue their own interests and file independent progress reports, such as the damaging report on the feasibility of phase III, which Mick Lewis presents to the Minister. Utzon appeals to his old friend Ove Arup: "I want your personal assistance (...) I did not engage this office for the Opera House (...) I engaged you personally (...) I have a perfect and ingenious scheme (...) I want that to be built and it needs your support (...) because your partners here do not even deal with the scheme and present an absolutely hopeless idea in a very amateurish way. (...) I would also like to inform you that the behaviour of your partners here is not professional. They are dealing directly with my client behind my back in spite of my telling them not to do so. I hope (...) that you are interested in interfering in this case. If not the situation

Hindernis für Utzon dar. Sie verfolgen ihre eigenen Interessen und erstatten ungehindert Bericht, wie zum Beispiel den vernichtenden Report zur Machbarkeitsfrage von Phase III, den Mick Lewis an den Minister schickt. Utzon appelliert daraufhin an seinen alten Freund Ove Arup: „Ich bitte um Deine persönliche Unterstützung (…) Ich habe nicht die Firma Ove Arup & Partners für das Opernhaus engagiert (…) ich habe Dich persönlich engagiert (…) Ich habe einen perfekten und genialen Entwurf (…) Ich will, daß das so gebaut wird, und dazu bedarf es Deiner Unterstützung (…) da Deine Partner hier nicht einmal auf den Entwurf näher eingehen und eine absolut hoffnungslose Idee auf höchst laienhafte Art und Weise präsentieren. (…) Darüber hinaus will ich Dir mitteilen, daß das Benehmen Deiner Partner hier unprofessionell ist. Sie agieren hinter meinem Rücken direkt mit meinem Bauherren, obwohl ich ihnen das ausdrücklich untersagte. Ich hoffe, (…) daß es Dir ein Anliegen ist, in dieser Sache einzugreifen. Falls nicht, so sehe ich mich unter Umständen gezwungen, mich von einem anderen Ingenieur beraten zu lassen, um dem Druck, den Dein Büro hier [auf mich] ausübt, zu widerstehen."[20] Aber diesmal stellt sich Ove Arup hinter seine Partner in Sydney, und Utzon erkennt – zu spät –, daß die Regierung den Statikern mehr vertraut als ihm. Erbost schreibt Utzon bereits nach seinem Rücktritt, am 16. März 1966, an Ove Arup: „(…) Aufgrund Deiner mangelnden Unterstützung und irreführenden Information glaubt der Bauherr, daß ich nichts weiter als ein Skizzenmacher bin (…)."[21]

Auch wenn Ove Arup das Sydney-Team in dieser Angelegenheit in Schutz nimmt, zeigt ein Brief an den Präsidenten der Königlichen Kammer der Architekten von NSW, M.R.A. Gilling, auch den Versuch, Utzon zurückzuholen: „Ich finde, man sollte Utzon zurückholen und ihm absolute Kontrolle über das Projekt einräumen. Wer den Entwurf kontrolliert (…), der kontrolliert die Architektur. Er wird einen ausgezeichneten Berater brauchen. Wir treten gerne freiwillig ab, falls er bessere finden kann. (…) Ich habe Mitleid mit Utzon. Ich habe [bereits] gesagt, daß er der beste Architekt ist, mit dem ich je zusammengearbeitet habe, und ich stehe dazu (…). Er ist ein äußerst sensibler Mensch und hat sehr unter den feindseligen Angriffen, einer verantwortungslosen Presse und politischen Machenschaften gelitten und die enorme Last fast alleine getragen."[22]

Nordansicht,
Untersicht Große Rampe,
Südansicht

North elevation,
under the superstructure,
South elevation

might arise that I have to take advice from another engineer in order to withstand pressure from your office here."[20] But this time Ove Arup backs his partners in Sydney and Utzon realizes — too late — that the government has more trust in the structural engineers than in him. An infuriated Utzon writes to Ove Arup on 16 March 1966, after his resignation: "(...) Because of your lack of support and misleading information, the client believes I am only a sketch maker (...)"[21]

Although Ove Arup protects the Sydney team in this matter, a letter addressed to the president of the Royal Chamber of Architects of New South Wales, M.R.A. Gilling, is proof of an attempt to bring Utzon back: "I think Utzon should be brought back and should be in complete control of the design. If you control the design (...) you control the architecture. He will need very good consultants. We will willingly stand down if he can find better ones. (...) I feel sorry for Utzon. I have said that he is the best architect I have worked with and I still say so... He is a very sensitive person and he has suffered from hostile attacks, from an irreponsible press, from political manipulations and he has carried an enormous burden almost single handed."[22]

However, the well-intentioned letter does nothing to change the fact that Utzon leaves and Arup & Partners remain. Jack Zunz, chief structural engineer of Sydney on Utzon's departure: "Utzon is a man of immense imaginative gifts. (...) But then the going got rougher and Utzon was pressed to produce drawings for the interiors. He didn't, couldn't, wouldn't have it, which way you will, and he resigned in '66, leaving behind hard feelings, chaos, controversy, but above all a shattered dream. (...) The truth is that he did walk out when information for the interiors and the glass walls was virtually non existent."[23]

Opinions are divided with regard to the feasibility and planning status of the detail drawings. To reach a definitive conclusion one would have to retrieve all the original plans from the archives and subject them to an evaluation from an independent jury.

In June 1966, Ove Arup was presented with the Royal Gold Medal for Architecture — the first to receive the award since Nervi — for his contributions to structural engineering in architecture. Since then, nearly every Ove Arup publication features the Opera House. This project allowed the London firm to win worldwide acclaim and to establish a reputation for realizing visions.

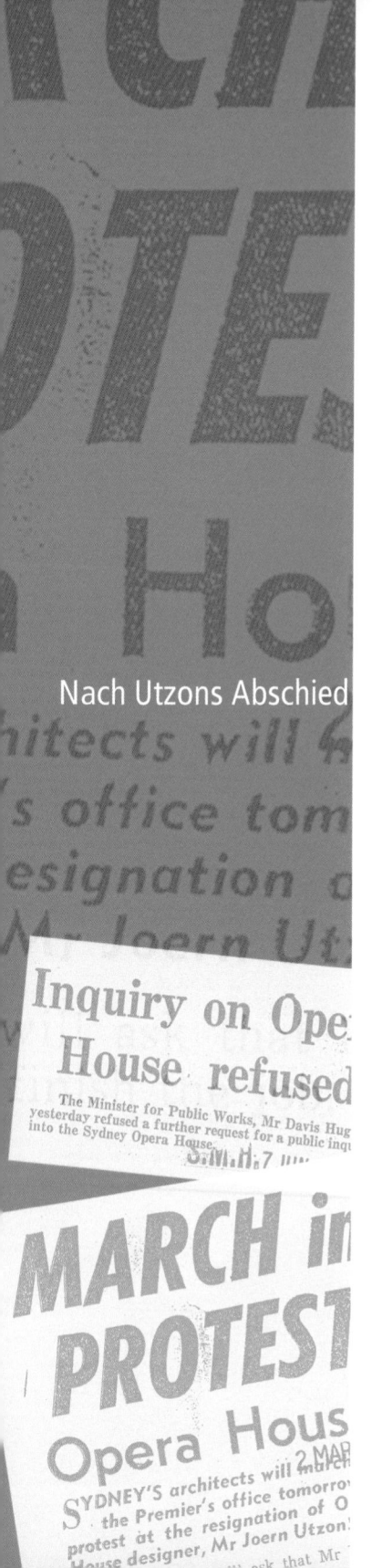

Der versöhnlich gemeinte Brief ändert aber nichts an der Tatsache, daß Utzon geht und Arup & Partners bleiben. Jack Zunz, Chefstatiker in Sydney, über Utzons Weggang: „Utzon ist ein Mann von unglaublicher Vorstellungskraft. (...) Aber dann ging's hart auf hart, und Utzon sollte Detailpläne für Innengestaltung abgeben. Er tat es nicht, konnte es nicht, wollte es einfach nicht, wie immer man das auch sehen will, und 1966 trat er zurück; er hinterließ verletzte Gefühle, Chaos, Kontroversen, vor allem aber einen zerbrochenen Traum. (...) Die Wahrheit ist, daß er zu einem Zeitpunkt ging, an dem es praktisch keinerlei Information bezüglich der Innenräume und der Glaswände gab."[23]

Bezüglich der Machbarkeit und dem Planungsstand der Detailpläne gibt es sehr unterschiedliche Auffassungen. Um eine definitve Aussage darüber zu treffen, müßten wohl alle Originalpläne aus den Archiven geholt und von einer unabhängigen Jury beurteilt werden.

Im Juni 1966 erhält Ove Arup nach Nervi die erste Royal Gold Medal for Architecture für seine Leistungen in Verbindung von Statik und Architektur. Seither ziert das Opernhaus beinahe jede Publikation von Ove Arup. Die Londoner Firma konnte mit diesem Projekt ihren Weltruhm – Visionen realisieren zu können – begründen.

Nach Utzons Abschied

Im März 1966 werden Demonstrationen, Petitionen und Unterschriftenaktionen organisiert. Harry Seidler, ein glühender Anhänger Utzons, gründet zusammen mit Peter Kollar das „Utzon-in-Charge"-Komitee und veranstaltet am 14. März ein Treffen im Rathaus, das tausende Besucher anzieht.

Das Royal Victorian Institute of Architects beschließt am 22. März 1966 eine Resolution, wonach es die Pflicht eines jedes Architekten sei, von einer Beteiligung am Projekt abzusehen, bis alle Umstände, die zu Utzons Kündigung führten, aufgeklärt seien.

Die weltbesten internationalen Architekten entfachen ein Feuer der Entrüstung und Solidarität mit Utzon. Am 29. März 1966 geht ein Brief an den Minister of Public Works of NSW, Mr. Davis Hughes: „In professionellen Kreisen ist man sehr besorgt, daß Jørn Utzon als leitender Architekt entlassen wurde. Das hervorragende Opernhaus in Sydney kann nur von Utzon selbst erfolgreich fertiggestellt werden. Das Schicksal dieses wichtigen Werkes liegt in Ihrer Hand. Die Unterzeichneten bitten Sie darum, Ihre Entscheidung zu überdenken." Namhafte Unterschriften zeichnen diesen Brief, der nie veröffentlicht wurde: Oscar Niemeyer, Lucio Costa, Brasilien; Ernst May, Hebebrand, Deutschland; Kenzo Tange, Japan; Eiler Rasmussen, Dänemark; Alvar Aalto, Finnland; Maxwell Fry, Großbritannien; Van den Brock, Van Esteren, Niederlande; Giedion, Roth, Steiger, Schweiz; Gropius, Neutra, Sert, USA etc.[24]

Die Architektenkammer von New South Wales hingegen macht der Regierung umgehend Vorschläge für Utzons Nachfolger. Am 18. März 1966 übergibt Utzon seine Pläne, und genau einen Monat später verläßt er für immer Australien. Utzon schätzte damals die verbleibende Bauzeit auf 18 Monate, die Kosten beliefen sich bis dahin auf 22 Millionen Australische Dollar.

After Utzon's Departure

In March 1966 demonstrations and petitions were organized and signatures gathered. Harry Seidler, a passionate supporter of Utzon, joined forces with Peter Kollar to found the "Utzon-in-Charge" committee, hosting an event at city hall that attracted thousands of visitors (14 March).

On 22 March of the same year, the Royal Victorian Institute of Architects passes a resolution that calls upon all architects to refrain from participating in the project until all the circumstances that led to Utzon's resignation are cleared up.

The leading architects in the world raise their voices in protest and in solidarity with Utzon. On 29 March a letter is delivered to the Minister of Public Works of NSW (New South Wales), Mr Davis Hughes: "The professional world is deeply concerned that Jørn Utzon should be dismissed as architect in charge. The outstanding Sydney Opera House can only be successfully completed by Utzon himself. The destiny of this important work lies in your hand. The undersigned ask you to reconsider your decision." This letter, never published, carries an impressive list of illustrous signatories: Oscar Niemeyer, Lucio Costa (Brazil), Ernst May, Hebebrand (Germany), Eiler Rasmussen (Denmark), Alvar Aalto (Finland), Maxwell Fry (Great Britain), Kenzo Tange (Japan), Van den Brock, Van Esteren (The Netherlands), Giedion, Roth, Steiger (Switzerland), Gropius, Neutra, Sert (United States) etc.[24] The Architects' Association of New South Wales, on the other hand, wastes no time in presenting the government with a list of names to choose Utzon's successor. Utzon hands over his plans on 18 March and leaves Australia precisely one month later.

At the time, Utzon estimated the remaining construction time to be eighteen months; the costs had risen to 22 million Australian dollars.

Obwohl er nach der Oper noch einige große Projekte umsetzte, zog er sich persönlich aus der architektonischen Öffentlichkeit zurück. Erst 25 Jahre später gibt er sein erstes großes Interview anläßlich eines Filmes von Daryl Dellora über die Geschichte des Opernhauses.[25]

Noch im April 1966 verkündet Davis Hughes Utzons Nachfolger: Eine Vereinigung von Architekten unter dem Namen Hall Todd and Littlemore[26], unter der Leitung des Regierungsarchitekten E.H. Farmer, soll das Opernhaus zu Ende führen.

Im Januar 1967 wird zwar die Fliesenverkleidung abgeschlossen, die weiteren Bauarbeiten werden aber bis zur Fertigstellung der neuen Pläne ausgesetzt.

Der Fernsehsender ABC präsentiert knapp nach Utzons Verlassen ein Papier mit spezifischen Änderungswünschen des Konzertsaals und droht im Falle der Nichtberücksichtigung, das Opernhaus nicht zu benützen. Die neuen Architekten versuchen, den Wünschen von ABC gerecht zu werden, und schlagen dem Minister eine radikale Änderung vor: Die Hallen sollen in ihren Funktionen vertauscht, die große Halle zur Symphony Hall, die kleine zum Opera Theatre umfunktioniert werden. Der Minister gibt zugunsten ABC nach. Das neue Design der Hallen stammt nun aus der Feder von Hall Todd und Littlemore.

Die speziell von Utzon entwickelte Bühnenmaschinerie, die bereits aus Wien eingetroffen und installiert war, wird als Altmetall verkauft. Die Kosten für das Entfernen belaufen sich auf 2,7 Millionen Australische Dollar. Weitere sieben Jahre sind notwendig, um die infrastrukturelle Reorganisation aufgrund der radikalen Änderungen durchzuführen. Die endgültigen Kosten belaufen sich 1973 auf 102 Millionen Australische Dollar – das Doppelte der höchsten, von Davis Hughes 1965 verkündeten Kostenschätzung.

Utzon, zwar nach Dänemark zurückgekehrt, setzt seine Arbeit ohne Entgelt fort. Er sucht unter anderem nach Lösungen für das Problem der Bestuhlung und der Sitzreihenabstände in der großen Halle, die

Große Halle (1973),
Aufgang zur Großen Halle

Major Hall (1973)
Corridor to the Major Hall

Although he realized some major projects after the Opera House, he withdrew personally from the public sphere of architecture. Twenty-five years passed before he gave his first in-depth interview in conjunction with a film by Daryl Dellora on the history of the Opera House.[25]

Davis Hughes announced his choice for Utzon's successor in April, the same month of Utzon's departure: a group of architects joined in a collective under the name of Hall Todd and Littlemore[26], under the managment of government architect E.H. Farmer, was chosen to complete the Opera House.

The tile covering was finished in January 1967, but the remaining work was put on hold until new plans were drafted.

Shortly after Utzon's departure, ABC (Australian Broadcasting Corporation) presents a paper with specific demands for changes to the concert hall, announcing that they would refuse to use the Opera House unless these wishes are granted. The new architects strive to meet ABC's demands and propose a radical change: reassigning the functions of the halls by refitting the Major Hall as the Symphony Hall and the Minor Hall as the Opera Theatre. The Minister concedes in favour of ABC. The new design for the halls is created by Hall Todd and Littlemore.

Utzon's customized stage machinery, which had already been shipped from Vienna and installed, is sold as scrap metal. The removal costs are 2.7 million Australian dollars. A further seven years would be required to implement the infrastructural changes necessary for the radical modifications. The final costs (1973) amount to 102 million Australian dollars – double Davis Hughes's maximum cost estimate announced in 1965.

Back in Denmark, Utzon continues with his work without remuneration. His efforts are directed, among other issues, at finding a solution for the seating and the distance between rows in the large hall, which were repeatedly criticized. In 1967 he writes to Davis

immer wieder kritisiert wurden. 1967 schreibt er an Davis Hughes über eine Möglichkeit, die Abstände zwischen den Reihen großzügiger zu halten. Die Antwort der Regierung ist knapp: „Die Regierung weiß von nichts, was bezüglich der Fertigstellung des Sydney Opernhauses Herrn Utzons Aufmerksamkeit bedürfte."[27]

Am 20. Oktober 1973 eröffnet die britische Königin Elisabeth II. das Sydney Opera House. Der Name von Jørn Utzon wird nicht erwähnt, und keine Tafel weist auf seinen Beitrag hin.

Es dauerte 20 Jahre, bis Utzon seinen ersten Preis – den Commemorative Sulman Award – von australischer Seite für seinen „Beitrag" zur Oper verliehen bekommt.

Anläßlich der 25-Jahr-Feier, 1998, werden Jørn Utzon die „Schlüssel der Stadt Sydney" übergeben. Im gleichen Jahr wird die Jørn Utzon Foundation gegründet, unterstützt vom State Government, dem Opera House Trust und dem Sydney City Council. Diese Foundation vergibt alle zwei Jahre einen Preis von 100.000 Australischen Dollar an besondere Leistungen im Bereich „Performing Arts" sowie jährlich einen Preis an Künstler aus dem Bereich „Oper".

Der Kreis schließt sich heute – über 30 Jahre später: Die Anerkennungen sind ihm zuteil geworden, der Erfolg des Opernhauses als Wahrzeichen von Sydney gibt Utzon in seinem Kampf um Visionen recht. Das Vorhaben, das Opernhaus in Zukunft nach Utzons architektonischen Leitlinien zu optimieren, ist eine späte Einsicht der Stadt Sydney und der Politik. Ungeachtet der Tatsache, daß einer der berühmtesten Bauten des 20. Jahrhunderts bis heute unvollendet ist und bleiben wird.

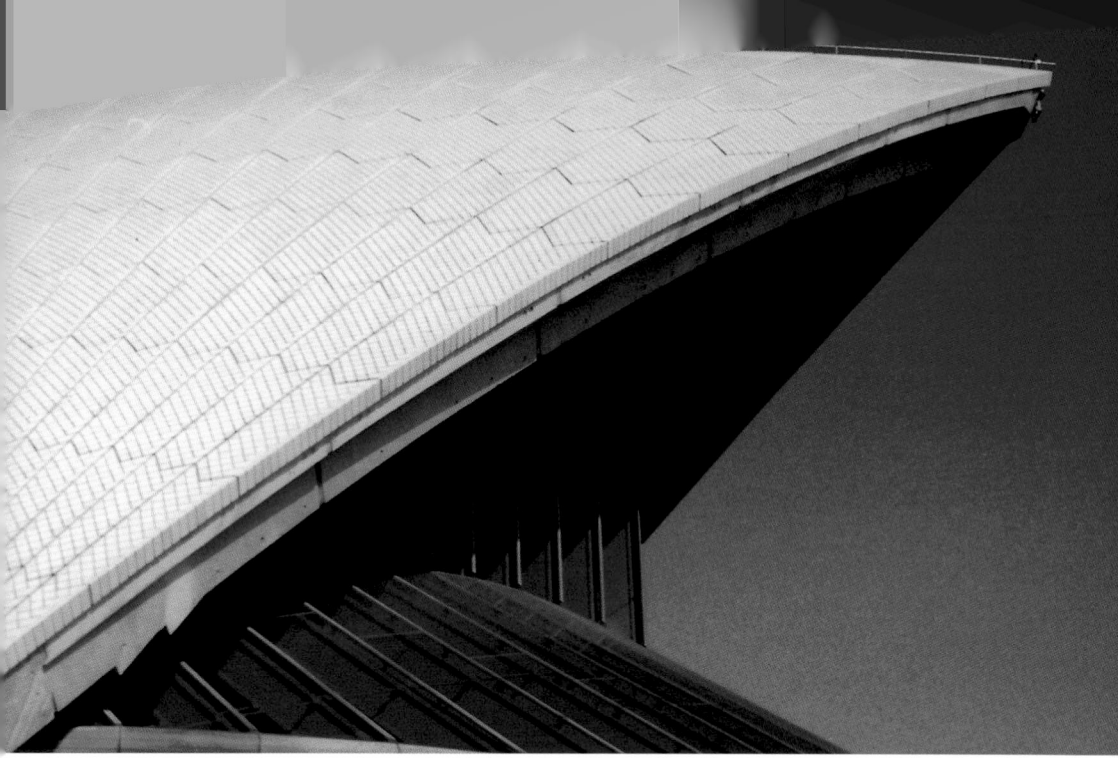

Hughes with suggestions for maintaining a more generous distance between the rows. The official reply is brusque: "The Government knows of nothing relating to the completion of the Sydney Opera House which requires Mr Utzon's attention."[27]

On 20 October 1973 Queen Elizabeth II officially opened the Sydney Opera House. There was no mention of Jørn Utzon and no plaque to commemorate his contribution.

Twenty years would pass before Utzon is presented with his first Australian award – the Commemorative Sulman Award – for his "contribution" to the Opera House.

On the occasion of the twenty-five year anniversary in 1998, Jørn Utzon was presented with the "keys to the City of Sydney".

The Jørn Utzon Foundation is founded in the same year, supported by the state government, the Opera House trust and the Sydney city council. This foundation awards 100,000 Australian dollars every two years for outstanding achievements in the performing arts, as well as an annual prize to artists working in opera.

Today, more than thirty years later, the story has come full circle. Utzon has received awards and recognition, and the success of the Opera House as a trademark of Sydney has vindicated the architect's fight for his vision. The plan to optimize the Opera House in the future in accordance with Utzon's architectural guidelines represents a late "coming to their senses" on the part of the city of Sydney and the politicians. Regardless of the fact that one of the most famous buildings of the twentieth century is still incomplete and will remain so.

Le Grand Louvre

Der mächtige Politiker/The Powerful Politician

Les Grands Travaux

Keine große Politik ohne bedeutende Architektur – das ist französische Staatspolitik, denn Architektur stellt als Akt der Repräsentation einen festen Bestandteil in der Führung und Gestaltung des französischen Staates dar. François Mitterrand, französischer Staatspräsident von 1981–1995, tritt in dieser Hinsicht in die Fußstapfen seiner Vorgänger, wie Georges Pompidou und Valerie Giscard d'Estaing, indem er bedeutende öffentliche Bauten unter die persönliche politische Entscheidung des Staatspräsidenten stellt. Diese Bauten gehen als „Grands Travaux" – als Staatsarchitektur – in die Geschichte Frankreichs ein. Sie dokumentieren die Symbiose von Macht und politischem Interesse zur Erneuerung einer Stadt. Gleichzeitig zeigt die Konzentration der bedeutendsten Kulturbauten Frankreichs, wie Le Centre Georges Pompidou (1972–77), Le Musée d'Orsay (1979–86), Le Parc de la Villette (1981–89), L'Institut du Monde Arabe (1983–87), La Défense mit La Grande Arche (1983–89), L'Opéra de la Bastille (1983–89), Le Grand Louvre (1983–93) und als jüngstes Beispiel die Grande Bibliothèque Nationale de Paris (1990–96), in der Hauptstadt das zentralistisch orientierte politische System Frankreichs dieser Zeit.

Der Louvre spielt dabei insofern eine interessante Rolle in Mitterrands Politik, weil er den maximalen Machtanspruch eines „Autokraten" widerspiegelt: Der Umbau des Louvre, dem ältesten Museum der Welt, soll auch zum größten Museum der Welt führen. Gleichzeitig stellt der Louvre ein historisches Denkmal im Zentrum von Paris dar und ist somit ein heikles Terrain für zeitgenössische Architekturplanung.

Der Louvre – 800 Jahre alt

Die ersten Teile des Louvre entstanden um 1202, als König Philippe Auguste eine mittelalterliche Festung – la Donjon – zum Schutz der Ile de France erbauen ließ, der heutigen Ile de la Cité in Paris. 200 Jahre später, ab dem Ende des 14. Jahrhunderts, ist die Festung Königssitz der französischen Monarchen. Von Karl V. bis Napoleon III. bewohnten die Könige über vier Jahrhunderte den Louvre. Im 16. Jahrhundert wird das Schloß „Château des Tuileries" im Park der Tuilerien, der dem Louvre vorgelagerten Gartenanlage, erbaut. 1871, als die Kommune – die republikanisch-revolutionären Kräfte des Landes – sich gegen die Regierung auflehnte und erbitterte Kämpfe gegen die französischen Regierungstruppen in Paris führte, wurden Teile des Louvre und das Schloß der Tuilerien in Brand gesetzt. Der Louvre wurde drei Jahre später wieder aufgebaut, die Ruine des Schlosses aber wurde 1882 endgültig abgetragen.

1792 werden sechs Kommissäre beauftragt, ein Louvre-Museum

No great politics without grand architecture – that is the national policy in France where representational architecture is understood as an integral component in governing and structuring the French state. In this respect, President François Mitterrand (1981-95) followed in the footsteps of his predecessors Georges Pompidou and Valerie Giscard d'Estaing by claiming the presidential right to making decisions about important public buildings. These buildings have become known as the "Grands Travaux" – state architecture. They document the symbiosis of power and political interests in the renewal of a city. At the concentration of significant cultural buildings in the capital – the Centre Georges Pompidou (1972-77), the Musée d'Orsay (1979-86), the Parc de la Villette (1981-89), the Institut du Monde Arabe (1983-87), La Défense with La Grande Arche (1983-89), the Opéra de la Bastille (1983-89), the Grand Louvre (1983-93) and most recently the Grande Bibliothèque Nationale de Paris (1990-96) – is a clear demonstration of the centralized political system in France during this period.

The Louvre occupies an interesting place in Mitterrand's political legacy as a perfect example of an "autocrat's" maximum claim to power: by converting and expanding the Louvre – the world's oldest museum – Mitterrand also created the world's largest museum. Yet the Louvre is also an historic monument in the heart of Paris and this means it is a delicate subject for contemporary architectural planning.

The Louvre – 800 years old
The earliest parts of the Louvre were created around 1202, when King Philippe Augustus built a medieval keep – the Donjon – for the protection of the Ile de France, today's Ile de la Cité in Paris. Two hundred years later, that is from the end of the fourteenth century onwards, the Donjon became the seat of the French monarchy and over the course of four centuries the Louvre was the main residence of kings, from Charles V to Napoleon III. The Château des Tuileries was constructed in the sixteenth century in the Tuileries, the gardens fronting the Louvre. In 1871, when the Commune – the country's revolutionary-republican factions – rose in revolt against the government and fought embittered battles against the national guard in Paris, sections of the Louvre and the entire Château des Tuileries burned to the ground. The Louvre was rebuilt three years later, but the ruins of the Château were demolished in 1882.

In 1792 six deputies were commissioned to create a Louvre museum for the display of the royal collections. The museum was inaugurated only one year later, on 10 August 1793. Since then, the Louvre has been open to the public.

Les Grands Travaux

1: Das Schloß von Philippe Auguste, um 1190
2: Das Palais du Louvre und das Château des Tuileries, verbunden durch die „Grande Galerie", um 1610
3: Um 1848
4: Le Louvre, 1981: Das „Château des Tuileries" wurde 1883 abgerissen

1: Philippe Auguste's castle, around 1190
2: The "Grand Gallerie" connecting the Palais du Louvre and the château des Tuileries, around 1610
3: Around 1848
4: Le Louvre, 1981: the Château des Tuileries was demolished in 1883

für die Präsentation der königlichen Sammlungen einzurichten. Nur ein Jahr später, am 10. August 1793, findet bereits die Eröffnung statt. Ab diesem Zeitpunkt ist der Louvre dem Volk zugänglich.

Die Idee
eines Politikers

Das Centre Georges Pompidou, das seit seiner Eröffnung 1977 mit steigenden Besucherzahlen große Popularität genießt, ist für Mitterrand ein Ansporn, auch dem Louvre neue Attraktionen zuzuführen.

Im September 1981 verkündet François Mitterrand die Notwendigkeit eines Louvre-Umbaus. Sein Ziel ist es, die Besucherzahlen zu erhöhen und vor allem den Louvre wieder in das Zentrum der nationalen Identität zu rücken. Der Gebäudekomplex wurde zu dieser Zeit nur zum Teil als Museum genutzt – sowohl Kulturministerium als auch Finanzministerium waren im Louvre untergebracht. Der Auszug des Finanzministeriums, das sich seit 120 Jahren im Nordflügel, dem Richelieu-Flügel des Louvre befindet, wird gleichzeitig als notwendige Maßnahme kommuniziert.

1982 nominiert Mitterrand Emile Biasini als Kopf der „Vorschlags- und Koordinationskommission zum Umbau des Louvre". Biasini bereist die größten Museen der Welt und trifft auf den sino-amerikanischen Architekten Ieoh Ming Pei, bekannt durch den Bau des Ostflügels der Washington Gallery und des Kennedy Memorials in Boston/USA.

Am 29. März 1983 findet eine erste Begegnung von Mitterrand und I.M.Pei im Beisein von Biasini statt. Pei drückt sich klar aus: Er möchte an keinem Wettbewerb mehr teilnehmen, ist jedoch an der „Louvre-Idee" sehr interessiert. Vier Monate später, am 27. Juli 1983, erhält I.M. Pei den Auftrag für den Umbau des Louvres und wird von Mitterrand als „concepteur du Grand Louvre" bestimmt.

Pei in einem Interview der Libération am 26. Januar 1984: „Die Direktbeauftragung ist eine große Ehre für mich. Meiner Meinung nach ist ein Wettbewerb nicht immer das Beste für ein Projekt. Ich arbeite mit zwei Partnerarchitekten, Michel Macary und Georges Duval, Chefarchitekt des Louvre, und vielen jungen Architekten zusammen. Im Grunde ist es ein französisches Projekt und steht durch seine dynamische und gleichzeitig statische Komposition in der Tradition von Le Nôtre."

Die Tatsache des Direktauftrages von Mitterrand an Pei wird als „le fait du prince" bezeichnet. (Mitterrand hatte den Spitznamen „le prince".)

Oben: Der Haupthof, Cour Napoléon, mit der Reiterstatue von Bernini – vor dem Umbau des Louvre, Stadtmodell mit Le Grand Louvre und der Pyramide

Above: The main courtyard, Cour Napoléon, with the equestrian statue by Bernini – before the rebuilding of the Louvre, city planning model with the Grand Louvre and the pyramid

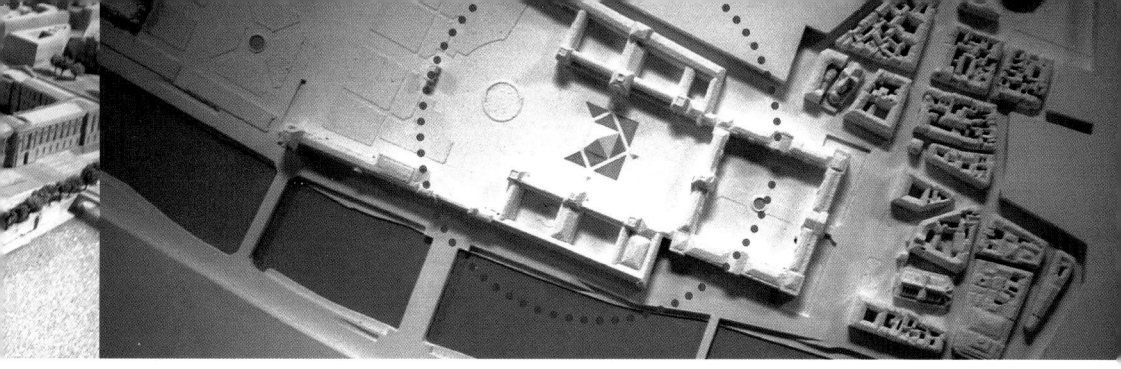

The Centre Georges Pompidou, which has been enjoying increasing numbers of visitors since its opening in 1977, is an incentive for Mitterrand to add new attractions to the Louvre.

In September 1981 François Mitterrand declared the need for a Louvre conversion.

His goal is to increase the number of visitors, and above all to reinstate the Louvre as the focal point of national identity. The complex was at that time only partly used as a museum, while the remaining space housed the Ministries of Culture and Finance. In conjunction with his plans for conversion, Mitterrand emphasizes that it is essential that the Ministry of Finance relocate from the Richelieu wing in the north section of the Louvre – its home for the past 120 years.

In 1982 François Mitterrand appointed Emile Biasini as chair of the "Committee for the Louvre Conversion and Proposal Coordination".

Biasini embarks on a tour of the world's largest museums and meets the Chinese-born American architect Ieoh Ming Pei, widely known for his design of the east wing of the Washington Gallery and the Kennedy Memorial in Boston, Massachusetts.

On 29 March 1983 Mitterrand and I.M. Pei met for the first time, with Biasini present. Pei very clearly stated that he no longer wished to participate in competitions, but that the "Louvre idea" intrigued him. Four months later, on 27 July 1983, I.M. Pei received the commission for the Louvre conversion. Mitterrand personally appointed him as "Concepteur du Grand Louvre".

In an interview with Libération Pei comments: "This presidential commission is a great honour for me. In my opinion, a competition does not always serve the best interests of a project. I am working with two architect partners, Michel Macary and Georges Duval, the chief architect of the Louvre, and many young architects. Basically this is a French project whose dynamic and yet static composition follows in the tradition of Le Nôtre." (26 January 1984)

Mitterrand's personal appointment of Pei is described as "le fait du prince". (Mitterrand's nickname was "le prince".)

A Politician's Idea

Preparations for the Conversion

The "Etablissement Public du Grand Louvre" – EPGL or Public Institution of the Great Louvre – was founded by official decree on 2 November 1983.

Its mandate is global in scope: creating a national cultural ensemble

Vorbereitungen für den Umbau

Durch ein offizielles Dekret wird die staatliche Einrichtung Etablissement Public du Grand Louvre – EPGL am 2. November 1983 gegründet. Ihr Auftrag erstreckt sich über das gesamte Areal: Entstehen soll ein nationales kulturelles Ensemble mit musealem Charakter. Dabei soll die Parkanlage Tuilerien mit dem Louvre verbunden werden. Dieser Gesamtkomplex soll den Namen „Grand Louvre" erhalten.

Anfang 1984 legt Pei seine Überlegungen zum Umbau vor. Er tritt für einen zentralen Haupteingang des Museums ein, der sich im Haupthof, dem Cour Napoléon, befinden soll.

Rund um diesen zentralen Eingang sollen die einzelnen Säle angeordnet werden. Die Wegführung innerhalb des Museums soll dadurch optimiert werden, daß die Sammlungen in einem logischen Zusammenhang innerhalb des Louvres angesiedelt und durch öffentliche Passagen, die der Information und als Ruhezonen dienen, voneinander getrennt werden. Das Finanzministerium soll aus dem Nordflügel des Louvre, dem „Aile Richelieu", ausquartiert werden und nach Bercy, einem Vorort im Osten von Paris, umziehen. Die Passage Richelieu könnte ausgebaut und für die Besucher nutzbar gemacht werden. Dadurch würden zudem zusätzliche Flächen frei, um Sammlungen, die aufgrund von Platzmangel bis dato nicht gezeigt wurden, der Öffentlichkeit zugänglich zu machen. Alle Flächen sollen mit einem durchgehenden Untergeschoß verbunden werden.

Als architektonische Umsetzung des Haupteingangs wählt Pei eine Glaspyramide.

„Die Pyramide", so I.M. Pei „ist keine architektonische Geste, sie hat funktionellen Anspruch, den Blick auf den Louvre selbst aus dem Inneren zu gewährleisten. Ich habe mich mit mehreren Formen auseinandergesetzt, und wenn ich mich für die Pyramide entschieden habe, so steht dies in keinem Bezug zu Ägypten, die Pyramide ist die reine und logische Form schlechthin." (In: Le Matin, 6.2.1984)

Pei präsentiert sein Projekt im Januar 1984 während eines dreitägigen Treffens in Arcachon (Südwestfrankreich) sämtlichen Chefkonservatoren des Louvre sowie dem Generalinspektor und Direktor der Museen Frankreichs und dem Direktor des Louvre. Alle stimmen für das Projekt.

Die Kritik

Als I.M. Pei sein Modell der Pyramide 1984 öffentlich präsentiert, bricht eine Welle der Kritik aus, die in vielen französischen Zeitungen als „la bataille de la pyramide" – die Schlacht um die Pyramide – betitelt wird. (beispielsweise in: Le Figaro, 3.2.1984, in: Le Matin, 6.2.1984, in: Nouvel Observateur, 17.2.1984)

Die Denkmalschutzkommission spricht sich 1984 mit 60 zu 40 Prozent gegen die Pyramide aus. Der Spruch der Gegner wird laut: „On ne touche pas au Louvre!" – „Finger weg vom Louvre!" (In: Le Matin, 6.2.1984)

Vorwürfe wie der, daß der neo-ägyptische Stil nicht mit dem Neo-Renaissance-Stil des Louvre zusammenpasse, werden erhoben. Daß

of museum-like character. The Tuileries gardens will be linked to the Louvre as part of this conversion and the entire complex is to be called "Grand Louvre."

In early 1984, Pei presented his ideas for the conversion.

His proposal envisions a central main entrance to the museum, to be placed in the main courtyard, the Cour Napoléon.

The various exhibition areas would radiate from this central entrance. Internally, the tour through the museum would be optimized by a logical arrangement of the collections within the Louvre, separated by public corridors that serve as information and resting areas. The proposal includes the relocation of the Ministry of Finance from the Louvre's north wing, the "Aile Richelieu", to Bercy, a suburb of Paris. The "Passage Richelieu" is earmarked for possible future conversion. This would free up additional space for exhibiting collections, which were previously out of sight in storage for lack of exhibition space. All areas are to be connected by a continuous lower level.

Pei decides to use a glass pyramid as the main entrance.

"The pyramid" Pei explains, "is not an architectural gesture, its function is to permit a view of the Louvre even from the inside. I have considered various shapes, and my choice of the pyramid. It is in no way a reference to Egypt; the pyramid is quite simply the purest and most logical shape." (In: Le Matin, 2 February 1984.)

At a three-day meeting held in the southwestern town of Arcachon in January 1984, Pei presented his project to the chief curators of the Louvre, the inspector general, the director of all French museums and the director of the Louvre. The vote for the project is unanimous.

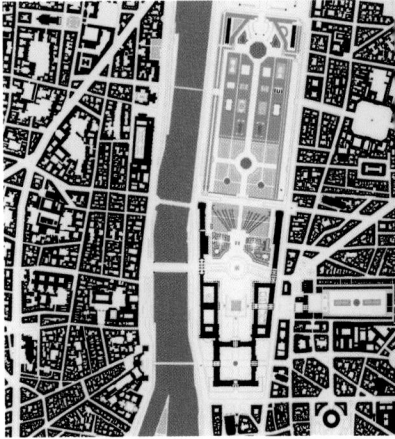

Lageplan: le Grand Louvre mit vorgelagerter Parkanlage „Les Tuileries"

Site plan: le Grand Louvre with the park "Les Tuileries" in front

Criticism

When I.M. Pei presented his pyramid model to the public in 1984, a wave of criticism swept through French newspapers, frequently referred to as "la bataille de la pyramide" – the battle of the pyramid. (e.g. in: Le Figaro, 3 February 1984, in: Le Matin, 2 February 1984, in: Le Nouvel Observateur, 17 February 1984).

In 1984 the Commission for Monument Preservation declared its opposition to the pyramid by a vote of sixty to forty per cent. The opposing voices became even more strident: "On ne touche pas au Louvre!" – "Keep your hands off the Louvre!". (In: Le Matin, 6 February 1984)

Accusations were raised – for example, that the neo-Egyptian style did not suit the Louvre's neo-Renaissance style. What the critics seemed to forget was that the Louvre is an agglomerate of various styles and that new sections had been added in each century.

Comparisons with the museum district in Vienna seem appropriate here: after the competition in 1990, critics and conservationists opposed the destruction of the "historical fabric" and the new buildings planned for the centre of the area. Yet the 1990 design merely envisioned tear-ing down sections that had been built after 1945. Here, as in Paris, critics had failed to fully investigate the architectural history, applying the term "historical fabric" to a random moment in time and extending it to include the whole area.

der Louvre ein Agglomerat verschiedener Stile ist und jedes Jahrhundert Bauten hinzukamen, ist von den Kritikern vergessen.

Vergleiche mit dem Museumsquartier in Wien bieten sich hier an: Kritiker und Denkmalschützer in Wien verwehrten sich nach dem Wettbewerb 1990 gegen eine Zerstörung der „historischen Bausubstanz" und gegen die geplanten Neubauten im Inneren des Areals. Der Entwurf von 1990 sah jedoch nur den Abriß jener Teile vor, die nach 1945 gebaut wurden. Hier wurde, wie auch in Paris, die Baugeschichte von den Kritikern ungenau studiert, der Begriff „historische Bausubstanz" auf einen willkürlichen historischen Moment eingefroren und auf das ganze Areal ausgedehnt.

Auch die Kritik, wonach die Pyramide die „historische Perspektive" zum Place de l'Etoile mit dem Arc de Triomphe versperre, wird durch historische Fakten widerlegt: Es gab nie eine unverbaute historische Achse, da das Schloß „Château des Tuileries" im Park der Tuilerien erst 1882 abgerissen wurde, es aber quer zu den Champs-Elysées stand und somit einen freien Blick versperrte. Hinzu kommt, daß der Louvre gar nicht auf der direkten Achse mit den Champs-Elysées und La Défense steht, sondern leicht nach Norden ausbricht. Dies hat seine Ursache darin, daß das Tuilerienschloß seinerzeit den Louvre westlich begrenzte. Die Pyramide liegt somit nicht auf der Achse Champs-Elysées – Arc de Triomphe.

Einen weiteren Angriffspunkt stellt die Einkaufspassage, Espaces du Carrousel, dar, die als unterirdische Verbindung vom Museumstrakt zur Tiefgarage fungieren soll. Sie wird von den Kritikern als „amerikanische Shopping Mall" entlarvt. Der Pyramide werden Spitznamen wie „Megamusée", „U-Bahn-Eingang", „Mitterramses I" gegeben. Auch in ihrer Funktion als zentraler Eingang wird die Pyramide kritisiert. Thomas Gaethgens schreibt am 5. Juli 1985 in „Die Zeit": „Statt den Touristenstrom von vornherein soweit wie möglich zu teilen, schafft man durch die unterirdische Haupteingangshalle einen zentralen Rummelplatz, von den Metrobahnhöfen kaum zu unterscheiden. (...)"

Sichtachse Arc de Triomphe – Louvre

Sight lines Arc de Triomphe – Louvre

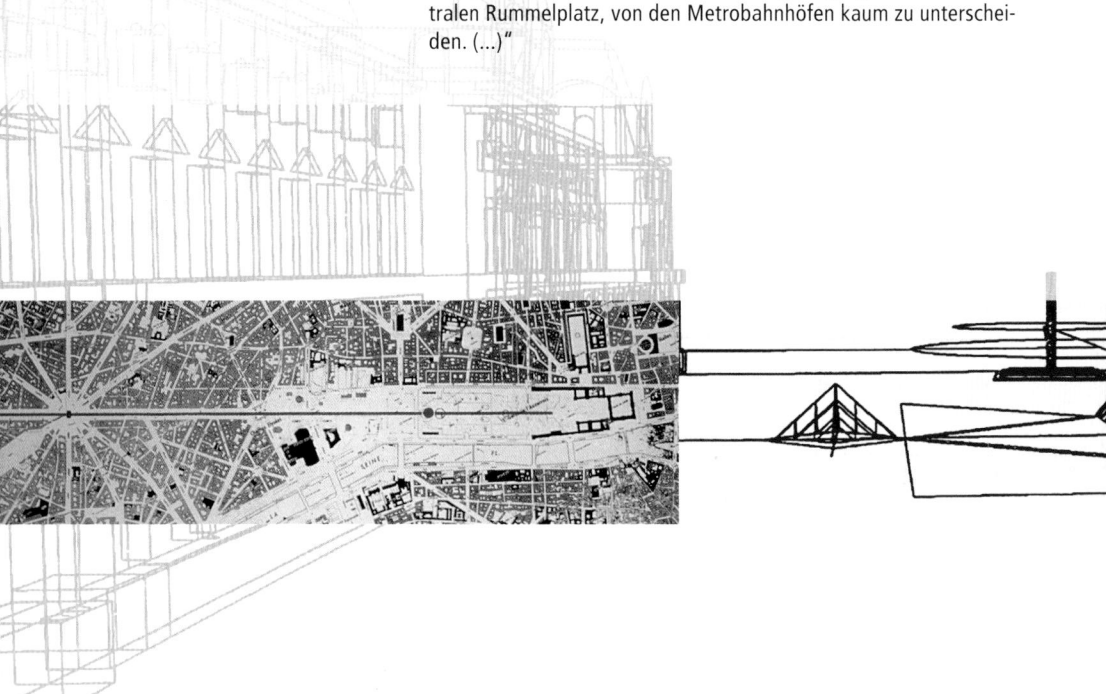

The criticism according to which the pyramid blocks the "historic view" of the Place de l'Etoile and the Arc de Triomphe does not stand up to scrutiny. There never existed an historical axis uncluttered by buildings, since the Château des Tuileries was demolished as late as 1882. Since it had stood at right angles to the Champs-Elysées, it blocked the free vista. One should note, too, that the Louvre does not even lie on the direct axis between the Champs-Elysées and La Défense, but veers slightly to the north. The reason for this is that the Château des Tuileries originally formed the western edge of the Louvre. Therefore the pyramid is not on the Champs-Elysées-Arc de Triomphe axis.

Another point of contention is the shopping arcade, Espaces du Carousel, which is intended to function as a subterranean link between the museum complex and the underground car park. Critics are quick to label it an "American shopping mall." Various nicknames are given to the pyramid, such as "Megamusée", "Subway entrance" and "Mitteramses I". Its function as the main entrance is also criticized. Thomas Gaethgens writes in Die Zeit: "Instead of dividing the stream of tourists right at the beginning, the underground main entrance hall creates a central fairground, which is barely distinguishable from the Métro station (...)" (5 July 1985).

The Initiatives

In 1984, Michel Guy, former state secretary of culture under Giscard d'Estaing (1974-76), led the way in founding an association "For the Restoration and Preservation of the Louvre" (together with Bruno Foucart and André Fermigier).

The association demands a 1:1 scale model of the pyramid and a full reconsideration of the entire programme. Within a few months of its foundation, the association has grown to 15,000 members.

This criticism is supported and intensified by several French newspapers and magazines, especially Le Figaro and Le Quotidien de Paris.

After I.M. Pei's proposal is made public, the daily Le Figaro makes

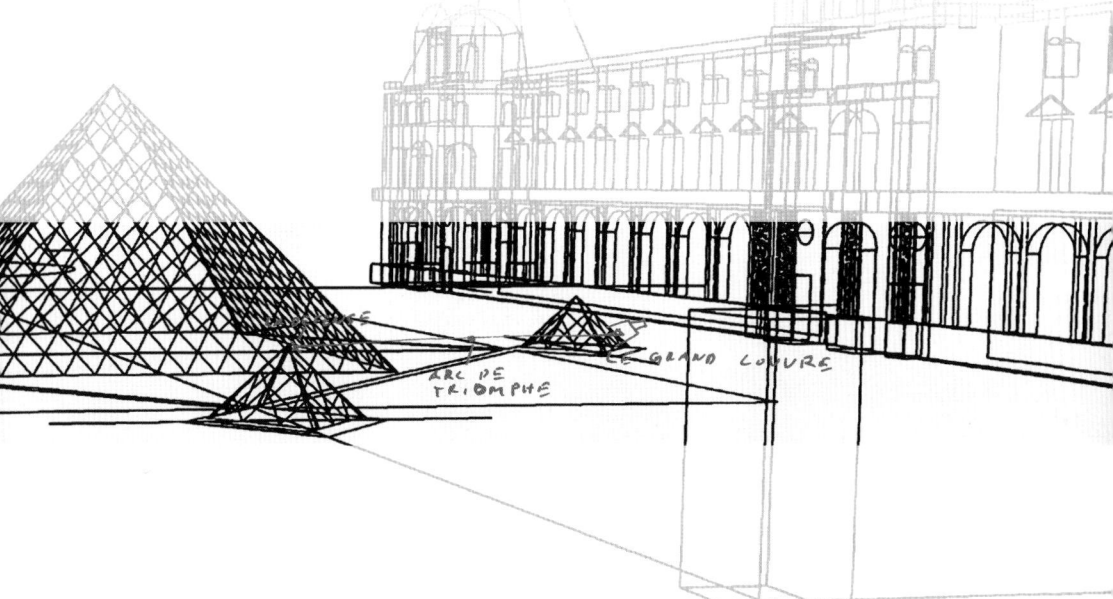

Die Initiativen

1984 formiert sich unter der Führung von Michel Guy, dem ehemaligen Staatssekretär für Kultur unter Giscard d'Estaing (1974–76), ein Verein „Für die Renovation und Erhaltung des Louvre" (gemeinsam mit Bruno Foucart und André Fermigier). Der Verein verlangt ein 1:1-Modell der Pyramide und ein Überdenken des Gesamtprogrammes. Bereits wenige Monate nach seiner Gründung zählt er 15.000 Mitglieder.

Unterstützt und forciert wird diese Kritik auch von mehreren französischen Zeitungen und Zeitschriften, allen voran die Tageszeitungen Le Figaro und Le Quotidien de Paris.

Im Februar 1984, kurz nach Bekanntwerden des Programmes von I.M. Pei, öffnet die Zeitung Le Figaro ihr Blatt den Lesermeinungen und betreibt eine offensive Gegenkampagne. Meinungen wie „Der Louvre ist kein Kaufhaus und braucht keine Signalwirkung" wird hier Platz geboten. (In: Le Figaro, 3.2.1984)

Zur gleichen Zeit startet die Zeitschrift Le Quotidien de Paris ihre Kampagne gegen den Umbau und veröffentlicht eine Umfrage unter der Pariser Bevölkerung – befragt werden 710 Personen (!) – , die ein klares „NON à la pyramide!" (In: Le Quotidien de Paris, 31.1.1985) ergibt. Bereits 1984 wird eine Unterschriftenaktion bedeutender Personen des öffentlichen Lebens ins Leben gerufen, die für das Projekt von Pei eintritt.

Zu lesen sind Namen wie Jacques Chirac (damals Bürgermeister von Paris), Jean Prouvé, Renzo Piano, Claude Pompidou (Witwe von Georges Pompidou), Jean Maheu (Präsident, Centre Georges Pompidou), Dominique Bozo (Direktor, Musée National d'Art Moderne), die Chefkonservatoren des Musée du Louvre etc.

Die Kritik am Umbau des Louvre liegt schließlich in Form eines Buches mit Pamphletcharakter im Februar 1985 in den Buchhandlungen auf: „Paris mystifié. La grande illusion du Grand Louvre." Herausgeber sind drei Kunsthistoriker: Sébastien Losta, Antoine Schnapper und Bruno Foucart, der auch einer der Mitbegründer des Vereins „Für die Renovation und Erhaltung des Louvre" war. Das Vorwort des Buches liefert Henri Cartier-Bresson.

Die Grünen der Region Ile de France rufen zu einer gemeinsamen Kampagne gegen die Errichtung der Pyramide und zu einer Petition auf.

Die Fronten verhärten sich, die Zeitschrift Le Figaro verschärft ihre Kampagne und schreibt am 4. März 1985: „DOUBLE non à la pyramide!" – „Doppeltes Nein zur Pyramide": Zwei Gründe für dieses doppelte Nein werden angeführt: Das Pyramidenprojekt sei nicht revolutionär genug, im Gegenteil, die Idee wäre zu altmodisch und somit das Projekt bald vergessen. Außerdem seien Teile des Louvre derzeit aus Geldmangel geschlossen, für den Bau der Pyramide aber wäre Geld vorhanden. „Da ist das wahre Skandalmaterial zu finden!" (In: Le Figaro, 4.3.1985)

Die Eröffnung der beiden Höfe Cour Carrée und Cour Napoléon wird von Le Figaro mit Charakterisierungen wie „kulturelle Diktatur" und „keine Kommunikation zwischen Regierenden und Regierten" versehen – bis hin zu „Die Pyramide ist eine geistige Verirrung". (In: Le Figaro, 16.3.1985)

its pages available for readers' opinions in February of the same year and launches an aggressive counter-campaign. The paper provides a forum for opinions such as: "The Louvre is not a department store and has no need to 'signal' its presence." (In: Le Figaro, 2 Feburary 1984)

The magazine Le Quotidien de Paris launches its own campaign against the conversion at the same time and publishes a poll of Parisians – although only 710 persons are asked (!) – which results in a resounding "NO to the pyramid!" (In: Le Quotidien de Paris, 31 January 1985).

On the other hand, a petition signed by leading figures in public life in 1984 demonstrates strong support for Pei's project. The list includes Jacques Chirac (then mayor of Paris), Jean Prouvé, Renzo Piano, Claude Pompidou (the widow of Georges Pompidou), Jean Maheu (president, Centre Georges Pompidou), Dominique Bozo (director, Musée National d'Art Moderne), the chief curators of the Musée du Louvre, and many more.

The criticism of the Louvre conversion culminates in a slim, pamphlet-like volume that appears in Parisian bookshops (February 1985): "Paris mystifié. La grande illusion du Grand Louvre." (Paris mystified. The grand illusion of the Great Louvre.) The work is published by three art historians: Sébastien Losta, Antoine Schnapper and Bruno Foucart, co-founder of the association "For the Renovation and Preservation of the Louvre." The foreword is provided by Henri Cartier-Bresson.

The Green Party of the Ile de France region calls for a joint campaign in protest against the erection of the pyramid and demands a petition.

The opposing groups entrench themselves further and further and the campaign waged by Le Figaro intensifies, culminating in the headline: "DOUBLE non à la pyramide!" – "Two Times NO to the Pyramid!" (4 March 1985): two reasons are given for this double No. First, the pyramid project isn't revolutionary enough; on the contrary, the idea is too old-fashioned and the project would soon slip into obscurity. And second, sections of the Louvre are closed because of a lack of funds, while money can apparently be found for the construction of the pyramid. "Here", the article continues, "is real material for a scandal!" (In: Le Figaro, 4 March 1985)

Le Figaro denounces the opening of the two courtyards, the Cour Carrée and the Cour Napoléon as "cultural dictatorship" and "a lack of communication between the governing and the governed," drawing the conclusion that "the pyramid is an intellectual aberration." (In: Le Figaro, 16 March 1985)

Ironically, Le Figaro would celebrate its tenth anniversary in the pyramid three years later, in 1988.

The Construction Phase, the 1:1 Model and Numerous Openings

For the construction of the Louvre project the French State had clearly stipulated that only French firms and contractors must be used. With the exception of two companies, this stipulation was fulfilled. Altogether, 110 companies participated in the construction and conversion. The conversion was divided into two stages (the first from 1983-89 and the second from 1989-93).

Ausgrabungsarbeiten im Hof „Cour Carrée" (links),
Baustellenetappen im Hof „Cour Napoléon", 1986, 1987 und 1988 (rechts)

Excavation works in the courtyard "Cour Carrée" (left page)
Construction phases in the courtyard "Cour Napoléon" in 1986, 1987 and 1988 (right page)

95

Pikanterweise feiert die Zeitschrift Figaro Magazine drei Jahre später, 1988, ihr 10jähriges Bestehen in der Pyramide.

Die Bauzeit, das 1:1 Modell und die zahlreichen Eröffnungen

Für die bauliche Umsetzung des Louvre-Projektes gab es die strikte Vorgabe seitens des französischen Staates, nur französische Firmen an dem Umbau zu beteiligen. Dies konnte, bis auf zwei Ausnahmen, auch tatsächlich eingehalten werden. Insgesamt waren 110 Firmen am Umbau beteiligt.

Der Umbau wurde in zwei Phasen aufgeteilt: Die 1. Phase, 1983–1989, umfaßt die archäologischen Ausgrabungsarbeiten, die Renovierung und den Umbau der beiden Höfe Cour Carrée und Cour Napoléon, sowie den Bau der Pyramide inklusive des Ausbaus des gesamten Untergeschosses. Der Umbau des Richelieu-Flügels wird in einer zweiten Phase von 1989–1993 vorgenommen.

Um Teile noch vor den Wahlen 1986 zu eröffnen, wird das Projekt unter den beteiligten Architekten aufgeteilt. Während I.M. Pei die Pyramide und das gesamte Erschließungssystem plant, sind Michel Macary für den Umbau des Richelieu-Flügels und Georges Duval, Chefarchitekt des Louvre, für die Restaurierung der Glasfassaden verantwortlich.

Aufgrund der zahllosen Debatten rund um den Bau der Pyramide verschieben sich die geplanten Fertigstellungstermine kontinuierlich nach hinten. Der ursprüngliche Termin für die Fertigstellung der Pyramide und des Cour Napoléon verzögert sich Ende 1987 um weitere eineinhalb Jahre.

Das Finanzministerium, seit 120 Jahren im Richelieu-Flügel, dem Nordflügel des Louvre, ansässig, soll in einen Neubau der Architekten Paul Chemetov und Borja Huidobro nach Bercy, einem Vorort im Osten von Paris, ziehen. Unter Finanzminister Pierre Bérégovoy erfolgt dieser Auszug auch teilweise, doch der neue Finanzminister Eduard Balladur weigert sich 1987, den Louvre zu verlassen – die bereits ausgezogenen Beamten kehren wieder in den Richelieu-Flügel zurück.

Die Arbeiten werden um Monate zurückgeworfen, und Pei meint dazu: „Es ist wie ein Körper mit nur einem Arm – es gibt Treppen, die nirgendwohin führen." (In: Libération, 4.3.1988.) Der umkämpfte Teil des Flügels erhält den Namen „Korridor von Danzig". (In: Libération, 14.10.1988.) Nach einem neuerlichen Wechsel des Finanzministers von Eduard Balladur zu Pierre Bérégovoy erfolgt letztendlich der Umzug im Februar 1989 – zwei Jahre später als geplant.

Jacques Chirac, Bürgermeister von Paris und einer der ersten Befürworter des Projektes, bremst 1985 plötzlich das „Unternehmen Pyramide". Er verlangt, von zahlreichen Gegnern des Projektes unterstützt, eine Simulation der Pyramide, um in Ruhe alle Für und Wider aufzuklären. Falls dies zu keinem Ergebnis führen sollte, müßte ein 1:1-Modell gebaut werden. Er bringt damit Mitterrand bewußt in Bedrängnis, der noch vor Ende seiner siebenjährigen Amtszeit die spektakuläre Pyramide, den „l'iceberg du Louvre", eröffnet wissen möchte. (In: Libération, 3.4.1985)

Emile Biasini, Leiter der Gesamtkoordination, beschließt, ein

Phase I comprised the excavation works, the renovation and conversion of the two courtyards, the Cour Carrée and the Cour Napoléon, as well as the construction of the pyramid including the completion of the underground level. Phase II focused on the conversion of the Richelieu wing.

To ensure that some areas would be ready for opening before the election of 1986, the project is divided among the participating architects. While I.M. Pei assumes the planning for the pyramid and the entire circulation and access system, Michel Macary is put in charge of the Richelieu wing conversion and Georges Duval, chief architect of the Louvre, takes on the restoration of the glass façades.

Due to the countless debates about the construction of the pyramid, the scheduled completion dates are constantly delayed. The original date for the completion of the pyramid and the Cour Napoléon is postponed by an additional one and a half years (in late 1987).

The Ministry of Finance, which has occupied the Richelieu wing, the north wing of the Louvre, for the past 120 years, is to move into a new building designed by architects Paul Chemetov and Borja Huidobro in Bercy, a suburb of Paris. The relocation was set in motion under finance minister Pierre Bérégovoy, but in 1987 the new finance minister, Eduard Balladur, refused to leave the Louvre and bureaucrats who had already moved out returned to the Richelieu wing.

The result is a setback of several months and Pei comments: "It's like a body with only one arm – there are stairs that lead nowhere" (In: Libération, 4 March 1988). The contested section of the wing is christened the "Gdansk corridor". (In: Libération, 14 October 1988)

When the portfolio of finance minister changed hands once again from Eduard Balladur back to Pierre Bérégovoy, the move was finally completed in February 1989 – two years later than originally planned.

Jacques Chirac, the mayor of Paris and one of the earliest supporters of the project suddenly put the brakes on the "pyramid enterprise" in 1985. With the support of many opponents to the project, he demands that a simulation model of the pyramid be created, which would explain the project once and for all to all its supporters and opponents. Should such a simulation still fail to produce a result, a 1:1 model would become necessary. This is a deliberate move on the part of the mayor to exert pressure on Mitterrand, whose greatest wish is to see the completion and inauguration of the spectacular pyramid, "l'iceberg du Louvre", before the end of his seven-year term in office. (In: Libération, 3 April 1985)

Emile Biasini, managing director of overall project coordination, decides to commission a "cable model". In May 1985, four arm-thick steel cables are rigged with a crane in the courtyard of the Cour Napoléon to represent the true scale and shape of the pyramid, and opened to the Parisian public for five days. 50,000 visitors are counted. After this presentation, the number of supporters rises and Chirac eases up on his criticism.

Finally, in August 1987, the skeleton of the pyramid was completed and the glazing work began five months later.

Von oben nach unten: Architekt I.M.Pei vor dem Louvre Modell und vor der realisierten Pyramide; Eröffnung am 29. März 1989, F. Mitterrand; Eröffnung am 29. März 1989, F. Mitterrand und I.M. Pei; Eröffnung Richelieu-Flügel am 19. November 1993, F. Mitterrand und J. Toubon

From top to bottom: Architect I.M.Pei in front of the model and the finished pyramid; Opening on 29 March 1989, F. Mitterrand; Opening on 29 March 1989, F. Mitterrand and I.M. Pei; Opening of the Richelieu wing on 19 November 1993, F. Mitterrand and J. Toubon

Pyramide mit Wasserbassins, 1993
(links),
1:1-Simulation der Pyramide, Mai 1985
(rechts)

Pyramid with pools, 1993 (left page)
1:1 simulation of the pyramid, 1985
(right page)

„Kabel-Modell" errichten zu lassen. Im Mai 1985 werden im Hof Cour Napoléon vier armdicke Stahlkabel von einem Kran zu einer Pyramide hochgezogen und fünf Tage lang der Pariser Bevölkerung präsentiert. 50.000 Besucher werden gezählt. Nach dieser Präsentation steigt die Zahl der Befürworter, und die Kritik seitens Chiracs verstummt.

Im August 1987 steht schließlich das Skelett der Pyramide, fünf Monate später wird mit der Verglasung begonnen.

Mitterrand möchte zwar den gesamten Umbau des Louvre noch in seiner Amtszeit verbucht sehen. Da er aber bereits 70 Jahre alt ist und die Präsidentschaftswahlen noch in die Umbauzeit fallen, muß er auf „Nummer sicher" gehen und beschließt, Teileröffnungen vorzunehmen. Dasselbe Vorgehen wird später bei der „Grande Bibliothèque Nationale de Paris" wiederholt. Es sollte Mitterrands letztes Projekt innerhalb der Grands Travaux werden – er stirbt am 8. Januar 1996.

Am 25. Juni 1986 wird der renovierte kleine Hof, der Cour Carrée, mit der Krypta Philippe Auguste eröffnet.

Am 14. Oktober 1988, zwei Jahre später, wird der Haupthof, der Cour Napoléon, eröffnet, obwohl die Bauarbeiten an der Pyramide noch nicht abgeschlossen sind.

Am 30. März 1989 schließlich findet die große Eröffnung der Pyramide und des Untergeschosses mit der „Hall Napoléon", der großen Empfangshalle unterhalb der Pyramide, und des „Place Carrousel" statt. Mitterrands Ausspruch „Wir haben die Schlacht um die Pyramide gewonnen!" drückt den Triumph eines Politikers aus, der ein Projekt gegen die Medien, gegen die Bevölkerung und gegen die eigenen Reihen durchgesetzt und es so zu seinem Projekt gemacht hat .

Am 18. November 1993, anläßlich der 200-Jahr-Feier des Louvre wird der Richelieu-Flügel feierlich eröffnet.

But Mitterrand would like to see the entire Louvre conversion and extension project completed while he is still in office. However, at seventy years of age and faced with a presidential election within the scheduled period of construction, Mitterrand must steer "a safe course" and decides to inaugurate the project piece by piece. The same approach is subsequently used for the "Grande Bibliothèque Nationale de Paris", which would become Mitterrand's last "Grand Travaux" project – he died on 8 January 1996.

On 25 June 1986 the small renovated courtyard, the Cour Carrée with the Philippe Augustus crypt was inaugurated.

Two years later, on 14 October 1988, the main courtyard, the Cour Napoléon was inaugurated even though the construction of the pyramid was still incomplete.

Finally, on 30 March 1989 there was the official grand opening of the pyramid and the underground level with the "Hall Napoléon", the great reception hall beneath the pyramid, and the "Place Carrousel". Mitterrand's exclamation: "We've won the battle of the pyramid!" is an expression of triumph by a politician who has successfully defended a project against the opinions of the media, the public and even his own ranks, thus making it into his project.

The Richelieu wing was inaugurated with great ceremony on 18 November 1993 on the occasion of the bicentennial of the Louvre.

The Pyramid: Stainless Steel, Aluminium and Glass

Pei in an interview with the daily Libération, on 26 January 1984: "The key issue in all my considerations was the problem of orientation. Visitors who arrive at the Louvre today have no reference point whatsoever and end up searching for the entrance. We need a symbol that will

Die Pyramide:
Rostfreier Stahl,
Aluminium, Glas

Pei in einem Interview mit der Tageszeitung Libération, vom 26. Januar 1984: „Das Wichtigste bei meinen Überlegungen war das Problem der Orientierung. Die Besucher, die heute in den Louvre kommen, haben keinerlei Anhaltspunkte und suchen den Eingang. Wir brauchen ein Symbol, damit wir uns zurechtfinden. Und dieses Symbol muß auch gleichzeitig der Haupteingang sein, so werden die Leute automatisch darauf zusteuern. Sobald sie die Pyramide betreten, werden sie von Rolltreppen ins Untergeschoß geführt – in die große Halle, dem zentralen, öffentlichen Platz. Um diesen Ort anziehend zu gestalten, braucht es zweierlei Dinge: Licht und Volumen. Viele haben gerade dieses kritisiert und gesagt: ‚Wozu brauchen wir eine Pyramide, um in den unteren Bereich zu gelangen?' Doch wie sähe das Resultat aus? Eine U-Bahn-Atmosphäre. Das wäre unmöglich. Ich habe die Pyramide gewählt. Sie wird das Herz des Louvre werden, exakt im Zentrum des Gebäudekomplexes. Die drei kleinen Pyramiden, je fünf Meter hoch, dienen zur zusätzlichen Belichtung der Rolltreppen, die in drei verschiedene Pavillons führen. Sie geben den Besuchern ein Gefühl der Orientierung. Das ist das Wichtigste in einem so großen Museum."

Trotz der geometrischen Einfachheit einer regelmäßigen Pyramide – regelmäßiges Vieleck mit der Spitze senkrecht über dem Mittelpunkt

provide orientation. And this symbol must at the same time be the main entrance; in this manner people will automatically move towards it. As soon as they enter the pyramid, escalators will take them down to the basement level – into the large hall, the central, public square. Two things are required to make this space attractive: light and volume. Many have criticized especially this point, saying: 'Why do we need a pyramid to reach the lower level?' But what would the alternative be? It would have the atmosphere of a subway station. That's unacceptable. I have chosen the pyramid. It will be the heart of the Louvre at the precise centre of the complex. The three small pyramids, each 5 m high, provide additional (natural) light for the escalators, which lead into three different pavilions. They provide a sense of orientation for the visitors. That is the most important factor in a museum of this scale."

Despite the geometric simplicity of a regular pyramid – a regular polygon whose peak is directly above the centre point of the base – the glass pyramid of the Louvre was preceded by an elaborate and involved planning phase.

The Louvre pyramid, with a total weight of 200 tonnes, rises to a height of 21.65 m, with 35-m sides and a footprint of 1250 square metres. The load-bearing structure of 128 stainless steel girders per side was based on computer calculations. The system of the spiderweb-like metal construction was realized in the Concorde workshops. The sixteen horizontal steel cables were prefabricated by a manufacturer in Boston,

der Grundfläche – ging dem Bau der Glaspyramide im Louvre eine gewaltige Planungsphase voran.

Die Pyramide des Louvre, mit einem Gesamtgewicht von 200 Tonnen, weist eine Höhe von 21,65 m, eine Seitenlänge von je 35 m und eine Grundfläche von 1.250 m² auf. Die Pyramidenträgerstruktur mit 128 Trägern aus rostfreiem Stahl pro Seite wurde mittels Computer errechnet. Das System der spinnwebenartigen Metallkonstruktion stammt aus den Werkstätten der Concorde-Produktion. Die 16 horizontal verlaufenden Stahlkabel wurden von einer Firma aus Boston vorgefertigt, die auf die Konstruktion von Hochsee-Segelschiffen spezialisiert ist. Alle beweglichen Teile wurden ein Jahr nach Fertigstellung überprüft und nachjustiert. Mit einem Kostenpunkt von 75 Millionen Francs bezeichnete die französische Tageszeitung Le Monde die Pyramide als „teuerstes Dach der Welt". (In: Le Monde, 20.1.1988)

Die staatliche Firma Saint Gobain entwickelte ein Spezialglas, das es bis dato nicht gab: Das Glas durfte nicht spiegeln und mußte achtzigprozentige Transparenz aufweisen. Produziert wurde ein Glas ohne Eisenoxid, der weiße Sand für die Glasherstellung kam aus Fontainebleau. Mit speziellen Lösungsmitteln vermischt, wurde es in Spezialöfen geschmolzen und bei 1000 Grad gewalzt. Poliert wurde es in England.

675 rautenförmige Glasteile à 150 Kilogramm werden mit einem Spezialsilikonkleber auf Alurahmen fixiert. Die gesamte Oberfläche der Pyramide weist keinerlei Vorsprünge auf, was eine problemlose Reinigung der Flächen ermöglicht.

Eine spezielle Klimaanlage sorgt das ganze Jahr hindurch für konstante Luftfeuchtigkeit und somit für eine perfekte Transparenz des Glases.

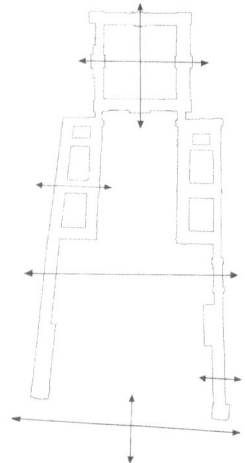

Fußgängerzirkulation, Achsen

Pedestrian circulation, axis

Das Raumprogramm des Grand Louvre

Die Pyramide im Hof Cour Napoléon[1], umgeben von sieben dreieckigen Wasserbassins aus anthrazitfarbenem Granit und drei kleineren Pyramiden, führt hinunter in die „Hall Napoléon", dem Zentrum des Louvre. Die Halle verfügt über eine größere Grundfläche als die Pyramide und ist um 45° gedreht – Motiv: Quadrat im Quadrat.

Von ihr geht die Wegführung in das Innere des Museums in drei Himmelsrichtungen: Nach Norden, Richtung Pavillon Richelieu, nach Osten, Richtung Pavillon Sully und nach Süden, Richtung Pavillon Denon. Die drei kleineren Pyramiden, die oberhalb dieser Zugänge angeordnet sind, dienen der Lichtzufuhr und der Orientierung im Inneren.

Die unterirdische Verlängerung des Hofes Cour Napoléon nach Westen bildet die „Passage du Carrousel", die zum „Place du Carrousel" führt – dem zentralen Treffpunkt der kommerziell orientierten Flächen des Louvre mit Geschäften, Cafés und Restaurants. Den Place du Carrousel markiert eine umgedrehte Pyramide, über die natürliches Licht ins Untergeschoß gelangt. Von hier gelangt man auch weiter in die gewaltige Tiefgarage mit einer Gesamtfläche von 25.000 m². Insgesamt wurde unterirdisch eine Fläche von sechs Hektar geschaffen.

specialized in building ocean-going yachts. All movable parts were tested and adjusted one year after completion. At a final cost of 75 million francs, the French daily Le Monde dubbed the pyramid as "the most expensive roof in the world". (In: Le Monde, 20 January 1988)

The state-owned company Saint Gobain developed special glass, a new prototype material: it had to be non-reflective and offer eighty per cent transparency. They produced a glass without iron oxide using white sand from Fontainebleau for the glass manufacturing process. Blended with special solvents, it was melted in custom furnaces and rolled at a temperature of 1000 degrees Celsius. The glass was polished in England.

675 rhomboidal glass sections weighing 150 kg each were attached to aluminium frames with a special silicon adhesive. The surface of the whole pyramid is completely smooth and even, which allows problem-free cleaning.

A custom air-conditioning system maintains constant air humidity levels throughout the year, and thus perfect transparency.

The pyramid located in the Cour Napoléon[1] is surrounded by seven triangular pools of anthracite-coloured granite and three smaller pyramids. It leads down into the "Hall Napoléon", the heart of the Louvre. The ground plan of the hall is larger than that of the pyramid and is rotated by 45 degrees. (Motif: square within square.)

From this point, paths lead in three directions into the core of the museum: to the north in the direction of the Richelieu pavilion, to the east in the direction of the Sully pavilion and to the south in the direction of the Denon pavilion. The three smaller pyramids above these entrances provide additional light and orientation in the interior.

The subterranean extension of the Cour Napoléon to the west is formed by the "Passage du Carrousel", which leads to the "Place du Carrousel" – the retail centre of the Louvre with shops, cafés and restaurants. The "Place du Carrousel" is marked by an inverted pyramid through which natural light enters into the basement level. This area also contains the access point to the enormous underground car park with a total area of 25,000 square metres. Altogether, six hectares of usable underground area have been created.

The large reception hall, the "Hall Napoléon" is surrounded by an auditorium with 450 seats, lounges, a café and the "Passage du Carrousel." The reception hall is nine metres below ground. Escalators lead to the mezzanine level and from there to the individual wings of the Louvre.

The hall ceilings – in part realized as coffered ceilings – are in white, surface-treated concrete. This produces a satin effect, a method which I.M. Pei had already used in the east wing of the National Gallery in Washington in 1978.

Another Pei trademark – the use of identical material for floors and walls – is also present in the entrance hall. Pei used sandstone from Burgundy to cover walls and floors, matte on the walls and polished on the floor.

The Spatial Programme of the Grand Louvre

Die Kosten

Die Umbaukosten des Louvres betrugen von 1983–2001 sechs Milliarden Francs

1. Bauphase:	2 Milliarden
(umfaßt Empfangsflächen, Cour Napoléon und Cour Carré)	
Cour Carrée:	225 Millionen
Cour Napoléon:	1,8 Milliarden
Pyramide:	75 Millionen

2. Bauphase:	1,2 Milliarden
(umfaßt die Arbeiten im Richelieu-Flügel)	
Zusatzkosten:	
Finanzministerium Bercy:	2,1 Milliarden
Brücken und Straßen:	500 Millionen

Costs

From 1983-2001 the conversion costs for the Louvre amounted to six billion francs.

1st construction phase:	2 billion
(includes reception areas, Cour Napoléon and Cour Carré)	
Cour Carrée:	225 million
Cour Napoléon:	1.8 billion
Pyramid:	75 million

2nd construction phase:	1.2 billion
(includes work in the Richelieu wing)	
Additional Costs:	
Ministry of Finance Bercy:	2.1 billion
Bridges and roads:	500 million

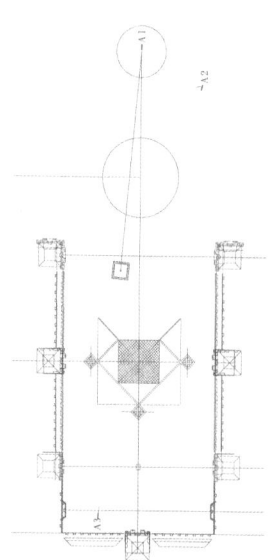

Oben: Sichtachsen; versetzte Reiterstatue
von Bernini und Glaspyramide
Von links nach rechts: Montage der Glasteile
der Pyramide; „Place Carrousel": umgedrehte Pyramide; Pyramide umgeben von drei
kleineren Pyramiden und sieben dreieckigen
Wasserbassins

Above: sight axis; removed equestrian
statue by Bernini and glass pyramid
From left to right: mounting of the glass
pieces; "Place Carrousel": inverted pyramid;
Main pyramid surrounded by three smaller
pyramids and seven triangular pools

Rund um die große Empfangshalle, die „Hall Napoléon", sind ein Auditorium mit 450 Sitzplätzen, Aufenthaltsräume, Sanitärbereiche, ein Café und die „Passage du Carrousel" angeordnet. Die Empfangshalle befindet sich neun Meter unterhalb der Erdoberfläche. Über Rolltreppen gelangt man in den eingezogenen Mezzanin und von dort zu den einzelnen Louvre-Flügeln.

Die Decken der Halle – teilweise als Kassettendecke ausgeführt – bestehen aus weißem, oberflächenbehandelten Beton. Dies hat einen Satin-Effekt zur Folge, eine Methode, die I.M. Pei bereits im Ostflügel der National Gallery in Washington 1978 angewandt hat.

Ein weiteres Markenzeichen Peis, Böden und Wände in ein und demselben Material zu halten, findet sich ebenfalls in der Eingangshalle wieder. Sandstein aus Burgund diente Pei zur Verkleidung von Wänden und Böden – matt eingesetzt an den Wänden, glänzend poliert am Boden.

Der Richelieu-Flügel beherbergt die Glyptothek – die Sammlung französischer Skulpturen. Die Dachverglasung dieses Flügels wurde von Macary und Rice-Francis-Ritchie entwickelt[2]. Die Passage Richelieu führt direkt zur Métro-Station Palais-Royal.

Die Terrasse der Tuilerien, der Parkanlage vor dem Louvre, wurde nach Originalplänen von Le Nôtre – Gartenbaumeister des 17. Jahrhunderts und Begründer des „Französischen Gartens" – wiederhergestellt.

Pei, Bewunderer dieser Zeit, stellt auch eine Kopie der Statue von Lorenzo Bernini aus dem Jahre 1685 wieder auf. Sie stellt Ludwig XIV. dar und steht heute genau in der Achse mit den Champs-Elysées. Sie bildet den Endpunkt der direkten Linie La Defense – Arc de Triomphe – Louvre.[3]

Die freigelegten Festungsmauern im Hof Cour Carrée von König Philippe Auguste und im Hof Cour Napoléon aus der Zeit Karl V. sind den Besuchern zugänglich gemacht worden. Die Krypta Philippe Auguste kann man zwischen neun Meter hohen Wällen durchwandern, die historischen Mauern des Hofes Cour Napoléon wurden in den Neubau integriert.

The Richelieu wing houses the sculpture gallery with a collection of French sculptures. The roof glazing for this wing was developed by Macary and Rice-Francis-Ritchie[2]. The "Passage Richelieu" leads directly to the Palais-Royal métro station.

The terraced Tuileries gardens around the Louvre were recreated in accordance with the original plans by Le Nôtre, the seventeenth-century landscape architect and originator of the "French garden".

Pei, an admirer of that era, also reinstated a reproduction of the statue by Lorenzo Bernini from 1685. It depicts Louis XIV and now stands precisely on the axis with the Champs-Elysées. The statue marks the termination point of a direct line leading from La Défense to the Arc de Triomphe to the Louvre.[3]

The excavated fortification walls – from King Phillippe Augustus' reign in the Cour Carrée and from Carl V's in the Cour Napoléon – have been made accessible to the public. Visitors can stroll through the Philippe Augustus crypt between 9-m-high walls, while the historic walls of the Cour Napoléon were integrated into the new construction.

The Louvre Today – and in the Future

In its eleven years of operation, the Grand Louvre has welcomed more than 60 million visitors. Conversion and renovation works will continue into 2005. The renovation and extension has increased the space for collections by fifty per cent.

Sections of the south wing "Aile de Flore" and the north wing "Aile Richelieu", where the French sculpture collection is housed, were completed in 2000. A separate exhibition space for the Mona Lisa will be opened in 2001.

A further 8250 square metres – of which 5550 square metres are exhibition areas – will continue to be under construction until 2005. 250 million francs have been set aside for the next ten years for façade and roof maintenance.

The main point of contention is still the pyramid in its role as central entrance and exit.

Der Louvre heute – und in Zukunft

Seit seinem nunmehr elfjährigen Bestehen kann der Grand Louvre mehr als 60 Millionen Besucher aufweisen. Die Umbauarbeiten werden noch bis 2005 fortgesetzt. Durch die Renovierung und die Erweiterung wurde eine bis zu fünfzigprozentige Raumgewinnung für die Sammlungen erzielt.

Teile des Südflügels „Aile de Flore" und des Nordflügels „Aile Richelieu", in dem sich die französische Skulpturensammlung befindet, wurden 2000 fertiggestellt. 2001 wird auch ein eigener Saal im Südflügel für die Mona Lisa eröffnet.

Weitere 8.250 m², davon 5.550 m² Ausstellungsfläche, werden bis 2005 Baustelle sein. 250 Millionen Francs sind für die nächsten zehn Jahre vorgesehen, um Fassade und Dach des Louvre instand zu halten. Hauptangriffspunkt bleibt die Pyramide als zentraler Hauptein- und -ausgang.

Das Erschließungskonzept von Pei, über einen zentralen Eingang in alle Bereiche des Louvre zu gelangen, wurde durch die Eröffnung eines zweiten Haupteinganges, Porte des Lions, im Südflügel „Aile de Flore" auf der Seineseite, im Mai 1999 durch Premierminister Lionel Jospin, erweitert. Dies ließ auch die Stimmen der Kritik, die sich an einem einzigen Haupteingang stießen, teilweise verstummen. Außerdem verfügt das Museum über zahlreiche Nebeneingänge.

Die letzte große Eröffnung eines Teilbereichs des Louvres war der ägyptische Pavillon am 19. Dezember 1999 durch Staatspräsident Jacques Chirac. Damit besitzt der Louvre mit 5000 antiken Schaustücken die weltweit bedeutendste Sammlung der ägyptischen Antike.

Im Sinne der französischen Streiktradition blieb und bleibt auch der Louvre von organisierten Kundgebungen seitens des Personals nicht verschont. Das Personal beschwerte sich über die „unzumutbaren Arbeitsbedingungen", die vor allem durch die schlechte Akustik in der Empfangshalle und die enorme Lärmbelastung, erzeugt durch das Volumen der Pyramide, entstanden.

Zahlreiche Streiks sind die Folge. 1999 sind zehn Prozent aller Säle geschlossen. Der Louvre verzeichnete in den letzten Jahren Streiks von einzelnen Tagen bis über drei Wochen, das bedeutet einen Verlust von 15.000 – 20.000 Besuchern täglich.

Es ist wie mit jedem anderen großen Museum oder Kulturbau heute, der einen langen Weg der Kritik hinter sich hat. Mittlerweile sind die Menschen stolz auf ihr Museum, es gehört zu den Wahrzeichen der Stadt.

Es ist aber auch ein Wirtschaftsbetrieb, der teils vom Staat, teils privat geführt wird. Dies führt zu einer schwierigen Gratwanderung zwischen wirtschaftlich erfolgreicher Führung und Öffnung des Hauses für „jedermann". Es stellt sich die Frage, ob der Louvre-Umbau dies bewerkstelligen kann.

So klassisch die Sammlung des Louvre auch ist, so paßt er sich dennoch in die zeitgenössische Museumslandschaft ein. Im Zeichen der heutigen Eventkultur präsentiert auch der Louvre seine „Stars": Nike, Venus von Milo und die Mona Lisa, Künstler wie Michelangelo, Vermeer, Géricaut, Ingrès etc.

Die Gesamtfläche des Louvre-Gebäudes beträgt 238.570 m², davon gehen 159.360 m² an das Musée du Louvre mit einer reinen Ausstellungsfläche von 59.860 m². (Bis 2005 werden 60.620 m² Ausstellungsfläche erreicht sein.)

Durch den Umbau konnten die Ausstellungsflächen gegenüber 1984 verdoppelt werden.

Insgesamt werden 35.000 Ausstellungsstücke gezeigt.

Die Empfangsflächen betragen insgesamt 22.300 m².

Das Gebäude des Louvre umfaßt neben dem Museum u. a. die Geschäftsflächen der „Espaces du Carrousel" (17.800 m²), die „Ecole du Louvre", Restaurierungswerkstätten, ein Recherchezentrum der „Museen Frankreichs", die Zentralvereinigung der „Arts Décoratifs" und Parkflächen von 25.000 m².

Pei's circulation concept of providing access to all areas of the Louvre from one central entrance was expanded by the creation of a second main entrance – the Porte des Lions in the south wing, the "Aile de Flore" overlooking the Seine, opened in May 1999 by prime minister Lionel Jospin. This silenced critics who had deplored the fact that there was only one main entrance. Moreover, the museum has a number of subsidiary entrances.

The final major inauguration of a Louvre section took place in December 1999, when President Jacques Chirac officially opened the Egyptian pavilion. The Louvre now boasts the most important collection of Ancient Egyptian art with a total of 5000 artefacts.

In keeping with the French tradition of labour disputes and strikes, the Louvre, too, has had and continues to have its share of demonstrations on the part of its staff. Employees complained about the "unbearable working conditions", in particular the poor acoustics in the reception hall and the high noise levels that result from the spatial volume of the pyramid.

Numerous strikes ensued. In 1999, ten per cent of all exhibition areas were closed. In recent years, the Louvre has had to cope with industrial action lasting anywhere from a few days to over three weeks, which translates into a loss of 15,000 to 20,000 visitors daily.

The story is identical to that of other major museums or cultural buildings, which have survived a long history of criticism. In the meantime, residents are proud of their museum, and it has become one of the landmarks of the city.

But it is also a business, operated in part by the state and in part privately. This leads to a difficult balancing act between successful

The Louvre covers a total area of **238,570** square metres, of which **159,360** are dedicated to the Musée du Louvre with a net exhibition area of **59,860** square metres. (By 2005, the total exhibition area will have grown to **60,620** square metres.)

The conversion has doubled the exhibition area in comparison to 1984.

A total of 35,000 exhibites are on view.

The reception areas cover a total of **22,300** square metres.

In addition to the museum, the Louvre also houses the retail areas of the "Espaces du Carrousel" (**17,800** square metres), the "Ecole du Louvre," restoration workshops, a research centre for the "museums of France," the central association of "Arts Décoratifs" and a parking area of **25,000** square metres.

Jährliche Kosten des Musée du Louvre:
775 Mio. Francs

Staatliche Subvention:
540 Mio. Francs (2/3 der Kosten).

Eigenmittel aus Einnahmen:
1/3 aller Kosten.
(2000: 150 Mio. Francs durch Ticketverkauf;
Anstieg um 50 Prozent gegenüber 1993
mit 100 Mio. Francs Einnahmen aus
Eintrittskartenverkauf.)

Die Idee und der Wunsch von Francois Mitterrand, den Louvre mit seinen Kunstschätzen den Franzosen näherzubringen, sind 12 Jahre nach Eröffnung der Pyramide mit rund 35 Prozent der Bevölkerung, die den Louvre zumindest einmal bereits besucht haben, zahlenmäßig vielleicht aufgegangen. Über 60 Prozent der Besucher kommen aber aus dem Ausland.

Zum Vergleich hat auch das Centre Georges Pompidou eine fünfjährige Schließungszeit hinter sich, in der das architektonische Gesamtkonzept überholt wurde. Seit dem Jahr 2000 kann der Besucher wieder beide Institutionen aufsuchen. Eine jährliche repräsentative Durchschnittsbesucherzahl wird man erst in zwei bis drei Jahren ermitteln können, wenn der Eröffnungsbonus nicht mehr relevant ins Gewicht fällt. (Im ersten Quartal 2000 zählte man 2,5 Millionen Besucher, die entweder Ausstellungen besuchten oder die Bibliothek frequentierten.)

Jedenfalls konnte Mitterrand sein Ziel erreichen, den Louvre zum größten Museum der Welt zu machen. Seine Staatspolitik hat die Kulturlandschaft in Paris wesentlich bereichert, obwohl seine zentralistische Machtausübung die Gemüter erhitzt hat und die Kritiker auf die Barrikaden brachte. Doch der unbedingte Machtanspruch von Mitterrand hat ihm geholfen, Architektur in den Vordergrund zu stellen, indem er prestigeträchtige Bauplätze wählte und so Denkmäler des 20. Jahrhunderts setzte – für die französische Bevölkerung und nicht zuletzt für sich selbst.

financial operation and making the institution accessible to the "common person". The question remains of whether the Louvre extension can meet this challenge.

Although the Louvre collection is classically orientated, it nevertheless fits into the contemporary museum scene. In keeping with today's event-focused culture, the Louvre also places its "stars" front and centre: Nike, Venus de Milo and the Mona Lisa, as well as artists such as Michelangelo, Vermeer, Géricault, Ingrès and others.

Twelve years after the opening of the pyramid, François Mitterrand's dream of bringing the Louvre and its art treasures closer to the French people has perhaps been achieved: nearly thirty-five per cent of the population have visited the Louvre at least once. Still, more than sixty per cent of visitors are foreigners.

By comparison, the Centre Georges Pompidou has just had to submit to a five-year closure during which the entire architectural concept was overhauled. Since 2000, both institutions have once again been open to visitors. It will take two to three years before average annual visitor figures are available, once the added attractions of recent openings no longer distort or inflate the figures. (In the first quarter of 2000, 2.5 million visitors were counted, frequenting either the exhibitions or the library.)

At any rate, Mitterrand succeeded in reaching his goal of transforming the Louvre into the world's largest museum. His national policies have considerably enriched the cultural landscape of Paris, even though his centralized approach to power sparked much heated debate and brought the critics onto the barricades. Yet Mitterrand's unconditional demand for power also helped him to push architecture into the foreground by selecting prestigious building sites and thus creating monuments to the twentieth century, both for the French people and for himself.

„Hall Napoléon": Eingangssituation, die über (Roll-)Treppen hinab in die Eingangshalle führt.

"Hall Napoléon": entrance, which leads–via escalators and stairs–down to the entrance hall.

Annual (operating) costs
of the Musée du Louvre: 775 million francs.

State subsidies:
540 million francs (2/3 of costs)

Museum income:
1/3 of total costs
(2000: 150 million francs from admission sales. An increase of 50 per cent by comparison to 1993 with 100 million francs income from ticket sales.)

Kultur- und Kongresszentrum Luzern

Der erfolgreiche Manager/The Successful Manager

Eine Stadt
stimmt ab

Luzern, idyllisch am Ufer des Vierwaldstättersees gelegen, umgeben von einem beeindruckenden Bergpanorama: die Tourismusmetropole der Schweiz. Mitten in der Idylle ein neues Objekt, sein weit über den See auskragendes Dach betont streng die Horizontale. Hier, im Herzen der Zentralschweiz, einer Stadt mit 60.000 Einwohnern, befindet sich das „Kultur- und Kongresszentrum Luzern" (KKL), ein Gebäude internationalen Zuschnitts mit einem der weltbesten Konzertsäle. Prominent am Ufer gelegen, Herzeigebeispiel zeitgenössischer Architektur, hat sich dieses Gebäude selbstbewußt seinen Platz geschaffen. Eine Stadt hat dafür gestimmt, ein Manager hat Überzeugungsarbeit geleistet.

Ausgangssituation

Anfang der achtziger Jahre existiert in Luzern eine vielfältige und blühende Kulturszene, die mit zunehmender Raumnot konfrontiert ist. Einer stark verankerten alternativen Szene stehen die weltweit anerkannten „internationalen Musikfestspiele" (IMF) gegenüber, die im 1933/34 von Architekt Armin Meili erbauten Kunst- und Kongreßhaus stattfinden. Dieses Gebäude befindet sich am Europaplatz in unmittelbarer Nähe des Bahnhofs, und es beherbergt auch das Kunstmuseum und die Stadthalle.

1986 startet die Stadt eine Kulturoffensive mit dem Ziel, die Raumsituation der Kulturszene Luzerns zu verbessern. Vor dieser städtischen Entwicklung hatten sich bereits die Kunstgesellschaft Luzern und der „Verein zur Erhaltung des Bourbaki-Panoramas" zusammengefunden und die Idee initiiert, Kunstmuseum und Bourbaki-Panorama in einem gemeinsamen Neubau am Löwenplatz unterzubringen.

Ein Architekturwettbewerb wurde ausgeschrieben, den die Züricher Architektengemeinschaft Kreis, Schaad und Schaad mit ihrem Projekt „Pro Arte" im Dezember 1987 gewinnen.

Die Stadt setzt eine Arbeitsgruppe ein, die sich mit einem umfassenden Umbau des bestehenden Kunst- und Kongreßhauses bei gleichzeitiger Ausquartierung des Kunstmuseums befaßt. Darauf melden sich auch die lokalen Musikvereine und die IMF zu Wort und fordern ihrerseits einen neuen Konzertsaal. Mit dem Ziel, den Neubau eines Konzerthauses durch Mittelbeschaffung, Öffentlichkeitsarbeit und Zusammenarbeit mit der öffentlichen Hand zu fördern, schließen sich IMF und AML (Allgemeine Musikgesellschaft Luzern) sowie lokale Musikvereine bis hin zum städtischen Blasmusikkorps, Banken, Firmen und Ein-

A City Casts its Vote

Lucerne is the tourist metropolis of Switzerland by virtue of its idyllic setting on Lake Lucerne and the imposing panorama of mountains. A new object has appeared at the centre of this idyll, its cantilevered roof projecting far into the lake in an uncompromising emphasis of the horizontal plane. Here, in a city of 60,000 inhabitants in the heart of central Switzerland, is the location for the Culture and Convention Centre (or CCC), a structure of international stature that boasts one of the best concert halls in the world. With its prominent site on the lakeshore, the building has confidently claimed a place for itself, becoming a showcase for contemporary architecture. An entire city cast its vote in favour of it and a dedicated manager undertook the necessary PR work.

Point of Departure

In the early 1980s Lucerne is home to a varied and flourishing cultural scene that is, however, faced increasingly with a dearth of performance and exhibition spaces. The deeply rooted alternative scene is complemented by the world-famous "International Music Festival" (IMF) that is held each year in the Art and Convention Centre built by architect Armin Meili in 1933/34. Located on Europaplatz in immediate proximity to the train station, the building also houses the art museum and city hall.

In 1986 the city launches an ambitious cultural campaign with the goal of improving the amenities for the arts in Lucerne. The art association of Lucerne and the "association for the preservation of the Bourbaki Panorama" had already joined forces prior to this municipal initiative, tabling the idea of housing the art museum and the Bourbaki Panorama under one roof in a new building on Löwenplatz.

A competition is held. In December 1987 the Zurich architects' cooperative Kreis, Schaad and Schaad are awarded first prize for their "Pro Arte" competition entry.

The city sets up a task force with the mandate to oversee the major conversion of the existing Art and Convention Centre and to relocate the art museum. Soon local music clubs and the IMF raise their voices, demanding a new concert hall. With the goal of promoting the construction of a new concert hall through fund raising, public relations and public funds, the IMF and the AML (Music Association of Lucerne), as well as local music clubs right down to the municipal brass band, banks, companies and private citizens all gather together to found the "Concert Hall Foundation."

Das größte Riesenrundgemälde der Welt mit 1.100 m² Fläche zeigt den Übertritt der französischen Ostarmee unter General Bourbaki bei Les Verrières in die Schweiz und deren Internierung während des Deutsch-Französischen Krieges 1870/71.

The largest panoramic painting in the world with 1,100 m² surface depicts the surrender of the French Eastern Army under General Bourbaki to Switzerland near Les Verrières and the internment during the German-French War of 1870/71.

Der Bahnhofsvorplatz mit dem
Meili-Bau in den vierziger (links)
und neunziger Jahren (rechts).

The forecourt of the Station with the
Meili building from the 1940s (left) and
the 1990s (right).

zelpersonen zusammen und gründen die „Stiftung Konzerthaus".

In dieser Situation der widerstreitenden Interessen, Umbau,- Neu-
bau- und Erweiterungspläne zieht die Stadt schließlich die Hayek
Engineering AG, Zürich, als Consultingunternehmen hinzu. Die Con-
sulter erhalten den Auftrag, eine Optimierungsstudie zur Schaffung von
Kulturräumen durchzuführen und das von der Stadt erstellte Leitbild
zu überprüfen. Im März 1988 wird die Hayek-Studie dem Stadtrat und
der Öffentlichkeit präsentiert. An der Erarbeitung wesentlich beteiligt
ist der Unternehmensberater Thomas Held. Die Ergebnisse sehen drei
Hauptpunkte vor:
> Das alte Kultur- und Kongreßhaus, der Meili-Bau, soll durch einen
Neubau am Europaplatz mit einem Konzertsaal, einer Stadthalle und
einer Kongreßinfrastruktur ersetzt werden.
> Das „Pro-Arte"-Projekt (am Löwenplatz) wird unterstützt; allerdings
bedarf es einer teilkommerziellen Nutzung, um die Finanzierbarkeit zu
gewährleisten.
> Eine zeitlich vorgezogene Bereitstellung neuer Räume für die Alter-
nativkultur wird vorgeschlagen. Die ehemalige Metallschlauchfabrik
Boa soll zum Kulturzentrum BOA für freies Theater, Tanztheater, Ausstellungen und Konzerte umgewidmet werden.

Der Stadtrat schließt sich größtenteils der Studie an und beschließt
im August 1988 ein Investitionsprogramm von 100 Millionen Franken,
das den Konzerthausneubau, das Zentrum für bildende Kunst am
Löwenplatz (Kunstmuseum und Bourbaki-Panorama) und die Boa-
Fabrik umfaßt. Allerdings gibt er nur ein Drittel der Boa-Fabrik frei, der
Rest soll weiterhin gewerblich genutzt werden. Das führt zur Gründung
der Boa-Initiative, die das gesamte Gebäude als selbstverwaltetes Kulturzentrum einfordert. Für den Stadtpräsidenten Franz Kurzmeyer ist
die Berücksichtigung der alternativen Szene auch ein wichtiges poli-
tisches Anliegen: „Bei uns dürfen keine Opernhauskrawalle stattfinden. Es ist auch eine Gerechtigkeitsfrage – man muß Vorleistun-
gen erbringen und Vertrauen schaffen. Man kann nicht 100 Millionen
in ein solches Projekt investieren und die alternative Szene mit nichts
abspeisen."[1]

Ein Wettbewerb mit mehreren Siegern

Um die Planung voranzutreiben, spendet die Verlegerin und Kunst-
mäzenin Alice Bucher 1988 der Stadt Luzern die benötigte Summe von
960.000 Franken für die Durchführung eines Architekturwettbewer-
bes „Konzerthaus". Diese Vorgehensweise entspricht aber nicht dem
Schweizer Verständnis von unmittelbarer Demokratie. Ein Referendum

Faced with this situation of competing interests, simultaneous plans for conversion, new construction and expansion, the city invites Hayek Engineering AG, Zurich, to act as consultants. The company is given the mandate to execute a feasibility study on the creation of cultural facilities and to analyse the model created by the city authorities. In March 1988 the Hayek study is presented to the city council and the public. Management consultant Thomas Held is a major contributor to the study. The findings emphasize three items:

> The old Art and Convention Centre, the Meili building, is to be replaced with a new building on Europaplatz, which will contain a concert hall, a town hall and convention facilities.

> The study supports the "Pro Arte" project (on Löwenplatz); however, partial commercial use is recommended to ensure financial viability.

> New space is to be made available to the alternative arts scene sooner than initially planned. The former metal tube factory Boa is to be converted into the BOA cultural centre for experimental theatre, dance theatre, exhibitions and concerts.

The city council reaches a majority vote in support of the study and adopts a resolution in August of 1988 to invest CHF 100 million in the new concert hall, the Centre for Visual Arts on Löwenplatz (art museum and Bourbaki Panorama) and the Boa factory. However, only one third of the Boa factory will be dedicated to cultural use with the remaining two thirds slated for continued commercial use. This leads to the founding of the Boa initiative, which demands that the entire structure be used as a self-governed cultural centre. Mayor Franz Kurzmeyer recognizes the consideration of the alternative scene as an important political issue: "We must not stoop to opera house rows. This is also a question of justice — we must be prepared to give in advance and to generate trust. It isn't right to invest 100 million in a project of this kind and leave the alternative scene empty-handed."[1]

A Competition with Several Victors

To speed up the planning process, publisher and art patron Alice Bucher donates CHF 960,000 to the city of Lucerne in 1988, the sum required to carry out the architecture competition for the "concert hall." But this procedure runs counter to the Swiss idea of direct democracy. A referendum is held in opposition to the use of the donation and on 5 March 1989 a vote is held for tendering the "Project Competition for a Cultural Centre on the Lake." The democratic process of the altogether seven referenda on the planned cultural centres is underway.

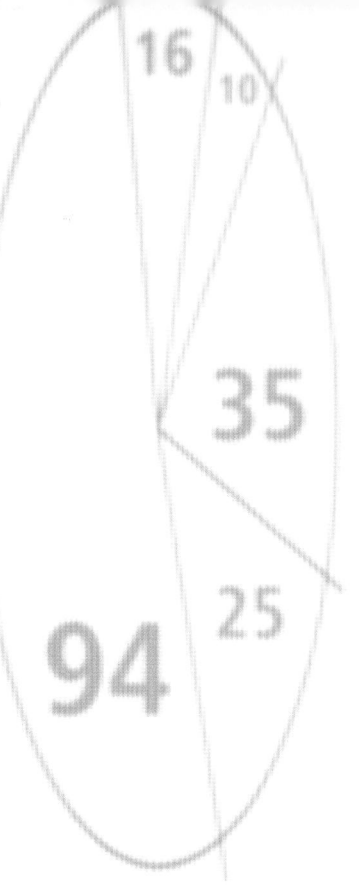

1991 werden Finanzierungsanteile der Trägerschaften festgelegt (in SFr)

In 1991 the sponsorship distribution is defined as follows (in CHF)

Stadt Luzern	**94 Mio.**
City of Lucerne	94 million
Kanton Luzern	**25 Mio.**
Canton Lucerne	25 million
Konzerthaus-Stiftung	**35 Mio.**
Concert Hall Foundation	35 million
IG Kongreßwesen	**10 Mio.**
IG Convention	
Management	10 million
Rest über Fremdfinanzierung	
Remainder through debt financing	

wird gegen die Verwendung der Spende eingebracht, und es kommt am 5. März 1989 zu einer Abstimmung über die Ausschreibung des „Projektwettbewerbs Kulturzentrum am See". Der demokratische Lauf der insgesamt sieben Volksabstimmungen über die geplanten Kulturzentren beginnt.

Eine Diskussion über Erhalt oder Abbruch des Meili-Baus entspinnt sich, wobei vor allem die Denkmalschutzkommission für den Erhalt eintritt. Mangels Einigung beschließt man, es den Wettbewerbsteilnehmern freizustellen, das alte Kunst- und Kongreßhaus zu belassen oder abzureißen. Die Ausschreibung des zweistufigen Wettbewerbes erfolgt noch im selben Monat – beschränkt auf das Land Schweiz sowie elf zugeladene ausländische Büros.

Von den 67 Einreichungen kommen neun Projekte in die zweite Runde. Die Jury ist sich uneinig, vergibt keine Plätze, sondern nur Ränge aus „ästhetischer Sicht":

> 1. Rang: „Opus", Jean Nouvel / Emmanuel Cattani, Paris. Ihr Vorschlag, den Meili-Bau mit Glas zu umhüllen und den neuen Konzertsaal schiffsheckähnlich in den See hinausragen zu lassen, verstößt jedoch gegen die Wettbewerbsbedingungen, da Seegrund nicht in die Planung einbezogen werden durfte.
> 2. Rang: „Argos", Rafael Moneo, USA. Da auch Rafael Moneo den Seegrund in die Planung miteinbezieht, ergeht nach neuerlicher Reihung der erste Platz an den Drittgereihten:
> 3. Rang: „Mauli Bay", Rudolphe Luscher, Lausanne.

Im Juni 1990 setzt der Stadtrat auf Vorschlag der Jury eine Projektführungsgruppe ein, die neue Rahmenbedingungen für die Weiterbearbeitung der ersten drei Projekte erarbeiten soll. Alle drei Architekturbüros akzeptieren diese Bedingungen. Während der Bund Schweizer Architekten das Projekt Nouvel/Cattani favorisiert, entscheiden sich der Luzerner Stadtrat und die Stiftung Konzerthaus für das drittgereihte Projekt, da es ihnen finanziell und planerisch am mach-

A debate begins on the merits of preserving or demolishing the Meili building, with the Commission for Monument Conservation making a strong case for preservation. Failure to reach a consensus leads to the decision to leave it up to each participant in the competition to decide whether the old Art and Convention Centre is to remain intact or be demolished. The tender for the two-level competition is released in the same month, restricted to Switzerland and eleven foreign invitees.

Of sixty-seven competition entries, nine projects are advanced to the second round. The jury is unable to agree: instead of awarding prizes, they decide to rank the entries based on "aesthetic merit."
> 1st rank: "Opus" by Jean Nouvel / Emmanuel Cattani, Paris. But the proposal to envelop the Meili building in glass and to cantilever the new concert hall into the lake in the manner of a ship's prow violates the competition rules, which specify that lake ground must not be included in the planning.
> 2nd rank: "Argos" by Rafael Moneo, USA. Since Rafael Moneo, too, incorporates lake ground into his proposal, the first place is awarded, after reconsideration, to the architect originally ranked third:
> 3rd rank: "Mauli Bay" by Rudolphe Luscher, Lausanne.

In June 1990, the city council follows the jury's recommendation to set up a project management team, whose task it is to develop new outlines for further development of the first three projects. All three architecture firms accept these conditions. While the Federation of Swiss Architects favours the project by Nouvel/Cattani, the Lucerne city council and the Concert Hall Foundation support the third ranked project, because it seems to be, in their view, the most feasible from a financial and a planning perspective. Nouvel/Cattani voice their protest. At the same time it becomes evident that the "Pro Arte" project cannot be realized for lack of financial support from the canton. The presidents of both the art association and the panorama association resign in protest over "this victory of musical circles over the [visual] arts." The confrontation in Lucerne is at its peak.

Jury member Mario Campi comments on the competition: "... while our recommendation is not legally binding, it is morally imperative if the city believes in the principle of architecture competitions. Should the third-rank project be chosen for further development, the architecture competition will degenerate into a farce."[2] Alice Bucher also criticizes the decision: "What is being planned is absolutely ridiculous and small-minded. It is depressing to be forced into watching this small-town farce."[3]

In March 1991 the dispute culminates in a civil lawsuit filed by Nouvel/Cattani against the city of Lucerne. Criticism comes from other

Wettbewerbsmodell Rudolphe Luscher (links) und Nouvel/Cattani (rechts) 1990, Alice Bucher (unten)

Competition model Rudolphe Luscher (left) and Nouvel/Cattani (right) 1990 Alice Bucher (below)

barsten erscheint. Das Büro Nouvel/Cattani protestiert. Zur gleichen Zeit stellt sich auch heraus, daß das „Pro-Arte"-Projekt nicht realisiert werden kann, da keinerlei finanzielle Unterstützung des Kantons einfließt. Die Präsidenten der Kunstgesellschaft und des Panoramavereins treten aus Protest „vor diesem Sieg der Musikkreise über die Kunstgesellschaft" zurück. Der Luzerner Eklat ist perfekt.

Mario Campi, Jurymitglied, über den Wettbewerb: „... unsere Empfehlung ist zwar nicht juristisch bindend, aber moralisch verpflichtend, wenn die Stadt an das Prinzip des Architekturwettbewerbs glaubt. Wird nun das drittrangierte Werk weiterverfolgt, wird der Architekturwettbewerb zur Farce."[2] Auch Alice Bucher kritisiert die Entscheidung: „Es ist absolut lächerlich und kleinmütig, was da nun geplant wird. Es ist deprimierend, diese kleinstädtische Posse mitansehen zu müssen."[3]

Entwurf Nouvel/Cattani (links),
Thomas Held (rechts)

Design Nouvel/Cattani (left)
Thomas Held (right)

Im März 1991 findet der Streit in einer Zivilklage von Nouvel/Cattani gegen die Stadt Luzern seinen Höhepunkt. Kritik kommt auch von anderer Seite. 1.000 Unterschriften werden von der sogenannten „Inseli-Initiative" gesammelt, die die weitere Verbauung des Europaplatzes verhindern will und für die Errichtung eines öffentlichen Parks eintritt. Die Initiative wird im Oktober 1991 von den Luzerner Stimmbürgern abgelehnt.[4]

Ein neuerlicher Vorstoß der städtischen Denkmalschutzkommission zur Erhaltung des Meili-Baus wird vom Stadtrat nicht unterstützt.

Der Stadtrat, die politische Repräsentanz von Luzern, erkennt, daß das Vorhaben nicht mit den eigenen Ressourcen bewältigt werden kann und setzt auf professionelles und externes Management. Die Wahl fällt auf den Unternehmensberater Thomas Held, der bereits durch seine Mitarbeit an der Optimierungsstudie von Hayek Engineering bestens mit dem Projekt vertraut ist. Er wird Geschäftsführer der Koordinationskonferenz Kulturraum (Koku). Seine Aufgabe ist die Erarbeitung eines konsensfähigen Gesamtkonzeptes und die Suche nach Partnern für Finanzierung, Betrieb und Öffentlichkeitsarbeit. Ein halbes Jahr später stellt er ein völlig neues Raumprogramm vor:

Er empfiehlt den Abbruch des Meili-Baus aus finanziellen, betrieblichen und ökonomischen Gründen. Das Kunstmuseum müsse in den Neubau integriert werden, wenn auch mit einer eigenständigen architektonischen Identität. Daraus folgt ein Gesamtkomplex am Europaplatz, bestehend aus Konzertsaal, multifunktionalem Saal, Kongreßzentrum, Kunstmuseum und Restaurants. Dieser Komplex solle von Rudolphe Luscher, dem drittgereihten des Wettbewerbes, umgesetzt werden.

Thomas Held macht sich im Verlauf auch für die Erweiterung der Projektierungsgesellschaft stark, die bis dahin nur aus der Stadt Luzern und der Stiftung Konzerthaus bestanden hatte. Man bindet nun auch den Kanton Luzern und die aus Hoteliers und Gewerbeleuten gebildete Interessensgemeinschaft Kongreßwesen ein. Die Finanzierungsanteile der einzelnen Trägerschaften werden festgelegt. Es wird entschieden, daß der Betrieb des künftigen Komplexes durch eine sich selbst tragende Betriebsgesellschaft nach privatwirtschaftlichen Maßstäben geführt werden soll. In einem weiteren wichtigen und richtungsweisenden Schritt werden die Nutzungsrechte der Luzerner Ver-

sources as well. 1000 signatures are gathered by the "Inseli Initiative," which seeks to prevent further densification of the Europaplatz and supports the creation of a public park. The initiative is rejected in October 1991 by Lucerne's electorate.[4]

Renewed efforts by the municipal Commission for Monument Conservation to preserve the Meili building fail to gain support from the city council.

The city council, the political executive of Lucerne, acknowledges that it is unable to realize the project with its own resources and decides to rely on professional and external management. Management consultant Thomas Held – already familiar with the project through his participation in the feasibility study carried out by Hayek Engineering – is selected for the task and appointed as managing director of the Task-Force for the Creation of Cultural Space (or Koordinationskonferenz Kulturraum (Koku)). He is charged with developing an overall concept capable of inviting consensus and actively seeking partners for financing, operation and public relations. Six months later, Held unveils a completely new programme. He recommends that the Meili building be demolished for financial, operational and economic reasons. The art museum should be integrated into the new building, albeit with an autonomous architectonic identity. The outcome is an integrated complex on Europaplatz consisting of concert hall, multi-functional auditorium, convention centre, art museum and restaurants. The complex is to be realized by Rudolphe Luscher, ranked third in the competition.

Thomas Held also actively pursues the expansion of the project group, hitherto composed of the city of Lucerne and the Concert Hall Foundation. Now the canton and the interest group Convention Management, whose membership includes hotel managers and business people, are asked to join. The financial responsibility of each sponsor is defined. A decision is reached that a self-sufficient company on a private enterprise basis will operate the future complex. In yet another and defining step the rights of use are determined for Lucerne's associations and non-profit organizations. Non-commercial events are to be made possible through special conditions and reduced rental fees. With this move Thomas Held achieves majority approval of the project.

Construction costs are estimated at CHF 180 million. A general manager will be charged with supervising the adherence to cost and construction schedules, while a general contractor will carry out the execution.

The principal parties – the city, the canton, the concert hall foundation and the convention and exhibition interest group – found a project development association, to which Thomas Held is once again appointed as managing director. Henceforth this association will be the client. Legal responsibility for the project is thereby transferred from the city to the project development association.

In January 1992 the executive city council ratifies the general concept, approving project financing to the tune of CHF 3.5 million for a preliminary project. The first stirrings of a conflict with Rudolphe Luscher

Die Anteile innerhalb der Projektierungsgesellschaft im Jahre 1992 (in SFr):

Equity distribution within the planning group in 1992 (in CHF):

Stadt Luzern	3,5 Mio.
City of Lucerne	3.5 million
Kanton Luzern	0,9 Mio.
Canton Lucerne	0.9 million
Stiftung Konzerthaus	0,2 Mio.
Concert Hall Foundation	0.2 million
IG Kongreß- und Ausstellungswesen	0,1 Mio.
IG Convention management	0.1 million

eine und nichtkommerziellen Organisationen festgelegt. Nichtkommerzielle Veranstaltungen sollen durch spezielle und vergünstigte Miettarife das Haus nutzen können. Damit erreicht Thomas Held eine breite Basis für die Zustimmung zum Projekt.

Die Schätzung der Baukosten beläuft sich auf rund 180 Millionen Schweizer Franken. Für die Gewährleistung der Kosten und Termine soll die Planung von einem Generalplaner, die Ausführung von einem Generalunternehmer erfolgen.

Die vier Hauptträger Stadt, Kanton, Stiftung Konzerthaus und IG Kongreß- und Ausstellungswesen gründen eine Projektierungsgesellschaft, in der wieder Thomas Held als Geschäftsführer eingesetzt wird. Diese fungiert fortan als Bauherrin. Damit geht die rechtliche Verantwortung für das Projekt von der Stadt auf die Projektierungsgesellschaft über.

Im Januar 1992 genehmigt der Große Stadtrat das Gesamtkonzept und bewilligt einen Projektierungskredit von 3,5 Millionen Schweizer Franken für ein Vorprojekt. Ein Konflikt mit Rudolphe Luscher bahnt sich an, der sich gegen die Einsetzung eines Generalplaners wehrt, da er sich in dieser Konstellation als Architekt abgewertet fühlt. Diverse Aussprachen zwischen ihm und Vertretern der Leitungsdelegation bringen keine Einigung. Thomas Held fühlt in Paris vor, ob es zu einer neuerlichen Zusammenarbeit mit Nouvel/Cattani kommen könne. Er hatte Erfolg: Eine offizielle Luzerner Delegation reist im März nach Paris und verabschiedet mit Nouvel/Cattani eine Grundsatzvereinbarung über deren Wiedereinstieg. Die Klage gegen die Stadt Luzern wird von Nouvel/Cattani zurückgezogen. Am Tag darauf wird Luscher mitgeteilt, daß er den Auftrag verloren habe.

Erst kurz vor der bevorstehenden Abstimmung am 17. Mai 1992 über den Projektierungskredit von 3,5 Millionen Schweizer Franken wird die Öffentlichkeit über diesen Architektenwechsel informiert. Die Stadträtin Laura Gallati reicht eine Stimmrechtsbeschwerde ein, da im Antrag, der Grundlage der Volksabstimmung ist, noch Rudolphe Luscher als Architekt angeführt ist. Die Beschwerde wird abgewiesen.

Mit einer deutlichen Mehrheit befürworten die Luzerner Stimmberechtigten dennoch den 3,5-Millionen-Kredit und somit den Beitritt der Stadt zur Projektierungsgesellschaft. Das Projekt Nouvel/Cattani kann damit beginnen.

Der neue Architekt und sein Entwurf

Noch im Oktober 1992 – fünf Monate später – präsentieren Nouvel/Cattani ihr Konzept für das Kultur- und Kongreßzentrum Luzern: Drei durch Wasserkanäle getrennte Gebäudeteile – Konzertsaal, Kongreßzentrum und Kunstmuseum – sollen durch einen gemeinsamen Infrastrukturtrakt verbunden werden. Ein weit auskragendes Flügeldach überspannt den Gesamtkomplex.

Ein überarbeiteter Entwurf im März 1993 zeigt sich durch die Vereinfachung in der Dach- und Fassadengestaltung und ein geringeres Foyervolumen wesentlich kompakter. Geschätzte Kosten jetzt: 194 Millionen Schweizer Franken.

are felt, for the architect is opposed to the appointment of a planning manager, feeling that this constellation devalues his own role as architect. Efforts at mediating between the architect and the representatives of the management delegation bring little success. Quietly and cautiously, Thomas Held begins to assess the situation in Paris in an attempt to gauge whether Nouvel/Cattani might be willing to reconsider the project. His efforts succeed: in March an official delegation travels from Lucerne to Paris, where an agreement in principle is signed with Nouvel/Cattani as to their reinstatement. Nouvel/Cattani retract their lawsuit. The very next day Luscher is told that he has lost the contract.

The public is informed of this change in architects shortly before the 17 May 1992 vote on the projected CHF 3.5 million financing. Councillor Laura Gallati submits a voting rights complaint, since the submission, which is the basis for the public referendum, still names Rudolphe Luscher as architect. The complaint is rejected.

Lucerne's electorate nevertheless supports the CHF 3.5 million credit with a clear majority, thus approving the membership of the city in the project development association. The Nouvel/Cattani project has thus been given the green light to proceed.

The New Architect and His Design

Five months later, in October 1992, Nouvel/Cattani present their concept for the CCC: three wings separated by water canals — concert hall, convention centre and art museum — linked by a common service tract. A winged roof, cantilevered far beyond the walls, spans the entire complex.

A revised design in March 1993 presents a far more compact structure as a result of a simplified approach to roof- and façade design and a smaller foyer. The estimated construction costs now stand at CHF 194 million.

Art historian Stanislaus von Moos undertakes a final effort to preserve the Meili building, entreating Jean Nouvel to review his plans one last time in the publication of the anniversary catalogue "60 Years Art Museum Lucerne in the Meili Building." Von Moos muses: "How

**Jean Nouvel, Franz Kurzmeyer
(Stadtpräsident von Luzern),
Aquarellstudie**

Jean Nouvel, Franz Kurzmeyer
(mayor of Lucerne)
Water-colour study

**Abbruch des Meili-Baus 1996
und Rohbau 1997**

Demolition of the Meili building
1996 and shell construction 1997

Ein letzter Vorstoß in Richtung Erhalt des Meili-Baus wird vom Kunsthistoriker Stanislaus von Moos unternommen, der im Jubiläumskatalog „60 Jahre Kunstmuseum Luzern im Meili-Bau" Jean Nouvel ersucht, seine Pläne nochmals zu überdenken. Denn: „Wie lange wird sich der waldstättische Knabentraum eines schweizerischen Sydney Opera House mit Flachdeckel halten können?"[5]

Der Akustiker Russel Johnson, der für den Konzertsaal der Birmingham Symphony Hall und des Meyerson Symphony Center von Dallas internationale Anerkennung fand, wird beauftragt. Sein Konzept geht von einer variablen Akustik durch Echokammern und einer in der Höhe verstellbaren Schalldecke, dem Canopy, aus.

Geplanter Baubeginn ist Frühjahr 1995. Um die Planungsarbeiten bis zur großen Volksabstimmung im Juni 1994 weiterführen zu können, werden weitere fünf Millionen Schweizer Franken benötigt, von denen drei Millionen durch private Donatoren zur Verfügung gestellt werden. Die restlichen zwei Millionen finanziert der Generalplaner Electrowatt Engineering mit seiner Tochtergesellschaft Göhner-Merkur AG vor und bekommt dafür im Gegenzug einen Totalunternehmervertrag.

Die Finanzierung

Karl Reichmuth, Luzerner Privatbankier und Vorsitzender des Sammelkomitees der Stiftung Konzerthaus, erreicht beim Regierungsrat des Kantons Luzern, daß die Donationen für das KKL von Steuern befreit werden. Das trägt zur Spendenfreudigkeit maßgeblich bei. Rund ein Drittel der Baukosten kann in jahrelanger Kleinarbeit von Stiftungen, Firmen und Privatpersonen zusammengetragen werden. Reichmuth erinnert sich „eisern jeden Abend drei Anrufe"[6] getätigt und dabei jedesmal Überzeugungsarbeit geleistet zu haben. Die Sammelaktion kann jedenfalls bis 1993 bereits 45 Millionen von privater Seite zusichern, was zu allgemeinem Erstaunen und Bewunderung in der Stadt Anlaß gibt.

122

long will this naive dream of a Swiss Sydney Opera House with a flat lid be sustainable?"[5]

Acoustic engineer Russel Johnson, internationally acclaimed for his work in the Birmingham Symphony Hall and the Meyerson Symphony Center in Dallas, is invited to participate. His concept is based on providing flexible acoustics by means of echo chambers and an adjustable sound ceiling, the canopy.

Construction is scheduled to begin in the spring of 1995. Another five million Swiss francs are needed to continue with the planning efforts until the large referendum in June 1994; three million are raised through private donations, while the remaining two million are provided by general contractor Electrowatt Engineering and its daughter company Goehner-Merkur AG, for which contribution the company receives an exclusive general contractor contract.

Financing

Karl Reichmuth, private banker in Lucerne and chair of the funding committee for the Concert Hall Foundation, manages to gain permission from the cantonal government for donations to the CCC to be tax deductible. This move greatly increases the flow of donations. Nearly one third of the construction costs are gathered throughout the following years through dedicated efforts in fund raising from foundations, companies and private citizens. Reichmuth recalls having "diligently made three calls every evening"[6], each time working hard to convince the correspondent on the other end of the line. By 1993 the fund-raising activities achieve a guarantee for CHF 45 million from private sources – a source of general amazement and admiration in the city.

In November the municipal endowment of CHF 11 million and a CHF 83 million construction fund are unanimously approved by the executive city council, followed a few weeks later by CHF 24 million from the canton, approved in the cantonal parliament with a majority vote of 133 to 2.

However, a final decision depends on the public referendum in June 1994.

Lucerne's hotel owners offer to contribute seven million Swiss francs. And thanks to a donation of two million Swiss francs, the art association can finally become a full member of the project development association.

An Inspired Marketing Concept – "Everything under one roof"

"Anyone who wishes to realize a larger building project today must enter into an intense dialogue with the public, regardless of the legal premise. ... In this day and age, individuals are perfectly able to halt a project without too much effort and at practically no risk. ... As a result of this state of affairs, the motto 'anything goes', which dominated the 1970s and 1980s, is no longer applicable to large construction projects; it has been replaced – at least in Switzerland – by a new motto: 'rien ne va plus!'"[7]

Im November werden die städtische Stiftungseinlage von 11 Millionen Schweizer Franken und der Baubeitrag von 83 Millionen vom Großen Stadtrat einstimmig und wenige Wochen später auch die kantonale Einlage von 24 Millionen Schweizer Franken vom Kantonsparlament mit 133 zu zwei Gegenstimmen angenommen

Eine endgültige Entscheidung darüber bedarf aber noch der Volksabstimmung im Juni 1994.

Die Luzerner Hoteliers garantieren sieben Millionen Stiftungseinlage. Die Kunstgesellschaft kann dank einer Spende von zwei Millionen nun auch in die Projektierungsgesellschaft aufgenommen werden.

„Wer heute ein größeres Bauvorhaben realisieren will, muß sich, unabhängig von der Rechtslage, intensiv mit der Öffentlichkeit auseinandersetzen. ... Einzelpersonen können heute ein Projekt ohne großen Aufwand und praktisch ohne Risiko verhindern. ... Als Folge dieser Entwicklung gilt für die Realisierung großer Bauvorhaben nicht mehr das ‚anything goes' der siebziger und achtziger Jahre, sondern – zumindest in der Schweiz – eher ein ‚rien ne va plus'."[7]

Thomas Held zeichnet sich im Verlauf des gesamten Projektes als der große Mediator aus, der die verschiedenen Interessen „an einen runden Tisch" bringt.

Bereits Anfang 1993 wird der überparteiliche „Infoverein Kultur- und Kongresszentrum" gegründet, um die Abstimmung am 12. Juni 1994 zu koordinieren. „Alles unter einem Dach", heißt das kultur- und tourismuspolitische Credo des Projektes. Im Juli 1993 wird erstmals eine perspektivische Zeichnung des Projekts in der Luzerner Tagespresse veröffentlicht, die von nun an als eine Art Logo weiterverwendet wird. Kurz darauf wird ein Modell im Maßstab 1:200 in der Ausstellung „Vorprojekt. Kultur- und Kongreßzentrum am See" einer breiten Öffentlichkeit präsentiert. Laufend werden Informationsbroschüren und Zeitungsbeilagen produziert, um die Luzerner auf dem neuesten Stand zu halten. Die PR-Arbeit setzt weniger auf großangelegte Medienkampagnen als vielmehr auf kleinteilige und zeitaufwendige „Face-to-face"-Arbeit. Unzählige Vorträge vor Vereinen und Organisationen sowie Diskussionen in Kneipen werden unternommen, um das Bauvorhaben zu erklären und allfällige Zweifel auszuräumen.

Vermittelt wird das Projekt über das anerkannte Aushängeschild der Internationalen Musikfestspiele (IMF), aber auch der „Pariser Stararchitekt Jean Nouvel"[8] dient als einzigartiges Markenzeichen. Um sich breite Akzeptanz zu sichern, sind die Versprechen, daß das neue KKL ein Haus für Rockkonzerte und Volkstümliches werde, daß die Vereine ein Nutzungsrecht zu günstigen Konditionen genießen werden, daß die Wirtschaft durch die Kongresse profitieren werde und das Zentrum kulturelle Impulse aller Art auslösen könne, von großer Bedeutung.

Nicht zuletzt bewirken auch die bis zur Abstimmung gesammelten Millionen – fast ein Drittel der Gesamtsumme! – einen enormen Druck,

Throughout the project, Thomas Held distinguishes himself as the great mediator who brings varying interests to "the round table."

As early as the outset of 1993 the non-party "CCC Information Association" is founded to co-ordinate the vote on 12 June 1994. The slogan to promote culture and tourism in the city through this project: "Everything under one roof." In July 1993 a perspective drawing of the project is published for the first time in Lucerne's daily paper, henceforth used as a kind of logo for the project. Shortly after, a model on a scale of 1:200 is presented to the public in an exhibition entitled "Preliminary Project: Culture and Convention Centre on the Lake." Numerous information brochures and newspaper inserts are produced to keep the residents of Lucerne up to date. Public relations focus less on large media campaigns than on detailed and time-consuming "face-to-face" work. Countless lectures in clubs and associations as well as public debates in pubs are organized to explain the building project and to eliminate any lingering doubts.

Public relations rely heavily on the fame of the International Music Festival (IMF), but the "star architect from Paris, Jean Nouvel"[8] is equally important for the project promotion. Promises of rock and folk concerts at the new CCC, of favourable conditions to allow local clubs to enjoy their rights of use, of benefits to the city's economy through the conventions held at the centre, and of cultural expansion, play an important role in securing widespread acceptance.

And finally there are the millions gathered through donations and contributions even before the referendum – nearly one third of the total cost! These, too, exert enormous pressure since they are contingent upon an affirmative vote result.

In the course of 1994 all parties, clubs and other organizations endorse the project and the financing plan. Only one dissenting voice remains: the association "Volkspark Inseli." A major public event is staged in the Meili building in May. A broad spectrum of performances (from the Handel choir to the town yodellers to the local gymnastics club) is intended to demonstrate the variety of uses to which the future CCC will be put.

Finally, the long-awaited day arrives: 12 June 1994, the day of the referendum. Lucerne's citizens vote by a 65.7% majority in favour of the CHF 94 million contribution, thereby approving the most expensive building project in the history of Lucerne.

This vote makes the city of Lucerne the principal sponsor of the project.

Construction calendar

Surveying begins the day after the referendum. In the same week the CCC sponsorship group is founded as successor to the project development association, entering into a contract with the general contractor. The group is now the owner of the CCC. Thomas Held is retained as managing director and Hanspeter Balmer is appointed president. The group is responsible for signing up contractors and for ensuring that the cost and construction schedules are carried out according to plan.

Einladungskarte zum „bunten Info-Abend" (links), Luzerner Neueste Nachrichten, 13.06.1994 (Franz Kurzmeyer, Jean Nouvel, Thomas Held)

Invitation card to a public information evening Luzerner Neueste Nachrichten, 13.06.1994 (Franz Kurzmeyer, Jean Nouvel, Thomas Held)

Prozent stimmten für den 94-Millionen-Beitrag der Stadt an ein neues Kultur- und Kongressze

Luzern glaubt an sich

(v. l. n. r.): Luzerns Stadtpräsident Franz Kurzmeyer, Architekt Jean Nouvel und Thomas Held von der Projektierungsgesellschaft.

Baukalender

1995

Januar	Baubeginn und zugleich erste Abbrucharbeiten am Ostflügel des Meili-Baus
April	Wagenbach-Brunnen steht an seinem neuen Standort
August	Start Aushub Baugrube
November	Start Rohbau Konzerthaussaal

1996

März	Eröffnung des äußeren See-beckens (Vierwaldstättersee um 800m² vergrößert)
Aug/Sept.	Letzte IMF im alten Konzertsaal
September	Abbruch alte Parkgarage
Oktober	Abbruch Westflügel Meili-Bau
November	Abschluß Montage Dach über Konzertsaal

1997

Januar	Start Ausbauarbeiten Konzert-saal
Februar	1. Aufrichtefest; Abschluß Rohbau Konzertsaal
März	Aushub Baugrube 2. Bauetappe
Juni	Start Rohbau 2. Bauetappe
Aug./Sept.	IMF im Zeltpavillon im Tribschen-Park
Oktober	Zwei 30 kg schwere Dachplatten der Unterseite fallen auf den Inseliquai. Erst mit neuer Siche-rungskonstruktion wird Arbeit wieder aufgenommen

1998

Februar	Abschluß Monatge Dach über Gesamtbau
Februar	2. Aufrichtefest; Gesamtrohbau ist abgeschlossen
Mai	Start Ausbauarbeiten 2. Bau-etappe
Juli	Ganze Fassade vollendet
August	Probekonzerte mit Publikum, um die Echokammern zu testen
August	18.-22., Eröffnungskonzerte (Berliner Philharmoniker unter Claudio Abbado)
Aug./Sept.	IMF im neuen Konzertsaal

1999

Juni	Abschluß Installationen
Juli	Abschluß Bauarbeiten
August	Übernahme Gesamtbau mit Museum, Start Probebetrieb

2000

März	24.-26., Eröffnungsfeier des KKLs (Luzerner Saal und Auditorium)
Juni	19., Eröffnung Kunstmuseum

Grundriß Niveau 0
Der Wagenbachbrunnen an seinem neuen Standort
Ostfassade mit Seebar

Floor plan level 0
Wagenbach-fountain installed at new site
East façade with sea bar

Construction calendar

1995
January	Start of construction and first demolition of the east wing of the Meili building
April	Wagenbach fountain installed at new site
August	Excavation of building pit starts
November	Shell work for concert hall begins

1996
March	Opening of outer lake basin (Lake Lucerne expanded by 800 m^2)
Aug/Sept.	Last IMF in old concert hall
September	Demolition of old parking garage
October	Demolition of west wing of Meili building
November	Completion of roof installation over concert hall

1997
January	Completion work on concert hall begins
February	First topping-out ceremony; completion of concert hall shell construction
March	Excavation of building pit for 2nd construction phase
June	Shell construction of 2nd construction phase begins
Aug./Sept.	IMF held in tent pavilion in Tribschen park
October	Two roof panels of the underside, each weighing 30 kg, fall onto the Inseli Quay. Work is resumed only after a new safety system has been put into place.

1998
February	Completion of roof installation across entire structure
February	Second topping-out ceremony; entire shell construction is complete
May	Completion works begin for 2nd construction phase
July	Completion of façade
August	Concert rehearsal in front of audience to test echo chambers
Aug. 18–22	Inaugural concerts (Berlin Philharmonics under Claudio Abbado)
Aug/Sept	IMF in new concert hall

1999
June	Completion of installation works
July	Completion of construction works
August	Acceptance of complex including museum, start of test operation

2000
March 24–26	Inauguration of the CCC (Lucerne Hall and Auditorium)
June 19	Art Museum Opening

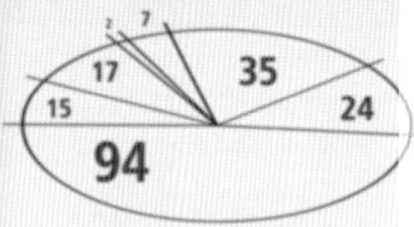

Nach der Abstimmung am 12. Juni 1994
sind die Anteile folgendermaßen (in SFr):

After the referendum on 12 June 1994
the distribution reads as follows (in CHF):

Stadt Luzern	**94 Mio.**
City of Lucerne	94 million
Kanton Luzern	**24 Mio.**
Canton Lucerne	24 million
Konzerthaus-Stiftung	**35 Mio.**
Concert Hall Foundation	35 million
IG Kongreß- und Ausstellungswesen	**7 Mio.**
IG Convention Management	7 million
Kunstgesellschaft Luzern	**2 Mio.**
Art Association of Lucerne	2 million
Fremdfinanzierung durch Hypotheken	**17 Mio.**
Debt financing through mortgages	17 million
Sonderbeiträge	**15 Mio.**
Spetial contributions	15 million

Der Plan „B"

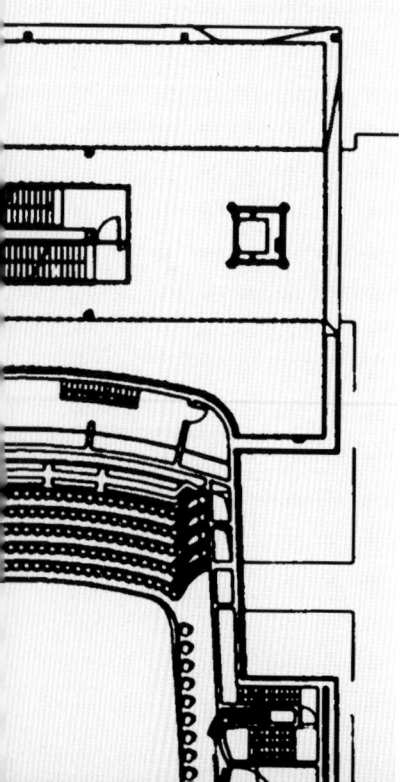

da diese Zusicherung an ein positives Abstimmungsergebnis gebunden ist.

Im Laufe des Jahres 1994 sprechen sich nach und nach alle Parteien, Vereine und sonstige Organisationen für das Projekt und den Hauptkredit aus. Nur der Verein Volkspark Inseli ist noch dagegen. Im Mai wird ein großangelegtes Informationsfest im Meili-Bau veranstaltet, bei dem ein breites Spektrum an Veranstaltungen (Händel-Chor über Stadtjodler bis zum Turnverein) die vielfältigen Nutzungsmöglichkeiten des künftigen KKL demonstrieren soll.

Der lang ersehnte Tag naht: der 12. Juni 1994, Tag der Volksabstimmung über den Projektierungskredit. Mit 65,7 Prozent stimmen die Luzerner dem 94-Millionen-Schweizer-Franken-Beitrag zu und damit dem teuersten Bauprojekt in der Geschichte Luzerns. Die Stadt Luzern wird somit Hauptaktionär der Trägerstiftung.

Baukalender

Bereits am Tag nach der Abstimmung beginnen die Vermessungsarbeiten. Noch in der gleichen Woche wird die Trägerstiftung KKL als Nachfolgerin der Projektierungsgesellschaft gegründet und tritt in den Vertrag mit dem Totalunternehmer ein. Sie ist nun Eigentümerin des Kultur- und Kongreßzentrums Luzern. Geschäftsführer bleibt Thomas Held, Präsident wird Hanspeter Balmer. Zu den Aufgaben der Trägerstiftung zählen insbesondere die Vergabe der Aufträge und die Einhaltung des Kosten- und Zeitplans.

Im August 1995 wird der Plan „B" offiziell. „B" steht für Beschleunigung, die Bauzeit soll um zwei Jahre verkürzt, das Kostenrisiko so minimiert werden, und die erste Teileröffnung soll bereits 1998 stattfinden. Entgegen des auch in die Abstimmung aufgenommenen Grundsatzes, wonach die Internationalen Musikfestwochen solange im Meili-Bau stattfinden sollen, bis der neue Konzertsaal fertiggestellt ist, einigt man sich in internen Verhandlungen über die Auslagerung der Musikfestwochen 1997 auf ein Provisorium.

Nach der Abstimmung vom 12. Juni 1994 beginnt auch die lange Suche nach einem geeigneten Betreiber für das Haus. Der Pächter soll wirtschaftliche Alleinverantwortung übernehmen, muß sich aber zugleich mit vielen Auflagen abfinden. Einschränkungen stellen zum Beispiel die Nutzungsrechte der IMF, AML und der Vereine dar. Lokale, nichtgewinnorientierte Veranstalter und Vereine können den Konzertsaal an 108, den Luzerner Saal an 72 und den kleinen Saal an 18 Tagen zu günstigen Konditionen mieten. Verhandlungen mit Mövenpick, der Schweizer Speisewagengesellschaft oder Swiss-International-Group scheitern an den Auflagen. Erst Ende 1996 können auf Betreiben des Stiftungspräsidenten Hanspeter Balmer fünf Luzerner Persönlichkeiten dazu motiviert werden, eine Gesellschaft, die MAG Management AG, zu gründen und den Pachtvertrag zu unterzeichnen. Allerdings gestaltet sich auch die Suche nach einem Generalmanager für die MAG als äußerst schwierig. Parallel dazu fordern die Luzerner Kulturschaffenden die Einrichtung eines Kulturbeauftragten, allerdings ohne viel Erfolg.

128

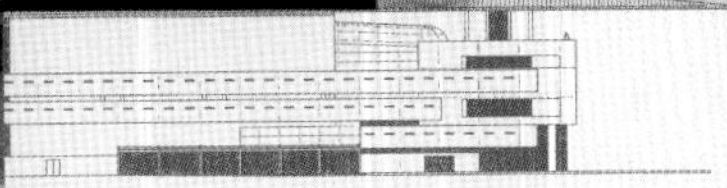

Plan "B" becomes official in August 1995. "B" stands for the German "Beschleunigung," that is, acceleration: construction is to be shortened by two years to minimize the risk of inflated costs and the first partial opening of the centre is brought forward to 1998. Contrary to the policy adopted during the referendum, which stipulated that the IMF would continue to be held in the Meili building until the completion of the new concert hall, a decision is made behind closed doors to move the festival to a temporary venue in 1997.

After the 12 June 1994 referendum, the long search for a suitable operator for the centre begins. The lessee is to assume sole fiscal responsibility while accepting many obligations and conditions. Some of the restrictions are, for example, the rights of use awarded to the IMF, the AML, clubs and associations. Local, non-profit organizers and associations are allowed to lease the concert hall on 108 days each year at reduced cost; they will enjoy the same privilege for the Lucerne hall on 72 days and in the small auditorium on 18 days. Negotiations with Mövenpick, the Schweizer Speisewagengesellschaft and Swiss-International Group founder because of these conditions. Finally, in late 1996, President Hanspeter Balmer succeeds in motivating five prominent Lucerne residents to found a company, the MAG Management AG, and to sign the lease. The search for a managing director for the MAG, however, turns out to be extremely difficult. At the same time the artists of Lucerne demand that an independent cultural representative be appointed, a demand that meets with little success.

IMF director Matthias Bamert and Martin Schwander, the director of the art museum, resign over the failure to meet these demands, protesting the lack of a "cultural conscience" and the unbridgeable chasm between artistic requirements and financial realities. In an open letter addressed to the new concert hall, Matthias Bamert expresses his concern about the many uses to which the hall is to be put: "Can

Plan "B"

Jean Nouvel mit Projektleiterin Brigitte Metra und Thomas Held, Schnitt CC

Jean Nouvel with project leader Brigitte Metra and Thomas Held
Cross section CC

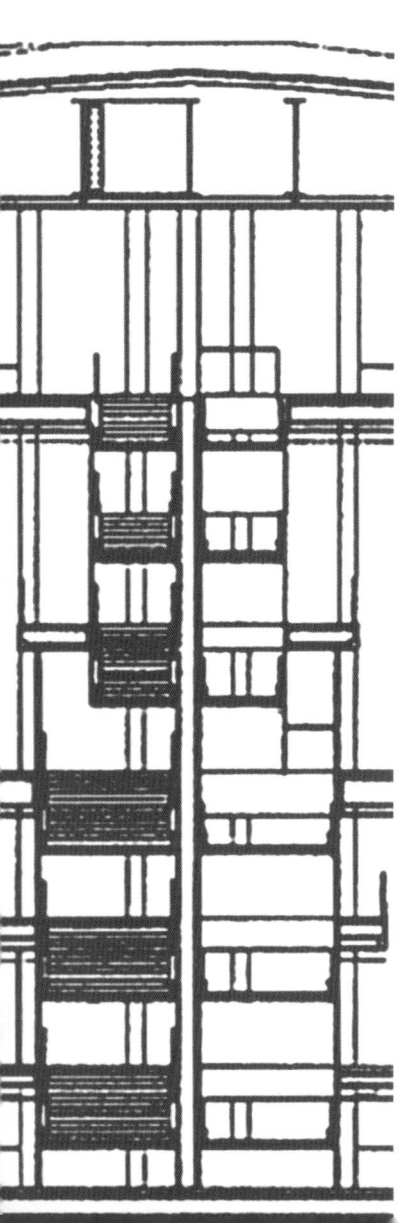

Matthias Bamert, Leiter der IMF, und Martin Schwander, Direktor des Kunstmuseums, kündigen nicht zuletzt deswegen ihre Verträge. Sie beklagen das Fehlen eines „kulturellen Gewissens" und halten die Schere zwischen künstlerischem Anspruch und finanziellen Realitäten für zu groß. In einem offenen Brief an den neuen Konzertsaal, in dem Matthias Bamert beklagt, wofür der Saal alles herhalten müsse, heißt es: „Ob das wirklich gutgehen kann, mein lieber neuer Konzertsaal? Ich habe Mitleid mit Dir, weil ich Dich so gut mag."[9]

In der Zwischenzeit wird die Boa-Fabrik zum Kulturzentrum für junge experimentelle Kultur ausgebaut und 1995 eröffnet. Im März 1996 stimmt die Stadt Luzern auch noch für die Erneuerung des Bourbaki-Panorama-Gebäudes[10], womit es Stadtpräsident Franz Kurzmeyer schließlich gelungen ist, seine drei Kulturprojekte „Grandes oeuvres" zu verwirklichen.

Erst im September 1997 findet sich ein Generalmanager, Michael Wittwer, der vor allem durch seine Kenntnisse im Kongreßmarketing hervorsticht. Bezüglich des Kulturauftrages gibt es allerdings noch keine Vorstellungen.

In einem Interview der Neuen Luzerner Zeitung mit Michael Wittwer wird unter anderem klar, wie sich die Fronten verteilen. Von Seiten der Kulturkreise wird Wittwer wiederholt ermahnt, nicht passiv auf Angebote zu reagieren, sondern aktiv Kulturpolitik zu betreiben oder eine Person beizuziehen, die dem Haus strategisch ein eigenes Profil vermitteln kann. Für Wittwer ist die MAG aber vorrangig ein Wirtschaftsunternehmen. „Der Kulturbeauftragte hat den Auftrag, Kultur zu machen. Dafür braucht er einen Topf, aus dem er das finanzieren kann. Und diesen Topf haben wir nicht."[11]

Außerdem sieht Wittwer die Suche nach einem Kulturbeauftragten nicht in seiner Verantwortung. Dies hätte bereits im Vorfeld von Seiten der Stadt geschehen müssen.

Auf Drängen der Kulturkreise erarbeitet die MAG ein Leitbild Kultur für den Betrieb des KKL, das sich wie folgt liest: „Das KKL strebt ein anspruchsvolles, breit gefächertes und innovatives Kulturangebot an. Dieses bereichert das kulturelle Leben, bezieht das bestehende Umfeld mit ein und besitzt eine weitreichende Ausstrahlung."[12]

In den ersten zwei Jahren des Betriebes verschlechtert sich das Image des KKL. Hauptgründe sind das fehlende inhaltliche Konzept und die mangelhafte Marketingstrategie.

Aber allen Unkenrufen zum Trotz ist das Haus voll. Das Programm ist vielschichtig – vom bayrischen Komiker über Gospelkonzerte bis hin zu erstklassigen Konzerten.

Die MAG steht unter großem Druck, da sich die Betriebskosten als enorm hoch herausstellen. Sie muß schwarze Zahlen schreiben und achtet daher kaum auf die Qualität der Produktionen, die sie ins Haus läßt. Auch die Luzerner Vereine, auf ihr Nutzungsrecht pochend, beanspruchen den Konzertsaal, da vorerst nur dieser zur Verfügung steht.

Lange Zeit sieht es so aus, als ob Stadt und Trägerstiftung mit dem Erreichen ihrer Aufgabe und ihres Zieles – der Fertigstellung des Hauses – alle Energie verbraucht hätten.

Doch lange steht die Trägerstiftung und allen voran Thomas Held

this really work out, my dear new concert hall? I feel sorry for you, because I do like you so very much."[9]

In the meantime the Boa factory is converted into a cultural centre for cutting-edge, experimental art and is opened in 1995. In March 1996 the city of Lucerne approves the renovation of the Bourbaki Panorama building[10], the final stage in mayor Franz Kurzmeyer's ambitious plan to realize three cultural projects, the "grandes oeuvres."

A managing director is finally found in September 1997 in Michael Wittwer, whose candidacy is impressive above all through his expertise in convention marketing. However, there are still no specific ideas with regard to the cultural mandate.

In an interview with Michael Wittwer in the Neue Luzerner Zeitung, Lucerne's daily newspaper, a clear image begins to emerge as to how the frontlines are being drawn. The artistic community repeatedly entreats Wittwer not to react passively to proposals, but to embark on a pro-active cultural policy or, failing this, to appoint someone whose task it would be to strategically develop an autonomous profile for the building. Yet Wittwer views the MAG primarily as an economic enterprise. "A cultural representative has the task of making culture happen. To do so, he needs a pot from which he can finance such an endeavour. And we have no such pot."[11]

Moreover, Wittwer does not regard the search for a cultural representative as part of his responsibilities, feeling that this should have been handled in the preliminary phases by the city itself. Acceding to pressures from the arts community, the MAG develops a cultural model for the operation of the CCC, which reads as follows: "The CCC aims to offer a discriminating, broad and innovative cultural programme. This enriches the cultural life [of the city], incorporating the existing infrastructure and has a widespread appeal."[12]

During the first two years of operation the image of the CCC suffers. The main reasons are the lack of a programming concept and the poor marketing strategy.

But the house is full, in spite of disapproval and criticism. The

„Geigenkasten" – Rohbau Konzertsaal (links), Konzertsaal mit geöffneten Echokammern, seewassergespeiste Kanäle zwischen den Bauteilen

"Violin case" – shell construction concert concert hall with opened echo chambers Lakewater-fed canals between building sections

dieser Vorgehensweise nicht tatenlos gegenüber. Eine behutsame Übernahme der Aktienmehrheit der MAG durch die Trägerstiftung wird lanciert, die im Sommer 2000 vollzogen wird. Die Trägerstiftung übernimmt nun selbst den Betrieb. Das Motto für die Zukunft: „Qualität statt Quantität."

Michael Wittwer geht – auf eigenen Wunsch. Neuer Verwaltungspräsident wird Rolf. E. Brönnimann, der interimistisch auch den Aufgabenbereich von Michael Wittwer übernimmt. Seine Devise lautet: „Das Preis-Leistungs-Verhältnis muß stimmen, und wenn es um Qualität geht, gilt: Nicht jeder Gast um jeden Preis." [13]

Aus der MAG wird die KKL AG.

Eine Arbeitsgruppe Kultur wird eingesetzt, die die Qualität der angebotenen Veranstaltungen anhand eines 5-Sterne-Rasters überprüfen soll.

Thomas Held ist es gelungen, ein Gebäude höchster architektonischer Qualität in Luzern zu verwirklichen und mit seinem Team eine Bevölkerung zu überzeugen, mit Stolz hinter einem Kulturbau zu stehen und dafür zu stimmen. Damit hat diese Stadt anderen Städten einiges voraus.

Das Marketingkonzept für die Errichtung dieses Baus wurde mit Erfolg an die Architektur geknüpft. Ein erfolgversprechendes Marke-

programme is multifaceted – from a Bavarian comedian to gospel concerts to world-class performances.

The MAG is under enormous pressure since operating costs prove to be excessive. Obliged to operate at a profit, the company pays little attention to the quality of the productions. Even Lucerne associations and clubs, insisting on their right of use, occupy the concert hall, since it is the only space available in the beginning.

For some time it looks as if city and foundation had spent all their energy in achieving their primary goal, the completion of the building.

But the foundation led by Thomas Held refuses to accept this state of affairs for long. A careful campaign of acquiring a majority in MAG shares is launched by the foundation and completed in the summer of 2000. The foundation now takes over the operation. The new motto: "Quality not Quantity."

Michael Wittwer resigns – voluntarily. Rolf. E. Brönnimann is appointed as new administrative director, also taking on Michael Wittwer's mandate in the short term. His credo: "The cost-performance ratio must balance and as regards quality we must adopt the maxim: not any guest at any price."[13]

The MAG is transformed into the KKL AG.

A cultural task force is set up to evaluate the quality of the event

Russell Johnson mit Projektleiter Eckhardt Kahle (links unten),
Schleusenbrücken in den Konzertsaal,
geöffnete Echokammern (rechts)

Russell Johnson with project leader
Eckhardt Kahle (below left)
Special ramps leading into the concert hall
Opened echo chambers (right)

tingkonzept für den Betrieb des Hauses muß sich aber über den Inhalt definieren. Der Inhalt muß der Hülle gerecht werden, und das bedeutet stringente Qualität.

Das Raumprogramm

„Ein guter Konzertsaal hat die Form einer Schuhschachtel."

Russel Johnson in: „KKL – die Geschichte seines Werdens, die Zukunft seiner Idee".

"A good concert hall is shaped like a shoebox."

Russel Johnson in: "KKL – die Geschichte seines Werdens, die Zukunft seiner Idee".

Der Konzertsaal, in der Mitte etwas zurückversetzt, der multifunktionale Luzerner Saal und daneben das Auditorium, die Kongreßnebenräume und im vierten Stock das Kunstmuseum sind zum Wasser hin symmetrisch angeordnet.[14] Seewassergespeiste Kanäle trennen die drei Bauteile voneinander. Ein Dienstleistungstrakt dient als verbindendes Rückgrat auf der dem See abgewandten Seite.

Das 2.500 Tonnen schwere Schwebedach[15] – mit spiegelnder Untersicht aus Aluminium-Verbundplatten – überragt alle Bauteile und kragt stützenfrei 45 Meter in den See hinaus. Die Fassaden der einzelnen Bauteile sind unterschiedlich gestaltet. Der Verwaltungstrakt wurde mit bronzegrünem Lochgitter verkleidet. Die dem See zugewandte Fassade besteht aus farbigem Blech und einer grün eingefärbten Glasfront im Bereich des großen Foyers. Die Glasfassade des Kunstmuseums wurde mit einer feinen metallischen, halb transparenten Außenhaut versehen.

Der Konzertsaal

Die Außenhaut des Konzertsaales ist aus speziell geschnittenem Ahornfurnier, das gebleicht und mit Wasserlack präpariert wurde. Sie wölbt sich in das Foyer wie der Bauch eines hölzernen Instruments.

Anfangs hatte Nouvel für den Konzertsaal blaue Wände, rote Balustraden und einen dunkelblauen Sternenhimmel als Decke konzipiert. Schwere Bedenken der Musiker gegenüber dieser Farbzusammensetzung führten schließlich in letzter Minute zu einer Änderung: Der „salle bleue" wird zum „salle blanche". Das Innere des Konzertsaales wird nun bestimmt durch das Weiß der Balustraden und Gipsreliefs der Akustikelemente, den verschiedenen Holztönen für Podium, Schalldecke, Boden und Bestuhlung und dem dunklen Sternenhimmel. Sind die schweren, doch beweglichen Türen zu den Echokammern geöffnet, schimmert indirekte rote Beleuchtung hervor.

Im zweiten und dritten Stock finden sich die Namen der Sponsoren eingraviert in den Fenstern wieder – die Spendenhöhe bestimmt die jeweilige Größe der Namensgravur. Im vierten Stock des Konzertsaales befindet sich eine Terrasse mit weitem Ausblick über den Vierwaldstättersee.

Die Akustik

Drei Jahre haben Jean Nouvel und Russel Johnson an dem Konzertsaal gearbeitet. Johnson bestand darauf, daß Höhe und Breite des Konzertsaales gleich sind, wodurch sich die Platzzahl verringerte: „Ein guter Konzertsaal hat die Form einer Schuhschachtel."

Um die „absolute Stille" im Saal herstellen zu können, wurde ein zweischaliger Baukörper konstruiert. Über abgedichtete Schleusenbrücken gelangt das Publikum in den Saal.

Die Echokammern wurden als zweite Wandschale rund um den

programme based on a five-star rating system.

Thomas Held has succeeded in realizing a building of the highest architectural quality in Lucerne and in convincing the public, with the help of his team, to support a cultural building with its vote. The city has thus gained a considerable advantage over others.

The marketing concept for the construction of the building was successfully linked to the architecture. Yet a promising marketing concept for the operation must be defined on the merit of content. The content must live up to the envelope and this means above all uncompromising quality.

The Spatial Design

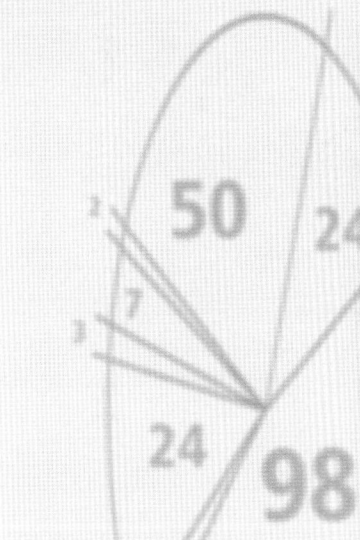

The concert hall, slightly recessed in the middle section, the multifunctional Lucerne hall and the adjacent auditorium, the convention facilities and the art museum on the fifth floor, are placed in symmetry to the body of water.[14] Lakewater-fed canals separate the three building sections from one another. A service wing creates a connecting spine along the rear of the complex, facing away from the lake.

The 2,500 ton suspended roof[15] – with a reflecting bottom view of aluminium composite slabs – spans all sections of the complex and projects forty-five metres into the lake without supports. Each façade of the building sections has a unique design. The administration wing is clad in a bronze-green perforated grid. The lakeside façade is encased in coloured plate and a green-tinted glass front in the area of the large foyer. The glass façade of the art museum has been fitted with a fine, semitransparent external metal skin.

The Concert Hall
The skin of the concert hall consists of custom-cut maple veneer, which has been bleached and treated with water lacquer. It curves into the foyer like the body of a wooden instrument.

Initially, Nouvel had envisioned the concert hall with blue walls, red balustrades and a dark blue starry sky for a ceiling. In response to concerns expressed by the musicians, this colour combination was modified at the last moment. The "salle bleue" was transformed into the "salle blanche." The white of the balustrades, the gypsum relief of the acoustic elements, the various wood hues on stage, sound ceiling, floor and seats and the dark starry sky now define the concert hall interior. Indirect red light flows into the space when the heavy, but movable doors to the echo chambers stand open.

The names of sponsors are engraved in the windows on the third and fourth floors – with the amount of donation reflected in the size of each engraved name. The fifth floor of the concert hall features a terrace with a sweeping view across Lake Lucerne.

The Acoustics
Jean Nouvel and Russel Johnson worked on the concert hall for three years. Johnson insisted that height and width of the hall should be identical, which reduced the number of seats: "A good concert hall is shaped like a shoebox."

Die effektiven Kosten belaufen sich 2000 auf 211 Millionen SFr.

In 2000, the true costs amount to CHF 211 million

Stadt Luzern	**98 Millionen**
City of Lucerne	98 million
Kanton Luzern	**24 Millionen**
Canton Lucerne	24 million
Konzerthaus-Stiftung	**50 Millionen**
Concert Hall Foundation	50 million
Kunstgesellschaft Luzern	**2 Millionen**
Art Association of Lucerne	2 million
Hotelierverein Luzern	**7 Millionen**
Hotel Association of Lucerne	7 million
Sonderfinanzierung	**3 Millionen**
Special financing	3 million
Fremdfinanzierung	**24 Millionen**
Debt financing	24 million
Finanzierungslücke	**3 Millionen**
Financial gap	3 million

Konzertsaal gebaut. Die 50 tonnenschweren Türen können in den Saal-
wänden geöffnet werden, um den Nachhallwert zu steigern. Dadurch
kann das 22.000 m³ umfassende Volumen auf 30.000 m³ vergrößert
werden.

An den Wänden und Türen zu den Echokammern sind Gipsreliefs
mit fünf verschiedenen Mustern angebracht, um das Vorherrschen einzelner Frequenzzonen zu vermeiden.

Über dem Podium befindet sich eine bewegliche Schalldecke, das
Canopy, deren zwei Teile dreistufig abgesenkt werden können, die für
zusätzliche akustische Feinabstimmung sorgt.

Das Kunstmuseum
Das Kunstmuseum liegt direkt unter dem Dach im vierten Stock des
westlichen, dem Bahnhof zugewandten Trakts. 19 großenteils fen-
sterlose, 5,5 m hohe Räume mit weißen Wänden und grauen Böden
aus geschliffenem Beton mit Basaltsplittern reihen sich sehr zurück-
haltend aneinander. Gedämpftes Tageslicht dringt durch ein kompli-
ziertes Filtersystem aus Metallblenden und Lamellen und kann gege-
benenfalls mit Kunstlicht angereichert werden. Nouvel, der zusammen
mit dem Basler Künstler Rémy Zaugg das Raumkonzept erstellte, spricht
von „nudité des espaces".

To achieve "absolute silence" in the hall, a double-leaf fabric was constructed. The public is guided into the hall across special ramps.

The echo chambers were erected as a secondary shell around the concert hall. The doors set into the walls, each weighing 50 tons, can be opened to increase the echo. In this manner, the 22,000 cubic metre volume can be increased to 30,000 cubic metres.

Gypsum reliefs in five different patterns are installed on walls and doors to prevent a predominance of any single frequency.

The canopy, a movable acoustic ceiling, is suspended above the stage, with two separate sections that can be lowered in three phases for additional acoustic fine-tuning.

The Art Museum

The art museum is located directly beneath the roof on the fifth floor of the west wing facing towards the train station. Nineteen, largely windowless 5.5-m-high exhibition rooms with white walls and grey floors of polished concrete inlaid with basalt chippings create a very understated enfilade. Muted daylight filters into the space through a complex system composed of metal panels and louvres, complemented by provisions for artificial lighting when required. Nouvel, who collaborated on this spatial concept with Basel artist Rémy Zaugg, speaks of a "nudité des espaces."

Museum Mönchengladbach

Der weitsichtige Direktor/The Visionary Director

Ein Besuch im
städtischen Museum
Abteiberg

Einem Direktor und seinem Architekten ist es gelungen, in einer Klein-
stadt wie Mönchengladbach trotz Rezession und Kulturmuffelei ein
Museum zu errichten, das zu einem Meilenstein in der Museumsdebatte
wurde. Ein aufsehenerregendes Projekt, das bereits in den siebziger
Jahren für den späteren Museumsboom in Deutschland neue Maßstäbe
setzte, an denen sich Museen nachfolgender Generationen messen
mussten. Aber was ist aus diesem Museum geworden, das einst Ziel
des internationalen Kunst- und Architekturtourismus war?

Der Architekturbonus nutzt sich mit den Jahren ab und die Grün-
dungsdirektoren ziehen sich nach einiger Zeit zurück. Das einstige
Wunschkind, als Motor der Imagewerbung errichtet, wird in schwie-
rigeren Zeiten zum ungeliebten Kind. Daraus resultierende Sparmaß-
nahmen machten es in Mönchengladbach dem Museum nicht leicht,
weiterhin ein anspruchsvolles Programm anzubieten. Sammlungen ver-
ließen das Museum. Die Stadt empfand die konsequente Hinwendung
zur Gegenwartskunst mit der Zeit als zu elitär und zu wenig publi-
kumswirksam, und die Direktorenwechsel brachten nicht den erhoff-
ten Umschwung in der Museumspolitik.

Fährt man heute nach Mönchengladbach, wird man nicht vom
architektonischen Charme dieses groß gewordenen Dorfs eingenommen. Selbst das Museum am Abteiberg ist in die Jahre gekommen, der
Garten gleicht einem kleinen Dschungel, Graffiti zieren die Fassaden,
das Leitsystem auf der Fußgängerplatte – die „Medialinien" – hin-
terlassen den Eindruck, Überreste einer ehemaligen Überdachung zu
sein.

Im Inneren des Museums sieht alles noch sehr ordentlich aus. Der
Eingang führt direkt in den großen Ausstellungsraum, der zugleich
Foyer, Kassabereich, Garderobe und Museumsshop beherbergt. Eine
freundliche ältere Dame erteilt Auskunft über die laufende Ausstellung.
Bei genauerer Hinsicht entpuppen sich alle vermeintlichen Museums-
besucher als freundliche ältere Damen, die hier die Funktion der Auf-
sicht übernehmen. Man hat das Haus praktisch für sich allein. Das
Museum, das in seinen Anfangsjahren bis zu 200.000 Besucher hatte,
kann heute nur mit Anstrengung 30.000 pro Jahr zählen. Dabei ist die
hauseigene Sammlung einen Besuch wert. Auch die Ausstellungen
folgen einer inhaltlich qualitativen Linie, nicht aber unbedingt dem
Publikumsinteresse. Und es liegt wohl auch daran, daß Architektur-
touristen immer den jeweils neuesten Meilensteinen im Museumsbau
folgen, die heute in Bilbao oder London zu finden sind.

Ziel war es damals, ein bürgernahes Museum zu schaffen. Mehrere
Zugangsmöglichkeiten sollten die Schwellenangst des Besuchers ab-
bauen, die Integration von Malklassen, Unterrichtsräumen, Film- und
Vortragsräumen und Cafeteria sollte die Nutzungsvielfalt erhöhen.
Diese Bereiche wurden mit den Sammlungsteilen verklammert. Das

„Ein Museum ist ein Museum.
Ein Museum ist kein
Dienstleistungsanbieter und
sollte daher auch nicht mit
anderen Dienstleistungsan-
bietern in Konkurrenz treten."

Johannes Cladders
in einem Interview mit den Autoren
am 22.11.2000, Krefeld

"A museum is a museum.
A museum is not a service
provider and shouldn't try to
compete with other
service providers."

Johannes Cladders
in conversation with the authors,
November 22, 2000, Krefeld.

A Visit to the Abteiberg Museum

In a small city like Mönchengladbach, a director and an architect overcame recession and cultural ignorance to build a museum that became a milestone in the museum debate. As far back as the early 1970s this project attracted much attention, setting new standards for the museum boom that was to follow in Germany and elsewhere and against which subsequent museum projects would be measured. What became of this museum, once upon a time a site of pilgrimage for international architecture and art tourists?

Architectural prestige can wear off with the passage of the years and founding directors eventually resign. The former dream child, erected as an engine for image advertising, became an unloved child when times turned lean and difficult. Budget cuts made it difficult for the museum in Mönchengladbach to continue to offer a discriminating exhibition programme. Collections moved out. The city gradually began to view the museum's dedication to contemporary art as elitist, lacking in public appeal; even changes at the helm through the appointment of new directors failed to deliver the hoped-for turnaround.

Driving through the Ruhr region to Mönchengladbach today, one is hardly captivated by the architectural charm of this oversized village. Even the Abteiberg Museum has begun to show its age, the gardens overgrown like a miniature jungle, the façades decorated with graffiti, the pathfinder lines on the pavement – the "media lines" – seem like remnants of a former roof structure.

The interior of the museum is still neat and organized. The entrance leads directly into the large exhibition space that houses the foyer, box office, wardrobe and museum shop. A friendly, elderly woman offers information on the current exhibition. Upon closer inspection all the apparent museum visitors are unmasked as friendly, elderly ladies who serve as museum guards. The rare visitor can more or less enjoy the museum on his or her own. The museum, which attracted up to 200,000 visitors per year at the beginning, has to work hard these days to coax 30,000 through its front door. And yet the permanent collection is truly worth a visit. The exhibitions, too, follow a discriminating programme, albeit not necessarily catered to popular tastes. And perhaps the change in visitor numbers is to some degree due to the fact that architecture fans tend to flock to the latest milestones, which today are found in Bilbao and in London.

At the time, the goal was to create a museum for the people. Several access routes were to help potential visitors overcome their fear of entering; the integration of art courses, class rooms, film screening and lecture rooms and a cafeteria would, it was hoped, increase the usability of the building. Each of these areas was integrated with the collection and exhibition areas. The concept of setting a café right

Leitsystem „Medialinien" auf der Fußgängerplatte (unten)

"Media lines" on the pedestrian plateau (below)

Jahre	Ausstellungs-etat* (in DM)	Ankaufsetat** (in DM)
1967	11.000	71.000
1970	30.000	71.000
1977	45.000	100.000
1982	340.000	100.000
1987	150.000	50.000
1992	130.000	50.000
2001	125.000	50.000

Durch Zuschüsse des Landes Nordrhein-Westfalen, Fördermittel des Museumsvereins, des Förderkreises, der Sparkassenstiftung und durch sonstige Spenden können vor allem die Ankaufsmittel jährlich auf 150 bis 300.000 DM erhöht werden.

*inkl. Kataloge, Werbemittel, Vorträge, Transporte
**inkl. städt. Mittel

damals plakativ neue Konzept, in die Museumsräume ein Café als Ort des kurzen Verweilens zu integrieren oder eine Buchecke zu schaffen, die sich hinter dem Kassabereich versteckt, griff ansatzweise dem heutigen Konzept des Museum-Events vor, wurde aber von der Welle des „Museums als marktwirtschaftlich orientierte Unterhaltungsmaschinerie" überrollt.

Von der damaligen Vorstellung, man ginge ins Museum, um dort mit Muße Kunst zu genießen, sind heute nur menschenleere Räume, ein geschlossenes Café und eine magere Buchauswahl übriggeblieben. Für Renovierungs- oder Umbauarbeiten fehlt es an Geld, und die Stadt Mönchengladbach leidet finanzielle Nöte. Das Museum kann sich mit den städtischen Mitteln kaum über Wasser halten und ist auf die Unterstützung des Museumsvereins angewiesen. Für Pressearbeit oder Marketingmaßnahmen gibt es weder Geld noch Personal.

Welche Persönlichkeiten waren damals vor Ort, um Mönchengladbach neben seiner Bekanntheit im Fußball zu einem Anziehungspunkt für Kultur zu machen? Dazu bedarf es der Geschichte – eben jenes Museumsdirektors und seines Architekten.

Erfolgsstory eines Direktors

Als Johannes Cladders im Jahre 1967 Direktor des städtischen Museums Mönchengladbach wird, besteht dieses aus einer kleinen 4-Zimmer-Wohnung. Das Museum verfügt über eine bescheidene heimatkundliche Sammlung sowie eine Auswahl expressionistischer Werke.

Gegründet 1904, hat das heimatkundliche Museum vorerst kein eigenes Museumsgebäude. In den zwanziger Jahren vermachen zwei Bürger ihre Häuser der Stadt: das Karl-Brandt-Haus (wird im zweiten Weltkrieg zerstört) und das Oskar-Kühn-Haus, das das Museum bis zur Fertigstellung des Neubaus beheimatet. Im Haus Brandt wird die Expressionistensammlung des gebürtigen Mönchengladbachers Walter Kaesbach (1879–1961) untergebracht, der 1928 seine Sammlung der Stadt stiftet und damit die entscheidenden Weichen für die Entwicklung zu einem Kunstmuseum stellt. Er kann nicht vorausahnen, daß seine Sammlung bereits 1937 im Zuge der Säuberungsaktion, die unter anderem der Ausstellung „Entartete Kunst" folgte, den Nationalsozialisten zum Opfer fällt.

Nach dem Krieg versucht die Stadt erneut eine Expressionistensammlung aufzubauen und beauftragt dafür Heinrich Dattenberg als ersten hauptamtlichen Direktor des Museums. Da das Budget alsbald den Ankauf expressionistischer Werke nicht mehr zuläßt, beginnt er sich der näheren Gegenwart der fünfziger und sechziger Jahre zuzuwenden.

Auch der Bauplan für ein neues Museum von dem Architekten Horst Log – das Haus Kühn samt Nachbargebäude abzureißen und auf dem vergrößerten Areal einen Neubau zu errichten – wird durch ein unerwartetes Ereignis verhindert. Das Lieblingskind der Stadt, die Kaiser-Friedrich-Halle, brennt 1964 ab, und alle Mittel der Stadt werden für den Wiederaufbau aufgewendet. Vorerst sind alle Museumspläne gestorben.

into the exhibition rooms as an invitation to linger and rest was truly innovative for its time, as was the intimate reading nook hidden behind the box office. These ideas were to some degree precursors of today's museum event, but they drowned in the wave of the "museum as an economically viable entertainment machine."

Of the original idea that one would enter the museum to enjoy art at leisure and in quiet, all that is left are empty rooms, a closed café and a diminished book selection. There are no funds for renovation or conversion and Mönchengladbach itself suffers from a lack of finances. The museum can barely stay afloat with the funds available to it and must rely on financial support from the museum association. There is neither money nor manpower for press releases and marketing campaigns.

Who were the personalities involved in the museum's beginnings, transforming Mönchengladbach – a town famous for its soccer club and little else – into a cultural mecca? To answer this question we need to look at the history of the museum director and his architect mentioned at the outset.

Ausstellung Joseph Beuys, 1967

Joseph Beuys Exhibition, 1967

A Director's Success Story

When Johannes Cladders became the director of the public museum of Mönchengladbach in 1967, it was housed in a small four-room apartment. The museum consisted of a modest collection of local history and a selection of Expressionist art.

Founded in 1904, the local history museum has no building of its own at first. In the 1920s, two residents bequeath their home to the city: the Karl Brandt House (destroyed in the Second World War) and the Oskar Kühn House, home to the museum until the completion of the new building. The Expressionist collection of local Walter Kaesbach (1879-1961) is placed in the Brandt House after Kaesbach donates his collection to the city in 1928, preparing the ground for the creation of an art museum. He cannot have anticipated that a few years later, in 1937, his collection would fall victim to the Nazi cleansing action following the exhibtion "Degenerate Art."

After the war the city tries to reconstruct the Kaesbach donation and appoints Heinrich Dattenberg as the first full-time director of the museum. The budget soon proves too limited for the acquisition of Expressionist art and the director turns his attention to more recent work from the 1950s and 1960s.

Architect Horst Log's plan for a new museum – which envisioned the demolition of Kühn House and the adjacent buildings to erect a new building on the larger site – is thwarted. In 1964 the city's pride and joy, the Kaiser-Friedrichs Hall, burns to the ground and all public funds flow into reconstructing it. Any plans for a museum are shelved.

Johannes Cladders arrives in Mönchengladbach in 1967. His first act is to curate the first feature exhibition on Joseph Beuys. Cladders sets the opening date to coincide with the art fair in Cologne, which draws an international public interested in art. His strategy succeeds. Visitors flock to the exhibition, curious about Joseph Beuys,

MUNICIPAL FUNDS FOR THE MUSEUM

Years	Exhibition budget* (in DM)	Acquisitions budget** (in DM)
1967	11,000	71,000
1970	30,000	71,000
1977	45,000	100,000
1982	340,000	100,000
1987	150,000	50,000
1992	130,000	50,000
2001	125,000	50,000

Additional grants from the state of North Rhine-Westphalia, sponsorship from the museum association, savings and loans endowments and other donations combine to raise the acquisitions budget in particular to DM 150 – 300,000 annually.

*incl. Catalogues, invitations, posters, lectures, transport **incl. Municipal funds

1967 kommt Johannes Cladders nach Mönchengladbach. Sein Auftakt ist die erste Einzelausstellung über Joseph Beuys. Cladders wählt den Eröffnungstermin so, daß zur selben Zeit der Kölner Kunstmarkt stattfindet und internationales, kunstinteressiertes Publikum anwesend ist – mit Erfolg. Das Publikum erscheint zahlreich und neugierig auf Joseph Beuys, von dem man zwar schon überall gehört, aber wenig gesehen hat.

Die Ausstellung löst in der Stadt einen Skandal aus. Die überregionale Presse jedoch ist begeistert, und die Stadt wird auf das Museum aufmerksam.

Auch die Folgeausstellungen des Museums finden Eingang in die Feuilletons der überregionalen Presse. Die Künstler, die Cladders ausstellt und ankauft, machen Karriere. 1970 kann die hauseigene Sammlung durch die Sammlung Etzold, die vorwiegend Werke aus dem Bereich der „Neuen Konkreten Kunst" und einige Werke zum „Konstruktivismus" umfaßt, erweitert werden. In den folgenden Jahren holt das Museum endgültig im Wettlauf des Kunstmarktes auf, und Werke aus Minimal Art und Concept Art wandern sozusagen direkt vom Atelier in die Sammlung.

Das Museum steht immer mehr im Rampenlicht des internationalen Kunstgeschehens und genießt den einmaligen Ruf, das richtige Gespür für zeitgenössische Kunst zu haben.

Cladders trifft auf Hollein

Eine neue Museumsidee wird geboren

Der kometenhafte Aufstieg Johannes Cladders fällt in eine Zeit, in der die Stadtgremien versuchen, der Wirtschaftskrise – verursacht durch die sterbende Textilindustrie – gegenzusteuern und auf den kulturellen Imagegewinn durch die Museumspolitik aufmerksam zu werden.

Ende der sechziger Jahre zählt Mönchengladbach nur 150.000 Einwohner. Durch die – für 1975 – geplante kommunale Neugliederung von Nordrhein-Westfalen, die einen Zusammenschluß mit der Stadt Rheydt und der Gemeinde Wickrath vorsieht, erhöht sich der Druck auf die einzelnen Gemeinden, prestigeträchtige Projekte zu realisieren.

Nach dem Wiederaufbau der Kaiser-Friedrich-Halle lebt die Museumsdiskussion wieder auf. Johannes Cladders findet im Kulturdezernenten Busso Diekamp einen wichtigen Mitstreiter, der sich politisch für das Projekt stark macht. Die Stadt läßt zuerst Johannes

of whom much has been heard but little actually seen.

The exhibition causes a scandal in the city. The national press, however, is enthusiastic and the city begins to take note of its museum.

The subsequent exhibitions are also discussed in editorials in the national press. The artists whose works Cladders exhibits and acquires are launched into successful careers. In 1970 the museum's collection is expanded with the Etzold collection, which contains mostly works from the "New Concrete" art movement and some "Constructivist" works. Over the course of the following years the museum finally succeeds in catching up with the racing art market, and works by Minimalists and Concept artists seem to flow directly from the artists' studios into the museum collection.

The museum is increasingly in the spotlight of the international art world and enjoys a unique reputation for having a "good nose" for contemporary art.

Cladders Meets Hollein

A New Museum Idea Is Born

Johannes Cladder's comet-like ascent comes at a time when city councils strive to counteract the economic crisis – caused by a declining textile industry – and are beginning to realize how much the city stands to gain through the museum's activities.

At the end of the 1960s Mönchengladbach had only 150,000 inhabitants. The restructuring of North Rhine-Westphalia, planned for 1975, envisions the incorporation of the city of Rheydt and the community of Wickrath into greater Mönchengladbach. The individual communities are increasingly under pressure to realize prestige objects.

Once the Kaiser-Friedrichs Hall reconstruction is completed, the debate surrounding the building of a museum takes on new life. In department head Busso Diekamp, Johannes Cladders has found an important supporter for his cause, willing to promote the project in the political arena. To begin with, the city invites Cladders to suggest appropriate sites for a museum. But his first choice, a central location, has already been assigned to the construction of a large department store. In turn, he is offered a site on the Abteiberg, located at the southern edge of the city centre.

In mid-1971 the administrative office of culture of Mönchengladbach launches an idea competition for the "Abteiberg" project. The

Gesamtansicht, Ausstellung Hans Hollein zum Thema Tod, 1970 (Mitte)

General view, Hans Hollein exhibition on the subject of Death, 1970 (middle)

Cladders geeignete Standorte für das Museum vorschlagen. Der von ihm auserwählte Platz in zentraler Lage ist aber bereits für ein großes Kaufhaus vorgesehen. Im Gegenzug bietet man ihm ein Areal auf dem Abteiberg am südlichen Rand der Innenstadt an.

Mitte 1971 schreibt die Kulturverwaltung von Mönchengladbach einen Ideenwettbewerb „Abteiberg" aus. Gefordert wird ein Bildungszentrum, bestehend aus Museum, audiovisuellem Zentrum, Bibliothek und Archiv, Volkshochschule, Musikschule mit Konzertsaal, Jugendzentrum, Schule und Wohnungen. Die Entwürfe bestätigten die Erwartungen: Das Bildungszentrum bedarf der engen Anbindung an die Schlagader des geschäftlichen Lebens, an die Hindenburgstraße. Für den Museumsneubau werden zwei mögliche Standorte nachgewiesen, darunter der – trotz des schwierigen Geländes und der ungünstigen Verkehrsanbindung – gewählte Standort an der Abteistraße oberhalb des Abteigartens und zwischen humanistischem Stiftsgymnasium im Osten und barocker Propstei im Westen.

Kulturdezernent Diekamp will zwar schnellstmöglich das gesamte Bildungszentrum verwirklichen, fordert aber im Sinne des finanziellen Engpasses stets die vorrangige Verwirklichung des Museumprojektes.

Der Kulturausschuß lädt Johannes Cladders ein, seine Vorstellungen zu einem Neubau darzustellen. Cladders versteht es wohl, Politiker für seine Ideen zu begeistern und ihnen die Sinnhaftigkeit bestimmter Vorgehen darzulegen. Er ist gegen einen Wettbewerb und erklärt dem zuständigen Kulturausschuß, daß man sich zunächst in der Architekturszene umsehen und sich einzelne Bauten ansehen müsste, um die jeweilige Handschrift eines Architekten zu erkennen. Diese unverwechselbare Handschrift sollte man dann für sein Museum auswählen und einen Vorentwurf ausarbeiten lassen. Denn ein Wettbewerb wäre teuer und das Ergebnis auch immer nur ein Vorentwurf.

Also wird Bildmaterial zur Architektur zusammengetragen, um sich über besagte Handschrift zu unterhalten. Cladders bringt unter anderem Material über Hans Hollein mit[1] – ein gewagter Vorstoß, da zu diesem Zeitpunkt nur das Kerzengeschäft Retti in Wien und die Feigen Gallery in N.Y. von Hollein realisiert waren, nicht unbedingt vergleichbare Bauten. Er hatte aber in seinen Gesprächen mit Hollein schon den richtigen Partner gefunden.

Der Vorsitzende des Kulturausschusses, Kurt Strahl, ein Mitglied der SPD, also der Oppositionspartei, und deshalb nicht gerade Unterstützer des Projektes, ist ein kulturbegeisterter Mann, und da der Ausschuß sich nicht in der Lage sieht, eine Beurteilung der eingereichten Vorschläge abzugeben, holt Strahl die Meinung von Cladders ein. Dieser will einen Neuling auf dem Gebiet des Museumsbaus, jemand, der sich von ganzem Herzen mit dem Projekt auseinandersetzt. Cladders wählt Hans Hollein und ihm vertrauend stimmen alle Mitglieder seiner Wahl zu.

1972 beauftragt der Kulturausschuß Hans Hollein, eine städtebauliche Studie und einen Vorentwurf zu liefern. Der städtebauliche Plan dient vor allem der Weiterverfolgung des Bildungszentrums, der Anbindungen der einzelnen Baumassen untereinander sowie an die Stadt. Der Vorentwurf enthält auch die Planung eines zweiten

specifications call for an education centre, consisting of museum, audiovisual centre, library and archive, adult education centre, music school with concert hall, youth centre, school and apartments. The design entries confirm the expectations: the education centre must be closely linked to the pulse of the commercial life of the city, the Hindenburgstrasse. Two possible sites are put forward, including the chosen location on Abteistrasse above the abbey garden, despite the challenges posed by the site and its poor links to public transport, between the Abbey High School for the Humanities to the east and the baroque abbey to the west.

While Diekamp is interested in realizing the entire education centre as soon as possible, he insists that the museum project must be given precedence in view of the financial restraints.

The culture committee invites Johannes Cladders to present his vision for the new building. Cladders is adept at winning politicians over for his ideas and in arguing convincingly for the logic of certain approaches. He is opposed to a competition and explains that the best course of action is to study the contemporary architectural scene and individual buildings, thus learning to understand the signature of particular architects. A unique signature should then be selected for his museum and developed into a preliminary design. For, his argument goes, competitions are expensive and the result is just the same: a preliminary design.

A catalogue of images and examples is gathered to discuss the aforementioned signature. Cladders contributes material on Hans Hollein, among others[1], – a daring move because at that time Hollein had only realized two projects, the Retti candle shop in Vienna and the Feigen Gallery in New York, not necessarily buildings ideal for comparison. However, in his dialogue with Hollein, Cladders had already found his ideal partner.

The chair of the cultural committee, Kurt Strahl, a Social Democrat and as a member of the official opposition not exactly a supporter of the project, is a man passionate about culture. Since the committee finds itself at a loss to evaluate the suggestions, Strahl turns to Cladders for his opinion. The latter speaks in favour of choosing a newcomer in the field of museum architecture, someone who will devote himself heart and soul to the project. Cladders suggest Hans Hollein and, trusting his judgement, all committee members endorse his choice.

In 1972 the cultural committee approves the plan and commissions Hans Hollein to deliver an urban development study and a preliminary design. The plan for urban development serves primarily to continue pursuing the education centre and to plan how the individual building fabrics will be linked to each other and to the city. The preliminary design also contains the planning for a second construction phase for future expansion.

Hans Hollein presents two alternatives: one is based on the concept of multi-use in a complex structure for the education centre, the other on a less dense development of individual buildings. Both concepts envision a continuous footpath that links the individual institutions to

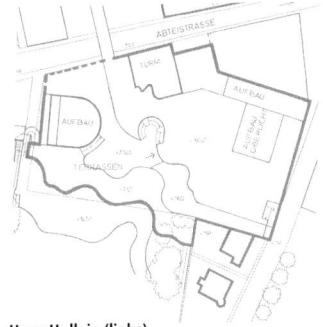

Hans Hollein (links)
Vorentwurf „Reisterrassen" (oben),
Vorentwurf „Maschine" (Mitte)

Hans Hollein (left)
Preliminary design "rice terraces"
(above), Preliminary
design "machine" (middle)

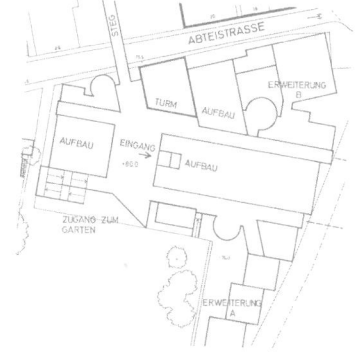

Bauabschnittes für eine spätere Erweiterung des Museums.

Hans Hollein legt zwei Alternativen vor: Die eine geht vom Konzept der Mehrfachnutzung in einem komplexen Gesamtbaukörper des Bildungszentrums aus, die andere von einer loseren Einzelbebauung. Beide Konzepte sehen eine durchgehende Fußgängerplatte vor, die die einzelnen Institutionen untereinander und mit der Hindenburgstraße verbindet. Letztere Alternative erhält den Vorzug, da die Realisierung über einen längeren Zeitraum hinweg geplant werden kann und somit erleichtert wird.

Auf Basis dieses Entschlusses erarbeitet Hollein in enger Zusammenarbeit mit Cladders zwei Vorentwürfe für das Museum, die unter den Namen „Maschine" und „Reisterrassen" dem Kultur- und Bauausschuß im Juni 1973 präsentiert werden. Lange kann kein Konsens gefunden werden, und wieder vertraut die Stadt auf Johannes Cladders, der zuerst Oberbürgermeister Bolzenius und dann alle anderen Mitglieder für die „Reisterrassen" gewinnen kann. Cladders entschied sich für diese Variante nicht zuletzt deshalb, da sie höhere Chancen hatte, vom Landeskonservator akzeptiert zu werden.

Der Spatenstich soll noch 1974 – im letzten selbständigen Verwaltungsjahr Mönchengladbachs – vollzogen werden. Eine erste Kostenschätzung von 16,8 Millionen DM wird erstellt.

Nach Bekanntgabe der Pläne werden sowohl Bauplatz als auch Architekt von der Bevölkerung mehrfach kritisiert. Der Grundtenor richtet sich gegen die stille und für die Öffentlichkeit nicht nachvollziehbare Wahl des Architekten sowie gegen den abseits gelegenen Standort.

Erweiterungspläne der Museumssammlung

Die Ausstellungen Cladders hatten über lange Zeit einen treuen, aber anonymen Besucher: Graf Giuseppe Panza di Biumo. Der Immobilienmakler und Kunstsammler aus Mailand bietet im Sommer 1973 plötzlich Teile seiner Sammlung für das geplante Museum als Dauerleihgabe an. Die Unterbringung der Leihgaben erfordert jedoch speziell

148

Modellserie: Draufsicht, Plattenebene, Ebene Abteistraße und Gartenebene (von links nach rechts)

Model series: top view, plateau level, Abteistrasse level and garden level (from left to right)

each other and to the Hindenburgstrasse. The latter is given preference since its realization is planned over an extended timeframe, which facilitates the process.

Based on this decision, Hollein enters into a close collaboration with Cladders to create two preliminary designs for the museum, which are presented to the cultural and planning committee under the names "machine" and "rice terraces" in June 1973. Despite lengthy deliberations the committee cannot reach a consensus and once again the city places its trust in Johannes Cladders, who is able to win over first the district mayor, Bolzenius, and then all other members for the "rice terrace" concept. Cladders chose this variation not least of all because it stood a better a chance of being accepted by the state commissioner.

The first turf is to be dug in 1974, the last year in which Mönchengladbach would have an independent administration. Preliminary costs are estimated at DM 16.8 million.

After the plans are released, the public criticizes both the choice of the site and the architect. The basic tenor of the protest is directed at the fact that the architect was chosen behind closed doors and at the museum's location off the beaten track.

Expansion Plans for the Museum Collection

Cladders' exhibitions enjoyed the loyalty of a faithful but anonymous visitor over many years: Count Giuseppe Panza di Biumo. In the summer of 1973, the real estate agent and art collector from Milan suddenly decides to offer some of his collection to the new museum as a

„Ich bin an die Planung dieses Museums als Architekt und als Künstler herangegangen. Als Künstler, der eine enge Beziehung zu den dort präsentierten Kunstwerken hat, als Künstler, der selbst Kunstwerke (die in Museen stehen) produziert, und als Künstler, der ein Bauprojekt als Kunstwerk auffaßt. Eine Dialektik zwischen dem Bauwerk, dem Raum und dem Kunstwerk ist angestrebt – nicht im Sinne einer Integration, sondern im Sinne einer Konfrontation, die das Potential der Objekte und des Raumes sichtbar und erlebbar werden läßt. Der Raum soll von einer komplexen Neutralität sein."

Aus dem Pressetext von Hans Hollein, 1982.

"I approached the planning of this museum as an architect and an artist. As an artist who is closely connected to the exponents displayed in the museum and as an artist who produces works of art himself (which are housed in museums), and finally as an artist who understands a building project as a work of art. A dialectic between building, space and artwork is the ultimate goal; not in the sense of integration but in the sense of a confrontation that renders the potential of the objects and of the space visible and experiential. The space should be characterized by a complex neutrality."

Excerpt from press release by Hans Hollein, 1982.

zugeschnittene Räume, da der Graf auf einer klaren räumlichen Abgrenzung seiner Sammlung besteht. Hollein erhält den Auftrag, die „Reisterrassen"-Variante in dieser Hinsicht zu überarbeiten. Das daraus resultierende Konzept läßt die Vorzüge des Raumprogrammes „Maschine" in den Entwurf „Reisterrassen" einfließen. Die Funktionen werden stärker in den Berg zurückgenommen, die Baumassen reduziert und das Museum über das begehbare Dach, von oben nach unten, erschlossen. Das Kleeblatt-System, eine Agglomeration kleiner geschlossener Raumzellen, soll den Ansprüchen der Panza-Leihgabe gerecht werden.

Im Juni 1974 genehmigen Kultur- und Bauausschuß einstimmig die neue Variante. Doch nun verzögern Finanzierungsprobleme einen raschen Baubeginn. Um das gesamte Bauvolumen zu verwirklichen, benötigt die Stadt weitere zwei Millionen DM. Schützenhilfe kommt von Prof. Hugo Borger, Verbandsvorsitzender der Museumsleiter des Rheinlandes, der sich für das Projekt politisch einsetzt. In einem Interview mit der Rheinischen Post[2] betont dieser: „Die sieben Kölner Museen haben im Jahr mehr Besucher als die Spiele der beiden Kölner Bundesligavereine. Das beweist, daß der Mensch Zielorte für seine Freizeit sucht. (...) Ich halte den Hollein-Plan für ausgezeichnet."

Die Stadt beantragt daraufhin Mittel aus dem Bundes-Fond „Aufbauhilfe für kriegszerstörte Museen".

Ende 1974 kommt es dann – gegen die Stimmen der SPD – zum Vertragsabschluß mit dem Grafen Panza di Biumo, wobei die Liechtensteiner Firma „Modern Painting Trust Reg." als Verleiher und die Stadt Mönchengladbach als Entleiher auftreten. 78 Hauptwerke, die den älteren Teil seiner Sammlung umfassen, sollen für 15 Jahre dem Museum Mönchengladbach als Leihgabe zur Verfügung gestellt werden, sobald der Neubau 1977 fertiggestellt ist. Die Werke hatte Panza kurz vorher in die Schweiz gebracht.

Mehrere Punkte des Vertrags, vor allem die Kündigungsrechte des Grafen, erregen Unmut in SPD-Kreisen und Bevölkerung. Danach ist die Stadt verpflichtet, die geplante Fertigstellung des Museums bis zum 31. Dezember 1977 einzuhalten. Findet die Privatsammlung nicht bis Ende 1978 in Mönchengladbach ihren Einzug, kann der Verleiher den Vertrag innerhalb von 6 Monaten kündigen.

Der Verleiher hat ein unmittelbares Mitspracherecht bei der Raumgestaltung für seine Sammlung. In den Räumen dürfen – auch nicht vorübergehend – keine anderen Kunstwerke präsentiert werden. Die Stadt verpflichtet sich, einem Vertreter des Trusts nebst Begleitperson jährlich bis zu acht Aufenthalte nebst Fahrkosten zu finanzieren. Schließlich behält Panza sich vor, im Falle finanzieller Schwierigkeiten vom Vertrag zurücktreten zu können. Die SPD prangert den Vertrag mit den Worten an: „Ein Museum für den Grafen, nicht für den Bürger."[3]

Im Dezember 1974 präsentiert Hollein den Ausschüssen und Graf Panza ein Modell im Maßstab 1:50, das allgemeine Zufriedenheit auslöst. „Art Aktuell" schreibt im Dezember, daß Mönchengladbach „mit dieser Sammlung das modernste moderne Museum Europas haben wird."

permanent loan. The condition: the exhibits require customized rooms since the count insists that his collection be clearly separated from other exponents in the museum. Hollein is asked to review the "rice terrace" option with these changes in mind. The resulting concept is a successful marriage of the advantages of the "machine" design and the "rice terrace" ideas. The functions are recessed further into the mountain, the overall building mass is reduced and the museum is made accessible via its promenade roof, from top to bottom. The clover-leaf system, an agglomeration of small, closed cells, is aimed at meeting the demands for the Panza loan.

In June 1974 the culture and planning committee votes unanimously in favour of the new design. However, financial difficulties threaten to prevent the start of construction. To realize the entire complex, the city requires an additional DM 2 million. Help arrives in the person of Professor Hugo Borger, the chair of the federation of museum directors of the Rhineland, who gives political support to the project. In an interview with the Rheinische Post[2] he states emphatically: "Cologne's seven museums attract more visitors each year than the matches of both of the city's football clubs. This proves that people are looking for leisure destinations. (...) In my view, Hollein's plan is excellent."

Following this endorsement the city requests financial support from the Federal Fund for "the reconstruction of museums destroyed in the war."

In late 1974 the contract is signed with Count Panza di Biumo, despite the opposition voiced by the Social Democrats. The Liechtenstein company "Modern Painting Trust Reg." is named as lender and the city of Mönchengladbach as borrower. Seventy-eight major works, representing the count's early years as a collector, will be made available to the museum in Mönchengladbach on loan for a period of fifteen years as soon as the new building is completed in 1977. Panza had transported the works to Switzerland shortly before signing the contract.

Several paragraphs in the contract, especially the cancellation rights granted to the count, are criticized in Social Democratic circles and among the public. The contract stipulates that the city must complete the museum by 31 December 1977. Should the private collection not find a home in the city by the end of 1978, the lender has the right to terminate the contract within a period of six months. The lender has a direct co-determination right in the design of the rooms that will house his collection. The rooms may not be used, even temporarily, for the presentation of other works of art. The city undertakes to pay for up to eight visits and travel expenses for one representative of the trust and one accompanying person. Finally, Panza reserves the right to withdraw from the contract in the eventuality of financial difficulties. The Social Democratic Party denounces the contract with the slogan "A museum for a count, not for citizens."[3]

In December 1974 Hollein presents a model on the scale of 1:50 to the various committees and to Count Panza. It is received with approval all round. In December "Art Aktuell" writes that Mönchengladbach "will have the most modern modern museum in Europe with this collection."

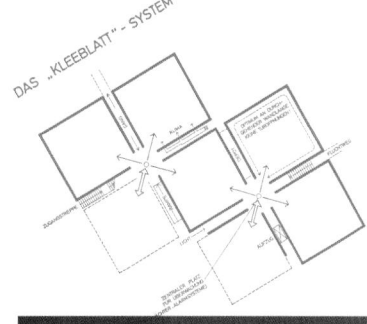

Hans Hollein, Johannes Cladders,
Graf Panza di Biumo (links),
Kleeblattsystem (rechts oben),
Hans Hollein, Graf Panza di Biumo, Thomas
van den Valentyn (Projektleiter) (rechts)

Hans Hollein, Johannes Cladders,
Count Panza di Biumo (left)
Clover-leaf system (above right)
Hans Hollein, Count Panza di Biumo, Thomas
van den Valentyn (project leader) (right)

Hoffnungsschimmer und Rückschläge

Der voraussichtliche Baubeginn ist nun September 1975. Das örtliche Architekturbüro Martin Gandke und H. P. Jensen übernimmt die Bauleitung und Durchführungsplanung.

Aufregung entfacht sich an einer geplanten 17tägigen Studienreise in die USA zwecks Besichtigung von rund 20 Museen, die Cladders und Hollein geplant haben. Über Wochen kann man in den regionalen Blättern die Erregung über 6.000 DM Reisekosten verfolgen. Der Rat reagiert und „verschiebt" die Reise.

Im April 1975 wird um die Baubewilligung angesucht, doch wenige Monate später debattiert man über eine neuerliche Verschiebung des Baubeginns, da die Mittel vom Land zwar vorgesehen, aber noch nicht bewilligt sind.

Zudem muß der Finanzhaushalt der drei Partnergemeinden stark nach unten revidiert werden. Zu guter Letzt werden der Stadt Mönchengladbach noch 20 Millionen DM Landeszuschuß aus dem Etat für das Jahr 1976 gestrichen. Der Finanzausschuß plädiert dafür, nur mit den bereits begonnenen kommunalen Baumaßnahmen fortzufahren, nicht aber mit neuen zu beginnen. Dem Museum droht endgültig der Finanztod. Die FDP fordert trotz verschlechterter Finanzsituation einen raschen Baubeginn. Mittels Flugblättern und an Infoständen wirbt sie für den Museumsneubau. Auch in der Bevölkerung nimmt die Zahl der Museumsbefürworter zu, die mangelnde Attraktivität der Stadt wird trotz des Fußballklubs Borussia angeprangert, und es wird eine starke Imageaufwertung der Stadt gefordert. Auch Johannes Cladders rührt unermüdlich in Vorträgen, Diskussionen und Radiosendungen die Werbetrommeln für sein Projekt.

Im November 1975 stimmt der städtische Kulturausschuß gegen die Stimmen der SPD schließlich für den Neubau und empfiehlt dem Finanzausschuß, für 1976 bereits die Mittel bereitzustellen. Die SPD geht mit der Mitteilung an die Öffentlichkeit, daß das Museum aufgrund der finanziellen Mißlage der Stadt nun durch Gebührenerhöhungen gedeckt werde, was die CDU sofort dementiert. Der Finanzausschuß genehmigt mit den Stimmen der CDU und FDP eine Mittelbereitstellung von drei Millionen DM für den Neubau im kommenden Jahr 1976.

Die Stimmung in der Stadt scheint plötzlich umzuschlagen. Den Verantwortlichen wird vorgeworfen, in dieser finanziell kritischen Lage über die Köpfe, Wünsche und Bedürfnisse der Bürger hinweg ein „Mausoleum der Kunst für eine kleine Bildungselite" zu errichten.[4] Das Jahr 1976 bringt noch einen weiteren Rückschlag. Der Bescheid des Bundes trifft ein und besagt, daß dem Museum kein Zuschuß aus dem Wiederaufbaufonds genehmigt wird, da – so die Argumentation – dieser nur „Museen mit bundesweiter Bedeutung" zusteht.

Zwei Jahre nach Antragsstellung genehmigen im August 1976 schließlich die drei zuständigen Landesministerien für Inneres, Finanzen und Kultur den Landeszuschuß von 5,9 Millionen DM.

Der geplante Baubeginn ist nun der 1. Dezember 1976. Die Kostenschätzung für den ersten Bauabschnitt beläuft sich mittlerweile auf 18,8 Millionen DM.

The construction is now scheduled to begin in September 1975. The local architectural firm M. Gandke and H.P. Jensen is asked to supervise and plan the building.

A seventeen-day study trip to the United States for the purpose of viewing some twenty museums planned by J. Cladders and H. Hollein stirs up a huge controversy. For weeks on end the local press expresses outrage at the DM 6,000 travel expenses. The committee responds by "postponing" the trip.

In April 1975 building permission is sought, yet only a few months later there is renewed discussion of a delay since federal support has been promised, but not approved.

In addition, the budget of the three partners has to be drastically reduced. To top it all off, DM 20 million is cut from the state grant for the city of Mönchengladbach's 1976 budget. The finance committee suggests that only those building measures already underway should be continued, while new projects should be put off. The museum is at risk of dying a financial death.

Despite the deteriorating financial situation, the Free Democratic Party calls for construction to begin as soon as possible. With flyers and information kiosks, the party actively promotes the museum project. Among the public, too, the number of supporters for the museum is beginning to grow, bemoaning the lack of attractions the city has to offer in spite of the local Borussia football club, and voices are being raised to improve the image of the city. Johannes Cladders is tireless in his efforts to promote his project through lectures, discussions and programmes broadcast on radio stations.

In November 1975, the municipal culture committee finally approves the new building, against the dissenting votes from the Social Democrats, issuing a recommendation to the finance committee that funds be made available for 1976. The Social Democratic Party goes public with the statement that the museum is being financed through an increase in rates due to the city's poor financial state; the Christian Democrats immediately deny any such allegation. With the combined Christian Democrat and Free Democrat vote the finance committee approves the release of DM 3 million for the new building in the following year, 1976.

Suddenly, the mood in the city takes an about-turn. The responsible authorities are being criticized for erecting a "mausoleum of art for a small educated elite" in times of financial crisis against the intentions, desires and needs of the public at large.[4] 1976 brings yet another setback: the state announces that the museum will not benefit from a subsidy from the reconstruction fund since, it reasons, the fund is only available to "museums of national importance."

Two years after the filing of the application, the three responsible state ministries (Interior, Finance, and Culture) approve a state subsidy of DM 5.9 million in August 1976.

Construction is scheduled to begin on 1 December 1976. The estimate for the first construction phase has climbed to DM 18.8 million.

In September 1976, the Christian Democrats and the Social

„Scheidung auf italienisch"[6]

Im September 1976 liefern sich CDU und SPD wieder harte Konfrontationen rund um den Museumsbau: 800.000 DM Zuschuß des Landschaftsverbandes Rheinland stehen zur Debatte. Durch den Neubau könnten die Bestände rheinischer Kulturgeschichte der Öffentlichkeit zugänglich gemacht werden. Nach harten Attacken wird die Mittelbereitstellung schließlich vom Kulturausschuß des Landschaftsverbandes genehmigt. „Im Bundesgebiet gehen jährlich 22 Millionen Bürger ins Museum. Das sind dreimal so viele wie zu Bundesliga-Fußballspielen", sagte Hans Rudolf Hartung, Kulturdezernent des Landschaftsverbandes. „Wenn 50 Millionen Mark für ein Stadion ausgegeben würden, rege das keinen Menschen auf."[5]

Just in dem Moment, da endlich alles seinen Lauf nimmt und scheinbar nichts mehr die geplante Realisierung des „modernsten Museums" hindern kann, tauchen vermehrt Gerüchte über Schwierigkeiten mit der Panza-Leihgabe auf. Panza beginnt, die Architektur zu kritisieren, bemängelt die Raumgestaltung, die Lichtqualität der Räume, bezichtigt die großen flexiblen Ausstellungsräume des „Charakters eines Modegeschäfts".[6] Er kündigt an, von seinem vertraglich festgelegten Kündigungsrecht Gebrauch zu machen, falls die Raumgestaltung für seine Sammlung nicht seinen Änderungswünschen angepaßt werde, und droht, seine Sammlung anderen Institutionen anzubieten.

Das Konzept wurde jedoch 1974 genau auf Panzas Wünsche hin zugeschnitten und seitdem nicht mehr geändert. Noch am 6. März 1974 hatte Panza nach Sichtung der letzten Pläne in einem Brief an Johannes Cladders geschrieben: „Nach Herrn Holleins neuesten Zeichnungen sind wir in der Lage, ein Museum auf höchstem internationalen Niveau zu errichten, und Mönchengladbach könnte zu einem Weltzentrum für Liebhaber der Gegenwartskunst werden."[7]

Es ranken sich nun viele Gerüchte um die wahren Hintergründe seines langsam beginnenden Rückzugs. Sicher ist, daß er zu dieser Zeit seine Sammlertätigkeit einstellte, da die anhaltende Rezession in Italien ihn zunehmend mit ernsthaften finanziellen Problemen belastete. Sicher ist auch, daß aufgrund von Gesetzesnovellen neue steuerliche Abgaben anfielen und Graf Panza sich entscheiden mußte, seine Sammlung zu verkaufen und das Geld nach Italien einzuführen oder aber die Kunstwerke selbst nach Italien zurückzubringen.

Die SPD nimmt die Entwicklung sofort zum Anlaß, die Vertragsauflösung zu fordern, beansprucht, die Schwierigkeiten mit Panza „schon lange kommen gesehen zu haben", und wehrt sich öffentlich gegen einen Vertrag, der „auf 15 Jahre die besten Ausstellungsräume exklusiv für sich in Anspruch nimmt."[8]

Obwohl Cladders und Hollein versuchen, soweit wie möglich auf die Wünsche von Graf Panza einzugehen, stellt dieser nun Forderungen, die sich nicht mehr auf seine Sammlungsräume allein beziehen, sondern auf das gesamte Museum. Allmählich dringen Gerüchte durch, wonach Panza bereits seit geraumer Zeit mit Dr. Werner Schmalenbach Gespräche führt, um denselben Sammlungsteil in den Neubau der

Democrats once again enter into a heated debate on the museum building. At issue: a DM 800,000 contribution from the Rhineland Federation. It is argued that the new building will make the stores of the Rhineland's cultural history accessible to the public. After heated discussion, the cultural committee of the Federation finally approves the release of the funds. "22 million citizens visit museums every year in this federal region. That's three times as many as the number of fans at the football matches of the Federal Football League," says Hans Rudolf Hartung, who held the culture portfolio in the Federation. "If 50 million Marks were spent on a stadium, no one would raise an eyebrow."[5]

"Divorce Italian Style"[6]

Just when everything seemed to be underway and nothing stood in the path of the planned realization of the "most modern museum," rumours begin to spread about difficulties with the Panza loan. Panza starts to criticize the architecture, pans the room design, the light quality in the rooms, comments that the large, flexible exhibition rooms have the "character of a fashion boutique"[6]. He announces that he intends to make use of his contractual right to withdraw should the room design not be adjusted to suit his wishes and threatens to offer his collection to other institutions.

Yet the concept had been adapted in 1974 to suit Panza's wishes and had not been changed since. As recently as 6 March 1974, Panza had written in a letter to Cladders after having studied the plans: "After these last drawings by Mr Hollein we are in a position to creat a top-class, international museum and Mönchengladbach could become the World attraction for the people interested in contemporary art."[7]

Rumours abound regarding the true reasons for his gradual retreat. The only thing certain is that he ceased his activities as a collector at around the same time, since the continuing recession in Italy increasingly puts financial stress on his own resources. Moreover, new legislation which resulted in new tax duties and affected foreign investments, i.e. the export of works of art, forced Count Panza to decide whether he should offer his collection for sale and import the money to Italy, or return the artworks to Italy.

The Social Democratic Party immediately seizes the opportunity offered by these developments to demand the annulment of the contract, claiming to have "long since predicted" these difficulties with Panza, and publicly opposing a contract "which claims exclusive use of the best exhibition rooms for the next fifteen years."[8]

Although Cladders and Hollein do their utmost to react to Count Panza's wishes, the latter now issues demands which are no longer restricted to the rooms housing his collection, but to the entire museum. Gradually rumours seep out that Panza has been in negotiation for some time with Dr Werner Schmalenbach regarding a new building for the Landesgalerie on Grabbe-Platz (Kunstsammlung Nordrhein-Westfalen) in Düsseldorf, to which he is offering to lend the same section of his collection.[9]

Flexibler Ausstellungsraum / Lichtsystem

Flexible exhibition room / Lighting system

Landesgalerie am Grabbe-Platz (Kunstsammlung Nordrhein-Westfalen) in Düsseldorf unterzubringen.[9]

Im Dezember 1976 scheitern schließlich die Verhandlungen Mönchengladbachs mit Panza. Ein rechtlicher Schwebezustand dominiert die kommenden Jahre, da die Stadt weiterhin auf Vertragserfüllung besteht und Panza als vertragsbrüchig bezeichnet.

Die Bevölkerung fühlt sich einmal mehr betrogen.

Es wird gebaut

Am 29. November 1976 findet der Spatenstich statt, geplanter Fertigstellungstermin ist Mai 1979. Die nach oben hin revidierte Kostenschätzung beträgt nun 22,9 Millionen DM.

Als besonders zeit- und kostenintensiv erweisen sich die Erdarbeiten. 18.000 Kubikmeter Erdreich müssen ausgehoben und für die Terrassierung mit 6.000 Kubikmeter Sand und Kies angefüllt werden.

Die Grundsteinlegung folgt am 26. August 1977. Kultusminister Gigersohn (SPD) lobt dabei den Mut der Stadt und wird dafür später aus den eigenen Reihen scharf kritisiert, da die SPD dem Projekt nach wie vor eine − oppositionsbedingte − kritische Haltung entgegenbringt.

Am 1. September 1978 feiert die Stadt ein großes Richtfest, das von dem Künstler Heinz Mack als „Licht-Richt-Fest" gestaltet wird. Anwesend ist − neben 20.000 Besuchern − Bundespräsident Walter Scheel.

Aufgrund des strengen Winters 1978/79 und einiger Konkurse am Bau beteiligter Firmen kommt es zu enormen Bauverzögerungen. Der Eröffnungstermin muß auf 1981 verschoben werden, der Kostenrahmen steigt auf 25,2 Millionen DM. Verzögerungen bedürfen immer eines Schuldigen, und so überhäufen sich erst der planende Architekt Hollein

In December 1976 Mönchengladbach's negotiations with Panza finally fall through. The following years are dominated by a legal quagmire since the city continues to insist on the fulfilment of the contract, citing Panza as being in breach of contract.

Once again the population feels cheated.

Ground is broken on 29 November 1976 with the completion date set for May 1979. The estimated cost has risen to DM 22.9 million.

The excavation works turn out to be especially time-consuming and costly. 18,000 cubic metres of earth have to shifted and 6,000 cubic metres of sand and gravel are required to build the terraces.

The cornerstone ceremony takes place on 26 August. Minister of Culture Gigersohn (Social Democrat) praises the courage of the city, for which he is later sharply criticized from his own party ranks since the Social Democrats continue to be critical of the project, in keeping with their role as official opposition. On 1 September 1978, the city celebrates a major topping-out ceremony, conceived by artist Heinz Mack as a "light topping-out party." Among the 20,000 guests: federal president Walter Scheel.

The extremely cold temperatures in the winter of 1978/79 and the bankruptcy of some participating companies greatly delay the construction. The opening has to be postponed to 1981, the estimated costs climb to DM 25.2 million. When such delays occur, a scapegoat is always sought and the planning architect Hollein and the executing architects Gandke and Jensen begin by accusing each other. This is followed by a demand from shell construction contractor Stengelmann for an additional claim of approximately DM 1 million.

Under Construction

Rohbauphase (Wechselausstellung, Sheddächer, Ausstellungsräume „Kleeblattsystem")

Shell construction phase (changing exhibtions, shed roofs, exhibition rooms "Clover-leaf system")

und die ausführenden Architekten Gandke und Jensen wechselseitig mit Anschuldigungen. Schließlich kündigt der Rohbau-Unternehmer Stengelmann auch noch eine Nachforderung von rund einer Million DM an.

Dieser sich länger hinziehende Streit wird – medienwirksam – mittels Leserbriefen zwischen Bauleitung und Bauunternehmer ausgetragen. Der Bauunternehmer erhöht seine Forderungen 1980 auf fast zwei Millionen DM, die Stadt erklärt sich zu einer Abschlagszahlung von 300.000 DM bereit. Stengelmann droht, gegen die Stadt zu klagen, und beantragt ein Konkursverfahren. Die Baustelle steht still, und der Bauskandal ist perfekt.

Die öffentliche Austragung der Schwierigkeiten bereitet den Kritikern des Projektes den gewünschten Nährboden. „Böse Zungen sagen, an dem Museum wird nicht gebaut, sondern gebastelt. Noch bösere Zungen meinen gar, daß die Baustelle vor ihrer Fertigstellung zum Denkmal gemacht wird."[10]

Eine Leihgabe kommt dazu, eine andere verabschiedet sich endgültig

Es bedarf an dieser Stelle eines kurzen Nachtrags. Durch den 1976 drohenden Verlust der Panza-Sammlung gerät Johannes Cladders in Bedrängnis. Die Lücke muß aufgefüllt werden. Im April 1978 kann er einen Teil der Sammlung Reinhard Onnasch als Dauerleihgabe sichern und so die Bereiche Pop- und Op-Art und Nouveau Realisme inhaltlich aufwerten.

Kurzfristig scheint es, als ob eine Vertragserfüllung Panzas bevorsteht. Mitte 1978 kehrt der Graf reumütig nach Mönchengladbach zurück und erklärt sich mit der Architektur plötzlich einverstanden. Grund dafür dürften auch seine mißlungenen Verhandlungen mit Düsseldorf sein, wie auch der zunehmende Druck der italienischen Regierung.

Bereits ein Jahr später aber ändert Panza wieder seine Meinung. Aufgrund der nicht termingerechten Fertigstellung hat er nun auch die rechtliche Handhabe und kündigt zum 30. Januar 1979 den Vertrag. Die Stadt prüft vorerst noch die rechtliche Substanz dieses Schrittes. Kulturdezernent Diekamp kommentiert die Panza-Verhandlungen so: „Wie in der Vergangenheit mehrfach, hat jetzt der Schriftwechsel mit Graf Panza seine Fortsetzung gefunden. Wir betreiben die Fortsetzung dieses Geplänkels nicht ohne Lust."[11/12]

Noch im Herbst 1981 hat Cladders keine Sammlung, die das Haus

The long-drawn-out dispute is fought, in best media fashion, by means of letters to the editor from the construction supervisor on the one hand and the general contractor on the other. The contractor raises his claim in 1980 to nearly DM 2 million and the city pronounces itself willing to offer a partial payment of DM 300,000. Stengelmann threatens to sue the city and initiates bankruptcy proceedings. The construction site grinds to a standstill; the situation has escalated into a full-blown scandal.

The public display of these difficulties provide the project's critics with the necessary fodder. "Evil tongues say that the museum isn't being constructed, it's being pieced together. Even more evil tongues have suggested that the construction site will be declared a monument before completion."[10]

A New Loan Arrives and the Other Bids Adieu

At this point a short postscript is in order. Johannes Cladders finds himself in a precarious situation through the loss of the Panza collection threatened in 1976. The gap must be filled. In April 1978 he succeeds in securing a part of the Reinhard Onnasch collection on permanent loan, greatly enhancing the museum's Pop- and Op-Art exhibits and adding to the content of its Nouveau Realisme collection.

For a short time it seems as if Panza may keep his contractrual obligations after all. In mid-1978 the count returns ruefully to Mönchengladbach and suddenly expresses his satisfaction with the architecture. This may have been due to his aborted negotiations with Düsseldorf and increasing pressure from the Italian government.

Yet within one year Panza again changes course. Owing to the delay in completion of construction he now has the necessary legal tool and declares the contract null and void as of 30 January 1979. At first, the city verifies the legality of this step. Minister Diekamp comments on the Panza negotiations by saying that, "as has occured several times in the past, the corrrespondence with Count Panza has been resumed. We undertake the continuation of this banter with some measure of amusement."[11/12]

By the fall of 1981 Cladders still does not have a collection to fill the house for the opening. Finally he contacts collector Erich Marx. Marx had originally hoped to house his collection in the Gropius building in Berlin, but ultimately decides to accept Johannes Cladders' offer.[13]

„Es ist ein Kunstwerk,
das Kunst beherbergt, kein Haus
also, das sich, seinen Anspruch
vertuschend, der Kunst grämlich
unterwürfe. Es ist stolz auf
seinen Inhalt, aber es ist
auch stolz auf sich selbst."

In: Die Zeit, am 18.06.1982

"It is a work of art that houses
art, not a building, therefore,
which is grudgingly subservient
to art denying its own claim. It is
proud of its content, but also
proud of itself."

In: Die Zeit, 18.06.1982

„Im Museum kulminiert dieser Konflikt. Es fängt ihn – und damit auch sich selbst – nur in dem Maße auf, in dem es sich selbst zum Kunstwerk erklärt. Das Museum ist das potentielle Gesamtkunstwerk des 20. Jhds. Es wird dazu in dem Maße, als es ihm gelingt, den räumlichen Anspruch der Architektur mit dem der Kunst zu vereinigen."

Aus dem Pressetext zur Eröffnung von Johannes Cladders, 1982.

"This conflict culminates in the museum. It absorbs it [the conflict] – and thus itself – only to the degree to which it declares itself as a work of art. The museum is the potential total work of art of the twentieth century. It becomes such a work to the degree to which it succeeds in uniting the spatial demands of the architecture with those of the art."

Excerpt from press release by Johannes Cladders on the occasion of the museum opening, 1982.

für die Eröffnung hätte füllen können. Schließlich bahnt er Kontakte zum Sammler Erich Marx an. Dieser hatte ursprünglich gehofft, seine Sammlung im Gropius-Bau, Berlin, unterzubringen, geht dann aber auf das Angebot Johannes Cladders ein.[13]

Eine letzte Verzögerung und die lang ersehnte Eröffnung

Johannes Cladders und Hans Hollein reisen unterdessen von einer internationalen Einladung zur nächsten, um ihr vielgerühmtes Projekt, daß im öffentlichen Interesse – neben dem Centre Georges Pompidou, Paris, der Staatsgalerie Stuttgart und der National Gallery Washington – rangiert, vorzustellen. Dabei dreht sich die internationale Debatte immer wieder um die Frage des Museums als „Tempel oder Forum" und um das gespannte Verhältnis von Architektur und Kunst. Cladders wie auch Hollein begegnen dieser Fragestellung mit dem Begriff des „Gesamtkunstwerkes". Der Rohbau zieht aber auch seinerseits viel Besuch an, Architekturinteressierte aus Europa, USA und Asien besichtigen das Gebäude bereits Jahre vor seiner Fertigstellung.

1981 muß die Fertigstellung nochmals um sechs Monate verschoben werden.

Nach sechsjähriger Bauzeit ist das Haus schließlich im Dezember bezugsfertig. Am 23. Mai 1982, kurz vor Beginn der „Biennale" in Venedig und der „Documenta" in Kassel, öffnet das Museum seine Pforten. Die Gesamtbaukosten belaufen sich auf über 31 Millionen DM.

Raumkonzept

Das Museum ist auf unterschiedlichen Wegen und Ebenen zu betreten: vom Fuße des Abteibergs den Abteigarten über die Terrassenwege zur Plattenebene hinauf, vorbei an schönen Einblicken in die Ausstellungsräume, oder direkt von der Abteistraße in die Ausstellungsebene. Die meistgenutzte Erschließung des Museums führt von der Oberstadtzone über einen schmalen Steg, der auf dem Museumsdach – der „Plattenebene" – mündet. Entlang des Steges führen „Medialinien" als Leitsystem direkt zu einem kleinen „Tempel" aus Glas und weißem Marmor, der auf den Eingang verweist.

Das Innere erinnert an einen „Raumschiff-Enterprise"-Aufzug – ein Kubus ohne offensichtliche Funktion. Der Eintretende muß sich um seine eigene Achse drehen, um die Glastür und die dahinterliegende, in das Museum hinabführende Treppe zu entdecken. Ein offener flexibler Ausstellungsraum offenbart sich, der zugleich auch Kassabereich, Garderobe und eine Buchhandlung beherbergt.

Das Haus hat zwei Hauptgeschosse, eines auf dem Niveau der Abteistraße, das andere auf dem Niveau der Gartenebene. Die Konzeption verlangte separate und neutrale Groß-Einzelräume (ca. 90 m²) für Einzelpräsentationen, kleinere Raumeinheiten (35 m²) sowie fließende Raumfolgen und -typen für größere Themenausstellungen, die versetzt angeordnet sind und teils über Oberlicht verfügen.

Das Innere schreibt keinen zwingenden Rundgang vor, die Räume fließen ineinander über, ständig ergeben sich neue Weggabelungen und bieten sich interessante Durchblicke. Glaubt sich der Besucher in

In the meantime Johannes Cladders and Hans Hollein travel from one international invitation to another to introduce the much-praised project, which has drawn public attention in the company of other illustrious projects: the Centre Georges Pompidou in Paris, the Staatsgalerie in Stuttgart and the National Gallery in Washington. The international debate returns again and again to the question of the museum as "temple or forum" and to the charged relationship between architecture and art. Cladders and Hollein answer this question with the term "total work of art."

But the shell construction also attracts much attention. Interested visitors arrive from Europe, the US and Asia to view the building years before its completion.

In 1981 the completion date has to be postponed one last time by another six months.

After six years of construction the building is finally ready for occupation in December. On 23 May 1982, just before the start of the Biennale in Venice and the Documenta in Kassel, the museum opens its doors to the public. Total buildings costs have risen to over DM 31 million.

Spatial Concept

Visitors can enter the museum from different paths and on different levels. At the foot of the Abteiberg, through the abbey garden across terrace paths to the plateau level, past beautiful views into the exhibition room or directly from the Abteistrasse into the exhibition level. The most frequently used access is provided by a narrow footbridge from the town on the hill onto the museum roof, the "plateau level." "Media lines" along the footbridge lead to a small "temple" of glass and white marble, marked as "entrance." The interior is reminiscent of an elevator in the "Starship Enterprise" – a cube without obvious function.

Anyone who enters must turn 180 degrees to discover the glass door behind which lies the stairway that leads down into the museum. The stairs end in an open, flexible exhibition space which simultaneously houses the box office, wardrobe and a book shop.

The building has two main floors, one at the height of the Abteistrasse and the other on the garden level. The concept called for separate and neutral large individual rooms (approximately 90 m^2) for feature exhibitions, smaller units (35 m^2), as well as flowing sequences of spaces and room types for thematic exhibitions on a large scale; the latter are staggered and partially lit with daylight from above.

The interior does not impose a specific parcours, the rooms flow into each other, at each turn new crossroads present themselves and offer interesting vistas. No sooner does the visitor fear that he may be lost in this maze of rooms than he finds himself once again in the large, central exhibition space, whose floor-to-ceiling glass walls offer a view onto the garden.

The administration building contains a delivery area, a warehou-

„Eingangstempel" und Fußgängerbrücke (links), überlagerte Geschoße (rechts)

"Entrance temple" and Footbridge (left), Overlapping floors (right)

BAUDATEN

Grundstücksgröße	4.081 m²
bebaute Fläche	2.925 m²
Gesamtnutzfläche	6.000 m²

davon:
für Bestandspräsentation	3.100m² (27 Räume)
und Wechselausstellung	400 m² (3 Räume)

weitere Einrichtungen:

Museums-Café
audiovisueller Einführungsraum
Vortragssaal (ca. 150 Plätze)
Unterrichtsraum (ca. 30 Plätze)
Malklasse (18 Plätze)
Präsenzbibliothek
Restaurierungswerkstätten

diesem Raumgefüge zu verlieren, gelangt er auch schon wieder in den großen zentralen Ausstellungsraum, der über raumhohe Verglasungen einen Ausblick in den Garten ermöglicht.

Das Verwaltungsgebäude beherbergt unter anderem einen Anlieferungsbereich, ein Lager, eine Bibliothek und das Archiv und überragt als einziger Bauteil die Plattenebene wesentlich.

Im äußersten Ostteil des Gebäudes liegen die Räume für die Wechselausstellungen mit Oberlicht und darunterliegend der Vortrags- und Filmsaal. Die Cafeteria kragt in den Garten und gewährt einerseits Ausblick auf das Münster und andererseits Einblick in die Ausstellung. Unter ihr befindet sich die Malklasse. Dort, wo das Gebäude mit dem Garten in Berührung tritt, zeichnet Hollein die Terrassenform im Inneren durch geschwungene Wände nach.

Die verschiedenen Bodenbeläge im Museum – von Marmor über Parkett bis Sisal-Teppich – deuten die inhaltliche Raumtrennung an und erleichtern zusätzlich die Orientierung. Verspielt wird Hollein erst in den Nebenräumen. Ein roter Audiovisionsraum, ein hellgrün karierter Vortragssaal und ein kreisrunder blau-roter Unterrichtsraum.

Für die Fassaden wurden vier Hauptmaterialien verwendet. Die geschlossene Fassade des Verwaltungsturms und die quadratische Halle der Wechselausstellungen sind mit hellem Sandstein verkleidet, die Ausstellungstürme einschließlich der Sheddächer mit grauem Titanzink. Alle Fensterfronten bestehen aus Aluminium und Glas. Die terrassenförmigen Wege zum Abteigarten sind mit Ziegelsteinen ausgeführt.

Der zweite Bauabschnitt ist nach wie vor im Gespräch. Hans Hollein hat erst 1998 eine neuerliche Studie vorgelegt. Die Realisierung hängt, wie so oft, von der Finanzierbarkeit und dem Mut einzelner Entscheidungsträger ab. All dies ist zur Zeit noch nicht in Sicht.

se, a library and the archive, and it is the only area of the complex to rise clearly above the plateau level.

The rooms for changing exhibitions with daylight ceilings are located at the eastern end of the building, with the auditorium and screening room below. The cafeteria juts into the garden and offers a view onto the abbey on one side and into the exhibition on the other. The art classrooms are located on the floor below. Wherever the building comes into direct contact with the garden, Hollein echoes the terraced shape with curved walls in the interior.

The many different floor coverings throughout the museum – from marble to parquet to sisal – indicate the functional division of the various spaces and facilitate orientation.

Hollein's design becomes playful only in the auxiliary rooms. A red audiovisual screening room, a lecture room in light-green checks and a circular blue and red classroom.

Four main materials were used for the façades. The closed façade of the administration tower and the square hall for the changing exhibitions are clad in light sandstone, the exhibition towers and their shed roofs are covered in grey titanium zinc. The windows are uniformly kept in aluminium and glass. The terraced paths to the abbey garden are laid in brick.

The second construction phase is still under discussion. As recently as 1998 Hans Hollein presented a new study. As so often, the realization is dependent upon financing and the courage of individuals with the power to make decisions. None is currently in sight.

BUILDING DATA

Plot size	4,081 m²
built area	2,925 m²
total usable area	6,000 m²
of which: for permanent collection	3,100 m² (27 rooms)
and changing exhibitions	400 m² (3 rooms)

additional facilities:
museum café
audiovisual screening room
auditorium (approx. 150 seats)
classroom (approx. 30 seats)
art studio (for 18 students)
library
restoration workshops

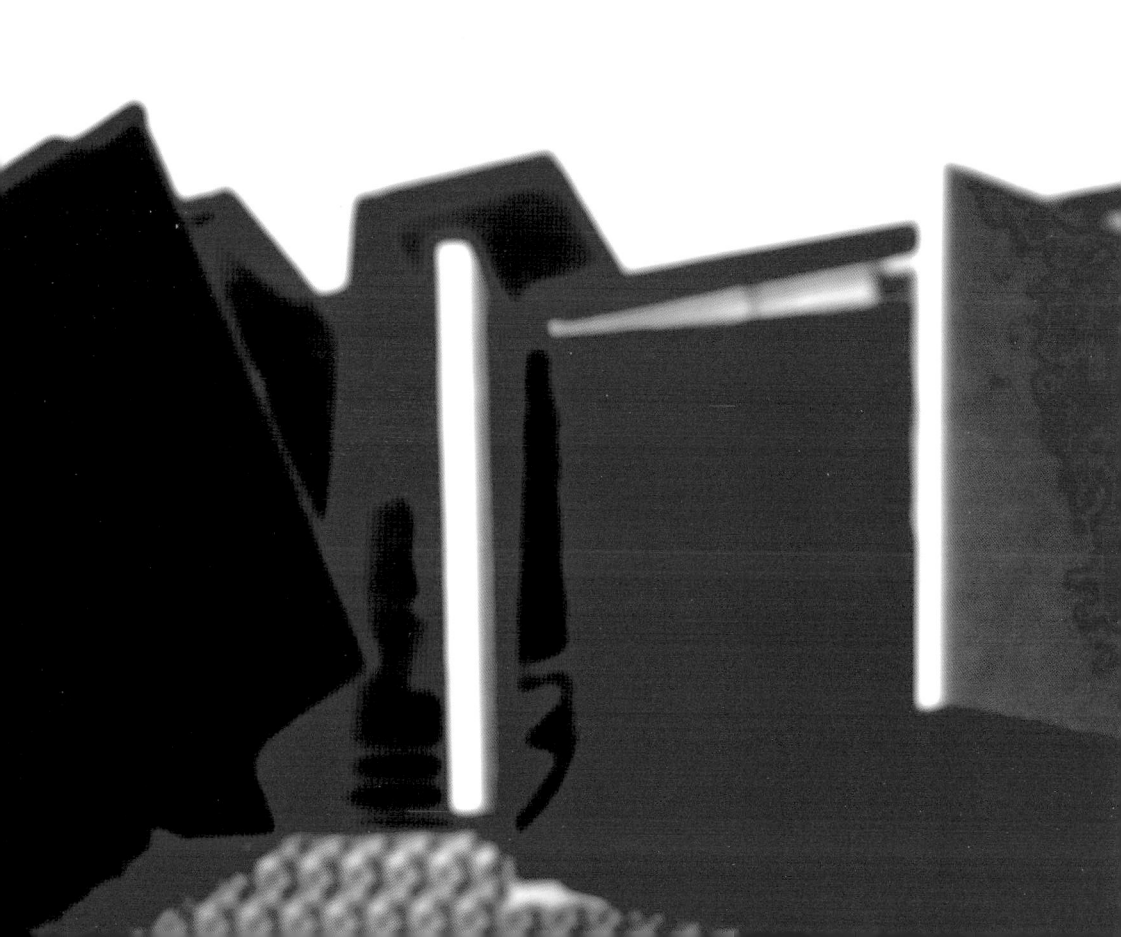

Groninger Museum

Der großzügige Sponsor/The Generous Sponsor

Disneyland im Hohen Norden

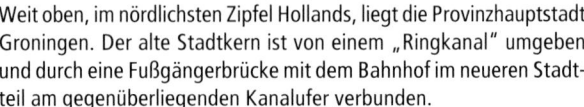

Weit oben, im nördlichsten Zipfel Hollands, liegt die Provinzhauptstadt Groningen. Der alte Stadtkern ist von einem „Ringkanal" umgeben und durch eine Fußgängerbrücke mit dem Bahnhof im neueren Stadtteil am gegenüberliegenden Kanalufer verbunden.

Mitten im Kanal „tummeln" sich sehr ausgefallene und bunte Bauten: das Groninger Museum. Dort, wo sich die Brücke zu einem ovalen Platz weitet, befindet sich der „goldene Turm" mit dem Museumseingang, der entlang der Brücke von einem hellgrünen und einem rosa Bauteil flankiert wird. An diesen zentralen Komplex sind in beide Flußrichtungen je zwei – übereinandergestapelte – Pavillons durch kleine Brücken angebunden. Der östliche „Stapel" besteht aus einem quadratischen Körper aus Ziegelstein, dem ein zylindrischer, mit Aluminium verkleideter Pavillon aufgesetzt ist. Der westlich gelegene Teil setzt sich aus einem bunt gemusterten Unterbau zusammen, dem eine dekonstruktivistische Architektur aus rot-schwarz gefleckten Stahlplatten mit Glaseinschnitten entspringt.

Der Gebäudegrundriß ist klar strukturiert. Jeder Pavillon ist vom Foyer im Turm aus separat begehbar.

Um der umfangreichen Sammlung gerecht zu werden, die die Bereiche Archäologie und Geschichte der Region, Kunsthandwerk, Gemäldesammlung und zeitgenössische Kunst umfaßt, legte der damalige Direktor Frans Haks großen Wert auf räumliche Trennung. Die einzelnen Bereiche sollten auch architektonisch zum Ausdruck kommen.

Im Inneren der Pavillons kontrastieren die Raumeindrücke: Einem nur mit Notbeleuchtung ausgestattetem großen Raum schließt sich ein Pavillon mit raumhohen fließenden weißen Vorhängen als Raumteiler an, die einzelne Vitrinen und Kunstgegenstände umhüllen. Der farbenreichste Bereich im mittleren Museumstrakt mit unterschiedlichen Raumgrößen und -typen erstreckt sich über drei Ebenen. Keine Wand ist weiß, alle sind in verschiedenen Pastelltönen gehalten. Nur der letzte Pavillon nimmt eine klare Gegenposition zur Farben- und Materialvielfalt der anderen Räume ein: Sichtbeton, Stahlplatten und Glas.

An die inhaltliche Konzeption von Frans Haks haben sich die nachfolgenden Direktoren nicht immer gehalten. Ein rascher Durchgang durch das Museum zeigt deutlich, daß mittlerweile fast alle Räume für Wechselausstellungen genutzt werden. Die historische und archäologische Sammlung wird nicht mehr präsentiert. Der als Gemäldegalerie konzipierte Pavillon wird ausschließlich für Rauminstallationen genutzt. Einzig der Kunsthandwerk-Pavillon ist noch im Originalzustand erhalten.

Dem derzeitigen Direktor Kees van Twist zufolge hat das ursprüngliche Präsentationskonzept nach Sammlungsbereichen nie wirklich funktioniert. Daß das Museum heute Besucherstatistiken um 200.000 Besucher pro Jahr aufweist – in einer Stadt, die 175.000 Einwohner hat –, ist auch das Ergebnis einer neuen Museumspolitik. 40 angestellte

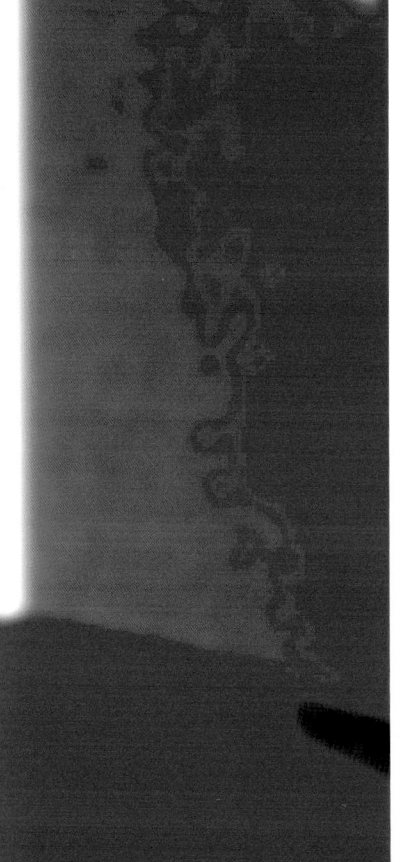

Disneyland in the Far North

The provincial capital of Groningen is located at the northernmost tip of Holland. A "ring canal" surrounds the historic town core, which is connected by a foot bridge to the railway station in the newer part of the city on the opposite bank.

A grouping of highly unusual buildings in vivid colours – the Groningen museum complex – animates the middle section of the canal. Where the bridge widens into an oval public space, a "golden tower" marks the museum entrance, which is flanked by a light green and a pink wing that run parallel to the bridge. A set of two pavilions, stacked one above the other, is connected to this central complex by small bridges, both upstream and downstream. The eastern "stack" consists of a square brick volume topped by a cylindrical, aluminium-clad pavilion. The western section has a brightly patterned substructure surmounted by a deconstructionist volume of red- and black-flecked steel plates with glass inserts.

The building has a clearly structured plan. Each pavilion is individually accessible from the foyer in the tower. Frans Haks, the museum's director at the time, set great store by spatial separation to do justice to each section of this vast collection, which comprises regional archaeology and history, arts and crafts, painting and contemporary art. The architecture was to give outward expression to the individual sections.

The pavilion interiors offer contrasting impressions. A large room equipped only with emergency lighting leads directly into a pavilion with flowing white floor-to-ceiling curtains, which act as room dividers by screening individual display cases and works of art. The most colourful area in the central museum wing encompasses three levels, with rooms of different sizes and types. None of the walls is white; all are painted in various pastel tones. With its exposed concrete, steel plates and glass, the last pavilion stands in marked contrast to the range

Mitarbeiter kümmern sich um Ausstellungsprogramm, Pressearbeit und Vermarktung des Hauses, inklusive Vermietung von Räumlichkeiten für Präsentationszwecke, Empfänge und Feste.

Subventionen von 11 Millionen Gulden ermöglichen eine großangelegte und äußerst erfolgreiche Ausstellungspolitik – ausgerichtet auf ein breites Publikum.

Das großzügige Geschenk

In Groningen hat auch die niederländische Gasunion „Gasunie" ihren Sitz. Als 1987 ihr 25jähriges Jubiläum bevorsteht, will sie der Stadt ein großzügiges Geschenk machen. Die Anforderungen, mit der Donation möglichst internationales Interesse zu wecken und dabei ein langfristiges Ergebnis zu erzielen, führen über ein Engagement im Kulturbereich zum alten Groninger Museum.

Das Museum hatte durch die Aktivitäten seines Direktors Frans Haks an nationalem wie internationalem Ansehen gewonnen, litt aber zunehmend an akuter Raumnot. Haks erhöhte die Ausstellungsaktivität des Museums, stellte dabei zeitgenössische Kunst und Design in den Mittelpunkt und weckte durch neue Präsentationsformen das Interesse eines breiteren Publikums.

Eine Erweiterung des Museums war schon jahrelang im Gespräch. 1984 liegen bereits fertige Pläne des Architekten Piet Blom vor, die aber wieder verworfen werden, nicht zuletzt weil Haks für einen Neubau eintritt. 1986 nimmt die Stadt schließlich einen Museumsneubau mit geschätzten Baukosten von 30 Millionen Gulden in ihr Programm auf – ohne gesicherte Finanzierbarkeit.

Frans Haks' persönliche Kontakte zu Ton Grotens, Direktor der Gasunie, leiten die Verhandlungen ein, die im September 1987 zu einer Schenkung von 25 Millionen Gulden an die Stadt führen.

172

of colours and materials of the other rooms.

Frans Haks's successors have not necessarily remained true to his original curatorial concept. A quick tour of the museum reveals that nearly all the rooms are now used for temporary exhibitions. The historical and archaeological collections are no longer on display. The pavilion intended for paintings is now used exclusively for installations. Only the Arts and Crafts pavilion remains in its original state.

Kees van Twist, the present director, feels that Haks's initial concept of presentation based on the various sections of the collection never really worked. And the museum's current record of 200,000 visitors per year — in a city of only 175,000 inhabitants — does seem to vindicate the new museum policy. A staff of forty deals with exhibition programming, public relations and marketing; the latter includes renting spaces out for presentations, receptions and festivities.

Subsidies of 11 million guilder allow for a generous and highly successful exhibition policy — geared towards a broad public.

Von links nach rechts:
Verbindungskorridore; Pavillon von Coop
Himmelb(l)au; hochgezogene Fußgänger-
brücke

From left to right: Connecting corridor;
Coop Himmelb(l)au Pavilion;
pedestrian bridge

A Generous Gift

The head office of the Dutch Gas Company "Gasunie" is also located in Groningen. On the occasion of its twenty-fifth anniversary in 1987, the company wanted to present a generous gift to the city. The idea of drawing international attention and at the same time providing a long-term result with the donation, inspired the company to look to the cultural sector and, ultimately, to the old Groningen Museum.

The museum had gained national and international recognition through the activities of its director, Frans Haks, but was increasingly hampered by a lack of space. Haks increased the museum's exhibition activities, with a focus on contemporary art and design, and succeeded in stimulating the interests of a broader public through innovative presentations.

173

Die einzigen Bedingungen der Gasunie sind, daß es bei einer einmaligen Zahlung bleiben muß und daß das neue Museum ein überregionales kulturelles Wahrzeichen werden sollte. Anläßlich der „Geschenk-Übergabe" sichert die Stadt zusätzliche fünf Millionen Gulden für die Realisierung zu.

Die Umsetzung beginnt auf verschiedenen Ebenen

Die drei Hauptpartner – Gasunie, Stadt Groningen und Groninger Museum – bilden eine Organisation, und Anfang 1988 wird eine „Vorbereitungskommission" gegründet, und die Mittel werden in eine Stiftung eingebracht. Mitglieder der Vorbereitungskommission, die als Auftraggeberin agiert, sind der Stadtplanungsdirektor sowie der stellvertretende Stadtdirektor von Groningen, Frans Haks vom Groninger Museum und Vertreter der Gasunie. Das Managementbüro Twijnstra Gudde unter Henk Weulink wird beauftragt, die interne Projektkoordination zu übernehmen. Henk Weulink, der bereits die Umbauarbeiten des Konzertgebäudes in Amsterdam überwachte, wird Projektmanager. Weulink über seine Bestellung: „Haks sagte zu mir: ‚Wir wollen den Eiffelturm von Groningen bauen', und ich wußte, worauf ich mich einließ."[1]

Aufgabe der Vorbereitungskommission ist die Erstellung eines Raumprogramms, die Suche nach einem Standort und die Wahl des Architekten. Da die Finanzierung des Baus bereits gesichert ist, glaubt man anfangs an einen raschen Baubeginn. Doch wird es zwei Jahre dauern, bis sich die Vorbereitungskommission, die Stadtpolitiker und Frans Haks auf Standort und Architekten einigen können, und weitere zwei Jahre, bis auch die Bevölkerung davon überzeugt werden kann.

Standortbestimmung

Die Stadt hatte bereits vorab, unabhängig von Plänen für ein neues Museum, an einem Masterplan für das Gebiet des Verbindungskanals gearbeitet. Der Verbindungskanal mit dem Wendebecken[2] verläuft ungefähr auf der Linie der ehemaligen Stadtbefestigungsanlagen, die 1874 abgerissen wurden.

Während das nördliche, der Altstadt zugewandte Ufer bald schon verbaut und eng mit der Innenstadt verwachsen war, bildete das südliche Ufer mit dem Bahnhof eine Grenze zu den neueren Stadtentwicklungsgebieten. 1986 beauftragt die Stadt zwei namhafte Architekten, Rem Koolhaas und Josef Paul Kleihues, mit der Erstellung eines Masterplans. Ziel ist eine stärkere Verschränkung der Stadtteile. Aufgrund ihrer unvereinbaren Architekturauffassungen teilen sie das Areal auf, wobei Koolhaas für den östlichen Bereich des Verbindungskanals und Kleihues für den westlichen Bereich inklusive Bahnhof und jetzigem

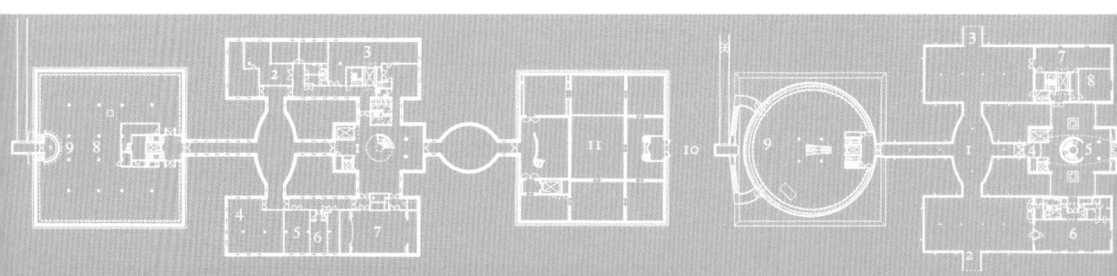

A museum expansion had been discussed for some years. As early as 1984, the architect Piet Blom presented a complete set of plans. These were rejected, however, not least of all because Haks was already campaigning for a new building.

Finally, in 1986, the city endorsed the idea of a new museum building, at an estimated construction cost of 30 million guilder – although financing had yet to be secured.

Frans Haks's personal contacts with Ton Grotens, the Gasunie director, set negotiations in motion, which, in September 1987, resulted in a gift of 25 million guilder to the city.

The only conditions imposed by the Gasunie were that this would be a one-time payment, and that the new museum should become a cultural landmark for the region. With the backing of this "gift" the city was able to secure an additional 5 million guilder for the construction.

The Implementation Begins on Various Levels

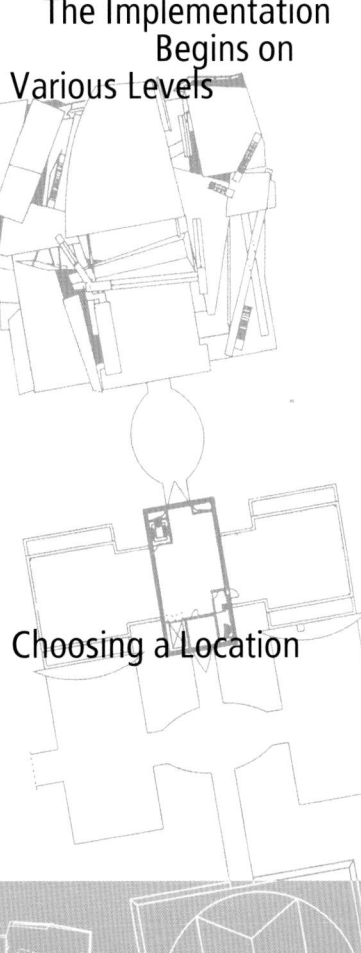

The three main partners – the Gasunie, the City of Groningen and the Groningen Museum – founded an organization, which appointed a "planning committee" and set up a foundation with the donation. Frans Haks of the Groningen Museum and representatives of "Gasunie", together with the chief city planner and Groningen's deputy mayor, were members of this committee, which assumed the responsibility of assigning contracts. The management consulting firm "Twijnstra Gudde," led by Henk Weulink, was commissioned to coordinate the project. Henk Weulink, who had already overseen the structural alteration of Amsterdam Concert Hall, was appointed as project manager. Weulink on his appointment: "Haks told me: 'We want to build Groningen's Eiffel Tower' and I knew what I was in for."[1]

The committee's brief was to create an agenda, locate a site and choose an architect. Since the financing was already secured, hopes ran high for an early start of construction. But two years would pass before the committee, the municipal authorities and Frans Haks agreed on the location and the architect, and a further two years before the city's inhabitants were also persuaded to accept their decisions.

Choosing a Location

Long before embarking on the museum project, the city had already worked on a masterplan for the area surrounding the canal. The canal with its turning basin[2] approximately follows the line of the former city fortifications, demolished in 1874. The north bank facing the old city was soon covered in dense urban development and closely integrated with the city centre; conversely, the south bank and the railway station formed a border to the areas of new city development. In 1986 the

Groninger Gezinsbode, 17.10.1987:
Erste Skizze der ortsansässigen Architekten
Das & Van Moehrlein für ein Museum im
Wendebecken; „Italienische Invasion im
Wendebecken"; Groninger Gezinsbode,
27.1.1989: Alessandro Mendini mit drei
seiner Mitarbeiter bei einer Bauplatz-
besichtigung.
Stadtplanungsmodell von Joseph Kleihues
mit Wohnbauten im Wendebecken (rechts)

Groninger Gezinsbode 17.10.1987:
preliminary design from the local architects
Das & Van Moehrlein for a museum in the
canal. "Italiaanse invasie bij Zwaaikom",
Groninger Gezinsbode 27.1.1989:
Alessandro Mendini with three co-workers
on a site visit.
Urban planning model with
apartment buildings in the canal by
Joseph Kleihues (right)

Nieuw museum in Verbindingskanaal?

Italiaanse invasie bij Zwaaikom

Museumsstandort zuständig ist. Auf Grundlage beider Masterpläne wurde das Gesamtareal weiterentwickelt.

Kleihues zeigt Möglichkeiten und Probleme des Wendebeckens auf und regt die Schaffung einer künstlichen Insel mit Wohnblöcken an. Dadurch bekäme der Verbindungskanal eine neue Funktion als Verbindungselement zwischen alt und neu mit eigener Identität. Er lädt den Architekten Georgio Grassi ein, diese Idee weiter auszuführen. Grassis Entwurf für die Wohninsel findet in Ypke Gietema, Ratsherr der sozialdemokratischen Partei von Groningen, einen starken Befürworter. Der Plan stößt jedoch sowohl in der Bevölkerung als auch in den anderen politischen Lagern auf vehementen Widerstand. Das historische Stadtbild würde zerstört werden, und eine Insel mit Wohnungen hätte sehr elitären Charakter. Der Plan fällt den Protesten zum Opfer.

Auch bei der Standortfrage für das Museum prallen unterschiedliche Interessen aufeinander – die Hauptkontrahenten sind Frans Haks und Ypke Gietema.

Frans Haks stellt sich einen grünen Bauplatz vor – in einem Stadterweiterungsgebiet am Rande Groningens.[3] Die sozialdemokratische Partei unter Ypke Gietema will das Museum im Stadtzentrum ansiedeln.

Die Vorbereitungskommission beginnt Anfang 1988 mit der Erstellung einer Studie zu möglichen Standorten. Neben einigen Vorschlägen im Stadtzentrum werden auch weitere „grüne Plätze" ausgewiesen. Innerhalb weniger Monate steigt die Zahl der Vorschläge auf 13. Ypke Gietema spricht sich vehement für eine zentrale Lage aus. Die erste Wahl fällt auf die „Aegon-Gründe", ein Bürogebäude der Versicherungsgesellschaft Aegon. Diese Variante wird jedoch frühzeitig publik, der Grundstückspreis steigt enorm, und die Idee muß fallengelassen werden. Auf politischer Ebene konzentriert sich bald jede Partei auf einen anderen Standort. Die Konservativen favorisieren weiterhin die Aegon-Gründe und die Christdemokraten den Westerhaven – ein Hafen im Westen des Stadtzentrums. Die Sozialdemokraten greifen schließlich die Idee der künstlichen Insel im Wendebecken wieder auf. Das Museum als öffentlicher Ort scheint die perfekte Alternative zu den Wohnblöcken von Grassi zu sein. Dafür fertigen zwei ortsansässige Architekten eine erste Skizze an.

Ein interner Kompromiß geht dem offiziellen voran. Haks will seinen langjährigen Wunscharchitekten Alessandro Mendini – Gietema das Museum im Wendebecken. Anläßlich eines Abendessens bei Frans Haks unterbreitet Gietema folgenden Vorschlag: „Du wählst den Architekten, aber dann bestimmen wir [Sozialdemokraten, Anm.] den Standort."[4]

Am 30.November 1988 einigt sich der Gemeinderat schließlich auf den Standort im Wendebecken. Die konservative Partei kann zu einer Zustimmung unter bestimmten Auflagen überzeugt werden. Demnach soll ein weiterer Stadtentwicklungsplan eingereicht werden und die endgültige Abstimmung erst auf Grundlage eines definitiven Entwurfs erfolgen.

Die Zeitung Nieuwsblad van het Noorden titelt: „Koalition der Zweckmäßigkeit"[5].

176

city commissioned two renowned architects, Rem Koolhaas and Josef Paul Kleihues, to develop a masterplan. The objective was to achieve greater integration of the various city districts. Because of the architects' fundamental differences in design philosophy, the area was divided into two sections: Koolhaas was assigned the eastern half with the canal and Kleihues the western half including the railway station and the present museum site. All developments undertaken since that time are based on these two masterplans.

In his proposal Kleihues highlights both the potential and the challenge of the turning basin, and suggests the creation of an artificial island with apartment blocks. As the connecting element between old and new, the canal would take on a new function – a unique identity. Kleihues invites architect Georgio Grassi to elaborate on this idea. Grassi's design for the residential island finds a strong supporter in Ypke Gietema, the Social Democratic city councillor for Groningen. But it is vigorously opposed by the general public and the other political factions, who agree that the proposed idea would destroy the historic townscape and that a residential development on the island would be too elitist in character. The plan falls victim to these protests.

Even the question of the museum site provokes a clash of interests — the main opponents are Frans Haks and Ypke Gietema.

Frans Haks envisions a green building location — in an urban expansion area on the edge of Groningen.[3] The Social Democratic Party, led by Ypke Gietema, supports a central location.

In early 1988, the planning committee begins to draft a study of potential sites.

Aside from several sites in the city centre, other "green" locations are also proposed. Within a few months the number of proposals rises to thirteen. Ypke Gietema vehemently defends a central location. The first choice falls on the "Aegon" site, an office building owned by the Aegon Insurance Company. When the information prematurely becomes public, the property value skyrockets and the idea has to be abandoned. Soon each political party begins to champion a different location: the Conservatives still favour the "Aegon" site; the Christian Democrats' choice is Westerhaven, a port west of the city centre; and the Social Democrats return to the idea of an artificial island in the turning basin. As a public space the museum seems to offer an ideal alternative to Grassi's apartment blocks. Two local architects prepare a preliminary sketch.

The public compromise is preceded by an internal one. Haks wants to bring his long-time favourite architect, Alessandro Mendini, on board – Gietema wants the museum in the turning basin. At a dinner hosted by Frans Haks, Gietema offers a deal: "You choose the architect, but we [Social Democrats, author's note] get to select the site."[4]

On 30 November of the same year, the city council finally decides on the location in the turning basin. The Conservatives decide to agree subject to certain conditions: another plan for city development must be submitted and the final vote must be based on a definitive design.

The newspaper headline in the Nieuwsblad van het Noorden reads: "A Coalition of Opportunism."[5]

177

Frans Haks' Museumsvision

Auf der Suche nach dem idealen Museumstyp besucht Franks Haks die verschiedensten Museen, wie das Stedelijk Museum in Amsterdam, das Guggenheim Museum in New York oder das Centre George Pompidou in Paris. Aber erst das Museum Mönchengladbach kommt seiner Vorstellung sehr nahe. Vor allem die Aufteilung in Raumzellen, die sich in Holleins Museum matrixartig aneinanderreihen und die den Besucher ohne Bevormundung auf eine Entdeckungsreise schicken, entsprechen Haks' Vorstellung von einem idealen Museum.

Haks will die Gebäudetypologie am inhaltlichen Programm ausrichten: Die mannigfaltige Sammlung soll zusammengehalten, eine Unterteilung innerhalb des Museums vollzogen werden. Vier große Untergruppen (Archäologie und Geschichte der Region; Kunsthandwerk; Alte Meister; Moderne Kunst und Design) werden festgelegt, die die Architektur widerzuspiegeln hat. Ein einfacher Grundriß und eine separate Erschließung der individuellen Sammlungsteile vom Eingangsbereich aus sollen dies gewährleisten. Um das Ergebnis zu optimieren, soll jeder Sammlungsbereich von einem anderen Architekten entworfen werden.

„Es war eine bewußte Entscheidung, das Museum für ein möglichst breites Publikum attraktiv zu gestalten – ein Anliegen, dem sich die wenigsten Museen widmen. Um dies zu erreichen, mußte es etwas Disneyland-Ähnliches aufweisen. (...) Es wäre ein Fehler anzunehmen, daß einander ähnliche, in identischen Räumen ausgestellte Exponate in der Lage seien, das Interesse der Besucher über Stunden hinweg aufrechtzuerhalten."[6]

Frans Haks hatte bereits 1986 damit begonnen, den geeigneten Architekten für seine Vision zu suchen. Wiederum dient ihm Mönchengladbach als Vorbild für die perfekte Zusammenarbeit zwischen Museumsdirektor und Architekt. Auch Haks sucht einen Architekten, der noch kein vergleichbares Gebäude realisiert hat. Er will ein architektonisch attraktives Museum mit klaren, nüchternen Ausstellungsräumen. Seine Wahl fällt auf Mendini, der Haks vor allem durch das Casa Alessi überzeugt.

Mendini zeigt sich sehr interessiert. Während ausgedehnter Reisen zu den wichtigsten Museen der Welt konkretisieren sie das Raumprogramm und legen Richtlinien fest. Unter anderem soll kein natürliches Licht in die Ausstellungsräume einfallen. Das Museum ist ein artifizieller Raum, der nur durch Kunstlicht konditioniert werden soll. Haks schreibt 1988 in sein Tagebuch: „Mendinis Museum wird eine Gruppenausstellung zur Architektur in einem einzigen Gebäude."[7]

Daß Frans Haks mit Mendini arbeiten will, ist ein offenes Geheimnis. Der Projektkoordinator Henk Weulink erstellt ein Anforderungsprofil, anhand dessen er das Büro Mendini prüft. Durch den Zusammenschluß Alessandro Mendinis mit seinem Bruder Francesco, der ein großes Architekturbüro unterhält, kann Mendini diese Auflagen erfüllen. Haks – dem Rat von Johannes Cladders[8] folgend, man solle eine Kommission nie mit mehreren Vorschlägen überlasten – stellt der Vorbereitungskommission nur Mendini zur Auswahl. Doch die Gasunie kann sich mit der Auswahl nur eines Architekten nicht anfreunden. Henk Weulink

**Alessandro Mendini,
Depotturm (rechts)**

Alessandro Mendini,
Depot tower (right)

178

In his search for the ideal museum type, Frans Haks visits a range of different institutions, such as the Stedelijk Museum in Amsterdam, the Guggenheim Museum in New York, and the Centre Georges Pompidou in Paris. But it isn't until he sees the museum in Mönchengladbach that he senses a kinship with his own vision. He is particularly taken with the spatial division into cells strung out into a matrix that allows visitors to embark on an unguided journey of discovery through the museum.

Haks wants the building typology to reflect the museum's programme, keeping the wide-ranging collection intact under one roof, with the necessary divisions taking place within the museum. Four major thematic sections are defined (Regional Archaeology and History, Arts and Crafts, Old Masters, Modern Art and Design). The architecture should express each of these sections by means of a simple ground plan and separate access to the individual parts of the collection from the entrance area. To optimize the results, a different architect will design each section.

"It has been a conscious choice to make the museum attractive to a very broad public, something most museums are unconcerned with. To achieve this it would have to have something of Disneyland about it. ... It is a mistake to think that similar subjects exhibited in identical rooms will hold the visitors' attention for hours."[6]

As early as 1986, Frans Haks begins to search for an architect who would be able to realize his vision.

Once again, the museum in Mönchengladbach serves as his model, this time with regard to the perfect collaboration between an architect and a museum director. Haks, too, is looking for an architect who has yet to design a building of this type. His vision is for an architecturally attractive museum, with clean, unadorned exhibition spaces. His choice falls on Mendini, whose design for the Casa Alessi strikes him as especially convincing.

Mendini shows great interest. On an extensive tour of the world's most important museums, they develop concrete ideas on the spatial programme and establish specific guidelines, stipulating, among other things, that the exhibition halls should be devoid of natural light. The museum is an artificial space and as such its only lighting source should also be artificial. A journal entry by Haks from 1988 reads: "Mendini's museum will become a group exhibition on architecture contained in a single building."[7]

Haks's desire to work with Mendini is an open secret. Henk Weulink, the project coordinator, drafts a requirements profile to assess the suitability of Mendini's firm. Mendini manages to meet the requirements by merging his smaller firm with that of his brother Francesco Mendini, who runs a large commercial architectural practice. Following Johannes Cladders' advice that one should never burden a committee with several proposals,[8] Haks presents Mendini to the planning committee as the only choice. But the Gasunie doesn't feel comfortable with the notion of narrowing the field down to one architect. Accordingly, Henk

erstellt eine Alternativenliste – mit Namen wie Fumihiko Maki, Rem Koolhaas, Tadao Ando and Frank Gehry. Haks ist erbost: „Nie, nur über meine Leiche werde ich über diese Liste diskutieren."[9] Die Gasunie gibt sich mit der Bereitstellung dieser „Alibi-Liste" bereits zufrieden. Am 4. Oktober einigt sich die Vorbereitungskommission einstimmig auf Alessandro Mendini. Die architektonische Umsetzung von Mendinis Entwurf übernimmt das niederländische Architekturbüro Team 4.

Nachdem im November 1988 eine vorläufige Entscheidung für das Wendebecken fällt, beginnt Mendini, sich mit dem Standort und insbesondere mit der Verknüpfung der verschiedenen Funktionen des öffentlichen Raumes – in Form der Fußgängerbrücke und des Museums – auseinanderzusetzen.

Die Zusammenführung von Standort und Architekten

Als die ersten Skizzen Mendinis der Öffentlichkeit präsentiert werden, lösen sie eine neue Welle von Protesten aus. Die erlaubte Gebäudehöhe werde überschritten, das Stadtbild zerstört, die Aussicht auf das Ufer verstellt. Vereinigungen wie „Schutz des wertvollen Stadtbildes" oder „Initiative breiter Verbindungskanal" bestehen seit der Zeit der Proteste gegen die Grassi-Wohnbauten. Ihnen gelingt, was die Politiker versäumen: Durch gezielte Informationskampagnen gewinnen sie Anrainer und Schiffer. Das Lokalblatt Groninger Gezinsbode unterstützt die Opposition und gibt ihr die nötige Öffentlichkeit. Zahlreiche Mittel werden eingesetzt, um die negativen Folgen des Museums aufzuzeigen. Binnenschiffer stellen die räumliche Ausdehnung des Museums am Wasser dar, Gasballone veranschaulichen die Gebäudehöhen etc. Der endgültige Entwurf Mendinis muß demnach das Hauptanliegen der Stadt, die Erhaltung der Blickachsen vom Bahnhof zum gegenüberliegenden Ufer, gewährleisten. Die Idee von Haks und Mendini, verschiedene Pavillons für die einzelnen Sammlungsteile zu verwirklichen, kommt diesem Anliegen entgegen.

Aufgrund der geforderten Nutzfläche wird ein Raumprogramm erstellt. Dieses übersteigt mit geschätzten Kosten von 40 Millionen Gulden aber bei weitem das Budget, da die Stiftungseinlage von 30 Millionen Gulden für die ursprünglich geschätzten Baukosten über einen Zeitraum von 4 Jahren „nur" 4 Millionen erwirtschaften wird.

Frans Haks besteht – neben der fixen Ausstellungsfläche für die Sammlungsteile – auf genügend Platz für Wechselausstellungen und spricht sich gegen Kürzungen aus. Schließlich einigt er sich mit Henk Weulink auf eine Unterteilung in zwei Bauabschnitte: Der Pavillon für die Alten Meister wird zwar geplant, eine Realisierung aber aufgeschoben, bis die nötigen Mittel gefunden sind.

Im Januar 1989 liegen die ersten Entwurfsvarianten vor – Mendini

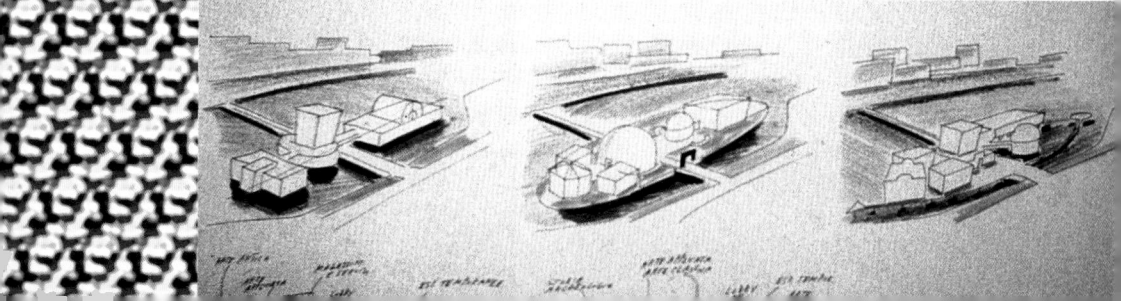

Weulink compiles an alternative list with names such as Fumihiko Maki, Rem Koolhaas, Tadao Ando and Frank Gehry. Haks is furious: "I will never discuss this list, except over my dead body."[9] However, the Gasunie seems satisfied by the mere existence of the list. On 4 October, the planning committee unanimously endorses the choice of Alessandro Mendini. The Dutch architectural firm Team 4 assumes executing responsibility.

In November 1988, a preliminary decision was passed in favour of using the turning basin.

Mendini begins to study the site in detail, paying particular attention to the challenge of integrating the various functions of the public space through the foot bridge and the museum.

Bringing the Site and the Architect Together

When Mendini's first sketches are presented to the public, they unleash a new wave of protests. The main points of contention are: the museum exceeds the prescribed building height, destroys the image of the cityscape and obscures the view of the riverbank. Citizens' associations, for example the group for the "protection of the cityscape" or the initiative "for the preservation of the wide canal," founded at the time of Grassi's proposal for apartment blocks, are still active. They succeed where the politicians had failed – namely in securing the united support of shoreline residents and boatmen through effective information campaigns. The local paper, the Groninger Gezinsbode, lends its support to this opposition and provides the necessary publicity. No effort is spared to advertise the negative ramifications of the museum project. In one elaborate publicity stunt barges are lined up along the water's edge to illustrate how much space the museum would occupy and helium balloons are floated to mark the projected building height. Mendini is forced to draft a final design to satisfy the city's chief demand of maintaining an unobstructed view from the railway station to the opposite bank. Haks's and Mendini's solution of creating a series of pavilions for the individual sections of the collection represents a concession to meet this demand.

A spatial programme is developed on the basis of the required floor space. However, at an estimated cost of 40 million guilder, this programme far exceeds the budget, since the foundation's investment of 30 million guilder for the original estimate of building costs will yield a "mere" 4 million guilder over the space of four years by careful management.

In addition to the exhibition spaces for the permanent collection, Frans Haks insists on creating sufficient room for temporary exhibitions and is vigorously opposed to cutting costs.

Erste Entwurfsvarianten, Januar 1989 (links)
Sichtachsen (rechts)

First variations of design, January 1989 (left)
sight lines (right)

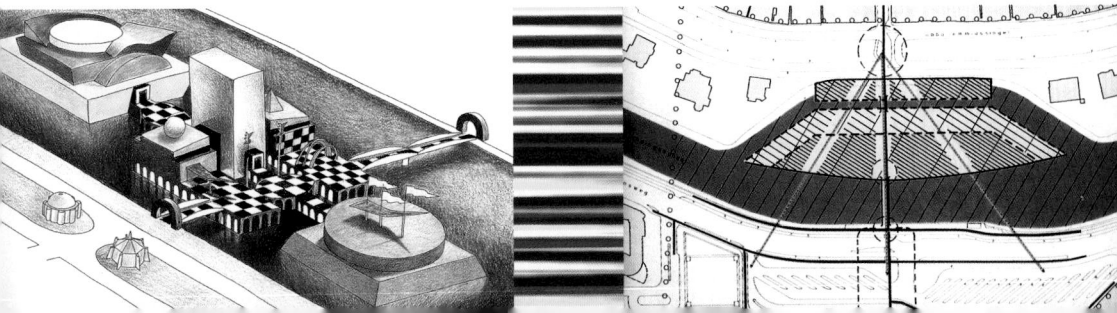

museum in het Verbindingskanaal

reed Overleg komt n
lfgemaakte tekening

Wordt het zo?

agiert erstmals mit einem offiziellen Auftrag der Stadt Groningen. Die Vorschläge reichen von einer engen Anbindung des Museums an das nördliche Ufer mit einer Vielzahl von kleinen Pavillons über die Variante einer richtigen Insel mit asymmetrischer Anordnung der Gebäude bis zur Variante des mittig im Kanal gelegenen Museums mit Pavillons, die untereinander durch Korridore auf Wasserniveau verbunden sind. Der Stadtplanungsausschuß favorisiert letztere Variante, da sie die Erhaltung der geforderten Sichtlinien am ehesten garantiert.

Die ersten Skizzen und Modelle werden im Februar 1989 im alten Groninger Museum ausgestellt. Mendini veranlaßt, daß nichts photographiert und damit publiziert werden darf, da es sich um vorläufige Studien handelt. Gietema verbietet sogar jegliches Photographieren in der Ausstellung. Er fürchtet eine negative Presse so sehr, daß auch die Gesichter der Ausstellungsbesucher schon zuviel verraten könnten. Eine solche Aktion schürt Mißtrauen. Als Reaktion fertigt die „Initiative breiter Verbindungskanal" ihre eigene Photomontage an, die in zahlreichen Veröffentlichungen erscheint.

In der Folge ergeben Meinungsumfragen, daß die Mehrheit der Groninger Bevölkerung gegen die Baupläne ist. Die Stadtverwaltung reagiert und legt die Baupläne zur Bürgerbeteiligung aus.

In der Zwischenzeit arbeitet Mendini weiter an den Entwürfen. Da die vielen einzelnen Bauteile das Budget übersteigen, werden die neuen Entwürfe immer kompakter, überschreiten die zulässige Gebäudehöhe und vernachlässigen die geforderten Sichtlinien.

Der sogenannte „Transparenzkonflikt" erreicht im März 1989 seinen Höhepunkt. Die städtische Behörde für Raumplanung und Wirtschaftsfragen teilt Mendini mit, er solle umgehend die Arbeiten einstellen. Henk Weulink fährt mit zwei Vertretern der Behörde nach Mailand. Aber Mendini bleibt hart. Einer Mitarbeiterin aus Mendinis Büro, Gerda Vosschaert, ist es zu verdanken, daß sich die Situation klärt. Sie fertigt Skizzen an, die sich auf die ursprüngliche Variante beziehen: fünf Bauteile, davon zwei kompakte und niedrigere Pavillons, ein Eingangspavillon und, vom Nordufer etwas abgerückt, der Turm. Die zwei kompakten Pavillons sind durch bogenförmige Brücken mit dem Eingangspavillon verbunden.

Aber auch diese Variante löst noch nicht alle Probleme. Vor allem die internen Verkehrswege zwischen Turm und Pavillons und die Anlieferung über die engen Brücken stellen ein Problem dar. Darüber hinaus ergeben Berechnungen Henk Weulinks, daß die geplante Gesamtfläche wiederum die Kosten übersteigt. Weulink erarbeitet daraufhin fünf mögliche Varianten und stellt sie Mendini zur Wahl. Dieser entscheidet sich schließlich für eine Variante strenger Geometrie: zwei Gebäudevolumen, ein Turm, eine Brücke für Passanten, die vor dem Eingang zum Foyer im Turm zu einem ovalförmigen Vorplatz wird und damit eine ungestörte Sicht zu beiden Ufern erlaubt. Die bogenförmigen Brücken zu den Pavillons werden nun zu Korridoren, die zur Hälfte unter dem Wasserniveau liegen. Im November 1989 einigen sich schließlich alle Parteien auf diese Variante.

Der Gemeinderat kann sich mit knapper Mehrheit zu einem positiven Beschluß durchringen. Mittels eines verkürzten Verfahrens soll

Finally, the museum director and Henk Weulink agree to divide the construction into two phases: the plan still includes a pavilion for Old Masters, but its realization is postponed until the necessary means are found.

The first variations of the design were presented in January 1989 – this was also the first time that Mendini acted "officially" for the city of Groningen.

The proposals run the gamut from tying the museum closely to the north bank with many small pavilions, to creating an artificial island with asymmetrically placed buildings, to placing the museum in the middle of the canal with pavilions that are linked by corridors at water level. The city planning committee is in favour of the last variation because it is the solution most likely to preserve the desired open view across the river.

In February of the same year, these sketches and models are exhibited at the old Groningen Museum. Mendini sees to it that no photographs are taken or published, arguing that these are only preliminary studies. And Gietema even goes so far as to impose a total ban on photographers in the exhibition; his fear of negative press reactions is so great that he worries that even expressions on the faces of visitors to the exhibition might be too revealing. But the secrecy only fans the flames of mistrust and the initiative "for the preservation of the wide canal" creates a photo collage of its own that is widely published.

Subsequent opinion polls show that the majority of Groningen's population is opposed to the building plans. The city administration responds by releasing the plans for public participation.

Meanwhile, Mendini continues to work on the designs. Because the idea of many separate buildings exceeds the budget, his new designs grow ever more compact, ignoring the building height requirements and the desired unobstructed sightline.

By March, the so-called "transparency conflict" reaches a critical point. Groningen's Department of Environmental Planning and Economic Affairs instructs Mendini to stop working on the project. Weulink travels to Milan accompanied by two departmental representatives. But Mendini refuses to budge. Thankfully one of Mendini's team members, Gerda Vosschaert, comes to the rescue by preparing new sketches that reprise the original concept: five building components, including two compact and low pavilions, an entrance pavilion and, slightly removed from the north bank, the tower. The two compact pavilions are linked to the entrance pavilion by arched bridges.

But even this variation doesn't solve all the problems. The internal circulation between tower and pavilions, and delivery access across the narrow bridges are particularly problematic. Furthermore, Henk Weulink's calculations reveal that the proposed total area once again exceeds the budgeted costs, and he works out five possible options (which meet budget requirements) from which Mendini is then asked to choose. In the end, the architect decides to go with a strictly geometric option: two building volumes, a tower and a foot bridge that widens into an oval forecourt in front of the tower's foyer entrance. This layout permits an unobstructed view of both shores. The arched

Photomontage der „Initiative breitere Verbindungskanal", veröffentlicht im Groninger Gezinsbode, am 20.2.1989 (links). Groninger Gezinsbode, 2.4.1990: Photomontage von Mendinis Projekt im Westerhaven; Nieuwsblad van het Noorden, 25.3.1991: symbolische „Ecksteinlegung" einiger Anhänger des Projekts (rechts).

Groninger Gezinsbode, 20.2.1989: Photo collage by the initiative "for the preservation of the wide canal" (left) Groninger Gezinsbode, 2.4.1990: Photo collage of Mendini's project on an alternative location in the Westerhaven; Nieuwsblad van het Noorden, 25.3.1991: symbolic "cornerstone ceremony" by a few supporters of the project. (right)

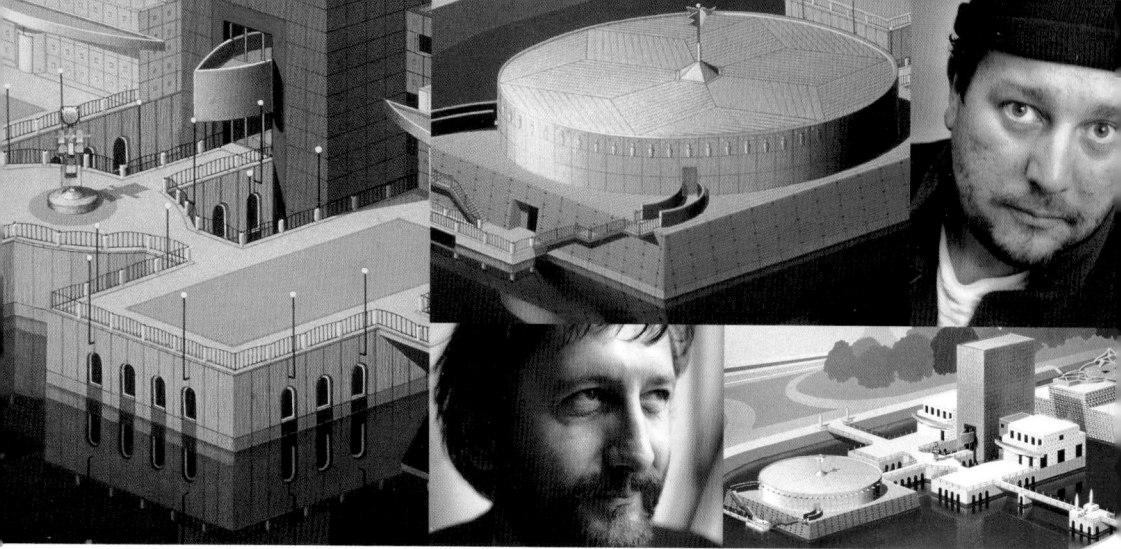

Ovaler Vorplatz; Pavillon von Philippe Starck
und Portrait von Philippe Starck (oben);
Portrait von Frank Stella und Gesamtansicht
mit Pavillon-Entwurf von Frank Stella
Pavillon von Coop Himmelb(l)au (rechts)

Oval public space; Philippe Starck Pavilion
and portrait of Philippe Starck (above);
Portrait of Frank Stella and drawing of the
museum with the pavilion design by
Frank Stella;
Pavilion Coop Himmelb(l)au (right page)

noch im Oktober 1990 mit dem Bau begonnen werden. Die einge-brachten Einwände der Opposition werden abgelehnt.

Doch es wird wieder quer geschossen: Der fast 80'jährige Anwalt Van Zaaijen, federführend in der Organisation „Schutz des wertvollen Stadtbilds" und Inhaber eines Büros am Ufer des Verbindungskanals, macht seinen Einfluß geltend und überzeugt den Staatsrat, alle Ein-wände der einzelnen Oppositionsgruppierungen einer eingehenden Prüfung zu unterziehen.

Im Januar 1991 setzt der Staatsrat die Baupläne der Gemeinde zeit-weilig aus, besteht auf ein vollständiges Flächenwidmungsverfahren und will die laufenden Prozesse gegen die Baupläne abwarten. Ypke Gietema denkt an Rücktritt. Der gesamte Planungsprozeß steht still.

Erst ein Jahr später, im Februar 1992, hebt der Staatsrat die Ein-stellung wieder auf. Gleichzeitig bewilligt er weitere drei Millionen Gulden für die zweite Bauphase.

Das Positive daran: Durch den langen Stillstand steigt die Stiftungs-einlage und Haks nutzt die Zeit, sein Projekt international zu präsen-tieren und zu vermarkten, um im eigenen Land den Druck zu erhöhen.

Die Gastarchitekten

Mendini beginnt bereits 1987, Gastarchitekten vorzuschlagen. Haks schweben junge Architekten vor, die sich in Form- und Material-sprache stark unterscheiden. Mendini aber kommt von der Idee der Architekten ab: „Er geht davon aus, daß die Erneuerung in der Architektur nicht so sehr von Architekten als vielmehr von ‚Out-sidern' kommen werde ... ."[10] Die endgültige Auswahl ist bereits im Juli 1988 (!) abgeschlossen.

Im November 1989 werden Philippe Starck und Michele de Lucchi für das Projekt gewonnen. Mendini tritt auch an den Künstler Frank Stella heran, dessen Arbeiten sich immer stärker mit Architektur befassen. Stella zeigt sich interessiert, drückt aber seine Haltung klar aus: „Euch ist natürlich bewußt, daß eure Sammlung nicht besonders bedeutend ist. (...) Ihr braucht daher eine Architektur, die das kompensiert (...)."[11]

bridges to the pavilions are modified into corridors that are partially below water level.

In November 1989 all parties finally agreed on this variation.

The vote passes in the city council with a narrow majority. An accelerated approval process is launched to start construction by the following year, in October 1990. The opposition's objections are summarily dismissed.

But another spanner is thrown into the works. The chief proponent of the association for the "protection of the cityscape," the nearly eighty-year-old lawyer Van Zaaijen, whose chambers are located on the canal bank, exerts his considerable influence and persuades the state council to revisit and carefully consider all the objections made by various opposing groups.

In January 1991, the state council imposed an injunction, temporarily halting the community's building plans.

The council insists on a complete investigation into the area dedication plans and decides to await the outcome of the actions launched against the building plans. Ypke Gietema contemplates a complete withdrawal. The entire planning process has come to a halt.

A full year passes before the state council lifts the injunction (in February 1992) and simultaneously grants an additional 3 million guilder for the second construction phase.

But there is a positive outcome as well: the investment has had time to grow during the twelve-month hiatus and Haks has used the time to present and market his project internationally, to increase his leverage on the home front.

The Guest Architects

As early as 1987, Mendini began to suggest that guest architects be invited. Haks envisioned a team of young architects with drastically differing views on form and materials. But Mendini soon abandoned the idea of working with architects. "His basic notion is that architecture will not be reformed by architects as much as by 'outsiders'... ."[10] By July 1988(!) a final selection list was ready.

In November 1989 Philippe Starck and Michele de Lucchi were persuaded to participate in the project. Mendini also approached artist Frank Stella, whose work was increasingly oriented towards architecture. Stella showed interest, but was boldly forthright in his attitude: "You must be aware that your collection is not particularly important. (...) That's why you will need an architecture to compensate for it (...)."[11]

De Lucchi is commissioned to design the western foundation pavilion which is to house the regional archaeology and history collection. He decides on a façade of dark-red brick — a familiar material for Groningen. The interior is divided into small sub-pavilions. Instead of general illumination, individual spotlights are used to draw the viewer's attention to special details. At Haks's express wish, there will be neither lead panels nor explanatory notes. Visiting the museum, he argues, should not be didactic but should arouse curiosity in the viewer.

Linke Seite: Pavillon von Alessandro
Mendini: ovaler Ausstellungsraum (oben);
vier Entwürfe zum Ausstellungsdesign
von Philippe Starck (unten links);
Raumplan für den Pavillon von Michele
de Lucchi (unten rechts)
Rechte Seite: Pavillon von Alessandro
Mendini: große Treppe – Zeichnung und
Umsetzung

Left page: pavilion by Alessandro Mendini:
oval exhibition room (above);
four exhibition designs by Philippe Starck
(below left);
Pavilion room plan by
Michele de Lucchi (below right)
Right page: pavilion by Alessandro Mendini:
grand staircase–
drawing and realization

Entwurfsreihe für den Pavillon von Frank
Stella (unten)

Design series of the pavilion
by Frank Stella (below)

De Lucchi wird beauftragt, den westlichen Sockelpavillon auszugestalten, der die Sammlung Archäologie und Geschichte der Region beherbergen soll. Er entschließt sich, die Fassade in dunkelrotem Backstein zu halten – ein für Groningen typisches Material. Der Raum wird in kleine Sub-Pavillons unterteilt. Statt einer allgemeinen Raumbeleuchtung sollen kleine Spots die Aufmerksamkeit des Betrachters auf spezielle Details lenken. Texttafeln und erklärende Beschriftung fehlen – auf Haks ausdrücklichen Wunsch. Der Besuch des Museums soll nicht belehren, sondern neugierig machen.

Philippe Starck wird für die Gestaltung des Kunsthandwerk-Pavillons hinzugezogen. Der flache, scheibenförmige Pavillon sitzt auf dem Unterbau von De Lucchis Pavillon. Raumhohe, weiße Vorhänge unterteilen ihn in Nischen. Schaukästen und im Boden eingelassene Vitrinen sind auf spezielle Schauobjekte zugeschnitten, die bewußt in Szene gesetzt werden. Dies wird als respektlos kritisiert. Haks und Starck argumentieren, daß der durchschnittliche Besucher kein Kunstexperte ist und die Präsentation daher attraktiv zu gestalten sei.

Frank Stellas erster Entwurf negiert fast alle Punkte der im Programm formulierten Anforderungen. Der Pavillon weist Fenster auf, die Fassade ist in gleißendem Weiß gehalten, überschreitet die erlaubte Bauhöhe um drei Meter und die Baukosten um fast das Dreifache (von geplanten drei auf acht Millionen Gulden). Trotzdem zeigt sich Frans Haks begeistert – Stella soll seinen Entwurf weiter ausarbeiten. Der erste Entwurf sieht Stützen und Balken aus Holz und Wände aus Teflon vor, für die schließlich Hersteller in der Schweiz und Deutschland gefunden werden. In der Zwischenzeit hat Stella sein Projekt zur Gänze umgeplant. Unüberwindbare Auseinandersetzungen treten auf, als Stella das Material Teflon auch für das Dach verwenden möchte. „Wenn ihr ein gewöhnliches Gebäude wollt, müßt ihr euch einen gewöhnlichen Architekten suchen."[12] Nach einem scheinbaren Kompromiß gibt Stella aber doch seinen Abschied bekannt: „Ich mach das nicht. Erstens glaube ich nicht, daß wir zu einem guten Ergebnis kommen, und zweitens glaube ich, daß ihr nur an einem ‚Stella' interessiert seid. Ich will euch vor einer falschen Entscheidung schützen."[13]

Der Ausfall Stellas setzt die Kommission unter enormen Zeitdruck.

188

Innenaufnahmen der Pavillons von
Alessandro Mendini und Philippe Starck

Interiors by Alessandro Mendini
and Philippe Starck

Philippe Starck is consulted on the design for the Arts and Crafts pavilion. This shallow, disk-like pavilion rests on top of De Lucchi's foundation pavilion. Floor-to-ceiling curtains divide the pavilion into niches; display cabinets and customized showcases, recessed into the floor, create a theatrical setting. This arrangement is criticized as "disrespectful," to which Haks and Starck respond with the argument that the average visitor is not an art expert, which is all the more reason to make the presentation as attractive as possible.

Frank Stella's first design ignores nearly every requirement formulated in the brief. His pavilion has windows and thus natural light, the façade is covered in dazzling white, the building exceeds the permitted height by three metres and the costs are almost three times too much (rising from 3 million to 8 million guilder). Nevertheless, Frans Haks reacts with enthusiasm and asks Stella to elaborate his design. The first design proposes wooden supports and beams, and Teflon walls, for which Swiss and German manufacturers are finally found after a long search. But by then Stella has come up with a completely different design. When Stella decides to use Teflon on the roof as well, insurmountable arguments arise. "If you want a conventional building, you will have to find yourselves a conventional architect."[12] At first it seems as if a compromise might be reached, but Stella nonetheless announces his resignation. "I won't do this. First of all, I don't believe the end product will be good, and secondly, I think you're only interested in having a 'Stella'. I want to protect you from making a wrong decision."[13]

Stella's departure places the committee under enormous pressure. Within a few days the Viennese firm Coop Himmelb(l)au is selected and the group responds with a new design in a very short time. Instead of Stella's filigree pavilion, their proposal envisions an explosion of steel and glass plates. Wolf Prix stated: "Our intention was to take the design method we had developed to extremes. This method starts from a drawing put on paper very spontaneously. It is then directly translated into architecture with the help of a model. (...) We never concerned ourselves with the works to be shown in the pavilion. (...) A museum only functions properly if it does not go into the art but instead creates art in an atmosphere of its own."[14]

Interne Konflikte

Startsein voor
nieuw museum

Inkomensverschillen
volgend jaar groter

Vier Jahre nach
„Geschenkübergabe"
wird gebaut

Die Wahl fällt innerhalb weniger Tage auf die Wiener Architekten Coop Himmelb(l)au. In kürzester Zeit präsentieren sie ihren Entwurf – statt des filigranen Pavillons von Stella eine Explosion aus Stahl- und Glasplatten. Wolf Prix: „Wir wollten die von uns entwickelte Entwurfsmethode auf die Spitze treiben. Ausgangspunkt dieser Methode ist eine äußerst spontan zu Papier gebrachte Zeichnung. Diese [Zeichnung] wird dann direkt, mit Hilfe eines Models, in Architektur umgesetzt. (...) Wir haben uns nie mit den Arbeiten, die im Pavillon ausgestellt werden sollten, auseinandergesetzt. (...) Ein Museum kann nur dann funktionieren, wenn es nicht versucht, auf die Kunst einzugehen, sondern selbst Kunst mit eigener Atmosphäre schafft."[14]

Während des ganzen Entwurfsprozesses muß Frans Haks auch museumsintern kämpfen. Zwischen ihm und den Kuratoren der einzelnen Sammlungsteile gibt es schon seit längerem größere Auffassungsunterschiede in bezug auf Präsentation und Sammlungspolitik. Für den Neubau will Haks seinen Anspruch nach Qualität gesichert wissen und fordert volle Verantwortung für Inhalt, Form, Präsentation und begleitende Publikationen. Doch Haks steht mit seiner Auffassung von Ausstellungspolitik alleine da und fühlt sich vom Museumsvorstand übergangen. Sein Entschluß, das Museum nach Fertigstellung zu verlassen, festigt sich. 1992 verliert Haks auch noch seine zwei wichtigsten Mitstreiter, da Ypke Gietema zurücktritt und Ton Grotens, Generaldirektor der Gasunie, nicht bis zur Eröffnung in seinem Amt bleiben wird.

Am 16.4.1993 titelt der Groninger Gezinsbode „1.000 Menschen zeichnen Petition gegen Haks", womit sie ihren Unmut über dessen Kunstpolitik zum Ausdruck bringen wollen. Das Museum dürfe nicht nur den letzten modischen Trends nachlaufen, sondern müsse auch der älteren und regionalen Kunst Platz bieten.

In seinem Tagebuch vom 1.8.1993 zitiert Haks den französischen Schriftsteller Gustave Flaubert: „(...) Es besteht eine permanente Verschwörung gegen alles Originelle (...). Je mehr Farbe, je mehr Profil du hast, um so mehr Anstoß wirst du erregen."[15]

Ein Gesetzeskonflikt bringt Frans Haks auch noch eine vorläufige Suspendierung als Direktor ein. Obwohl er sich glimpflich aus der Angelegenheit retten kann, scheint sein Ruf endgültig angeschlagen. Er vereinbart mit der Gemeinde, per 1. Juli 1996 zurückzutreten.

Als auch die letzten Berufungsverhandlungen abgeschlossen sind, wird vier Jahre nach der Beschlußfassung über ein neues Museum der Baubeginn gefeiert. Mit einer großen Lasershow wird am 25. April 1992 der erste Pfahl in den Grund des Wendebeckens gerammt. Die Finanzierung der zweiten Bauphase ist sichergestellt.[16] Die Errichtung des Komplexes schreitet rasch und unter enormem Druck voran. Bereits am 29. Oktober 1994 wird das neue Museum anläßlich der 100-Jahr-Feier des Groninger Museums von Königin Beatrix eröffnet. Das Ergebnis beschreibt Haks wie folgt: „Das Museum ist eine Mischung aus Schinkels

Throughout the design process Frans Haks also had an internal struggle with his colleagues at the museum. The director and his curators had been in disagreement for some time with regard to presentation and museum policy. Haks wanted some assurance that his demands for quality in the new building would be satisfied and campaigned to be given sole responsibility for content, form, presentation and museum publications. But his ideas on exhibition policies weren't shared by his colleagues. In the end, he felt isolated and determined to resign once the museum had been completed. When Ypke Gietema resigned from office in 1992, and the chief executive of the Gasunie, Ton Grotens, announced that he would be retiring before the museum's opening, Haks lost his two best allies.

On 16 April 1993 the headline of the Groninger Gezinsbode proclaimed: "1000 signatures against Haks." At issue was the public's criticism of Haks's art policies. The museum, they demanded, should not pander to every new trend, but also provide space for older, more traditional and regional art.

In his diary entry 1 August 1993, Haks quotes the French writer Gustave Flaubert "(...) There is an ongoing conspiracy against all that is original (...). The more colourful you are, the higher your profile, the more offence you will give."[15]

On top of all this, Frans Haks is faced with litigation and temporarily suspended from his position as museum director. Although he emerges from the affair without blame, his reputation seems to have suffered a fatal blow and he announces his resignation for 1 July 1996.

When the last appeal hearings were completed, the start of construction was finally celebrated only four years after the decision to build a new museum had been made. The first piling was driven into the bottom of the turning basin on 25 April 1992 to the accompaniment of an impressive laser show. Financing for the second phase of construction had been secured.[16] Construction of the complex proceeded rapidly and under enormous pressure. Queen Beatrix presided over the official opening of the new museum on 29 October 1994, the centennial of

Internal Conflicts

**Nieuwsblad van het Noorden, 25.4.1992:
Fest zum Baubeginn mit Lasershow (links),
Pavillon von Coop Himmelb(l)au im Bau;**

Nieuwsblad van het Noorden 25.4.1992:
laser show accompanying the
construction start (left)
Coop Himmelb(l)au pavilion
under construction

Construction begins
four years after
"handing over the gift"

Innenaufnahmen Pavillon von
Coop Himmelb(l)au

Interior Coop Himmelb(l)au pavilion

Einfachheit, Mönchengladbachs Labyrinth und Disneylands Vielfalt geworden. Meiner Ansicht nach befriedigt es somit alle bestehenden Anforderungen."[17]

Das neue Museum

„Protzig und tuntig", „aufregend und kitschig", „sexy und glamourös"[18]. Die nationale und internationale Presse geht auf ungewöhnliche Begriffssuche – und ist sich ob der architektonischen Qualität uneinig. Von absolut vernichtenden Aburteilungen bis zu hochjubelnden Besprechungen ist alles zu lesen.

Die Zeitschrift Eigenhuis & Interieur schreibt im Februar 1995: „Im Groninger Museum wird nicht nur der Unterschied zwischen Architektur und Design aufgehoben, sondern auch jener zwischen Museum, Möbelmesse, Geschäftslokal, Schauraum und Galerie."

Charles Jencks wiederum lobt das Museum laut Eigenhuis & Interieur als „das wichtigste Gebäude dieses Jahrhunderts".

Ed Mellet schreibt über den Pavillon von Coop Himmelb(l)au: „Wenn Architektur brennen soll, wie Prix einmal forderte, dann glimmt der Dachpavillon höchstens ein bißchen vor sich hin."[19]

Anfangs sind auch die Stimmen aus der Bevölkerung noch sehr unterschiedlich. Kritisiert werden beispielsweise die minimalen historischen Begleittexte, die unzureichende Ausschilderung der Wege, die schlechte Beleuchtung im De-Lucchi-Pavillon, die auch zu einigen kleineren Unfällen führt.

Auch die kurze Bauzeit hinterläßt ihre Spuren. An regnerischen Tagen beginnt sich der Bodenbelag im Erdgeschoß zu lösen.

Der Coop-Himmelb(l)au-Pavillon kann zwar bis zur Eröffnung unter extremem Zeitdruck fertiggestellt werden, präsentiert sich aber nur als leerer Raum. Mangelnde Dichtung und Klimaanlage verursachen häufig Probleme. Die Eröffnung für die Gemäldesammlung wird mehrere

the old Groningen Museum. Haks described the finished complex as follows: "The museum has become a mixture of the simplicity of Schinkel, the labyrinth of Mönchengladbach and the variety of Disneyland. In my view, it thus meets the existing needs."[17]

"Ostentatious and prissy," "exciting and kitschy," "sexy and glamorous"[18] – the national and international press is united in their quest for unusual descriptions, but they cannot agree on the architectural quality. The reviews range from abject condemnation to jubilant praise.

The February 1995 issue of the magazine Eigenhuis & Interieur announced that "The Groningen Museum not only abolishes the distinction between architecture and design, but also any distinction between museum, furniture fair, office, showroom and gallery."

Charles Jencks, on the other hand, also quoted in Eigenhuis & Interieur, declared the museum as "the most significant building of the century."

Ed Mellet panned the Coop Himmelb(l)au pavilion, quipping that "...if architecture should burn, as Prix once demanded, then the roof pavilion is, at best, quietly smouldering away."[19]

To begin with, public opinion was just as divided. Some criticized the sparse historical notes, the lack of signage, the poor lighting in the De Lucchi pavilion, which even caused a few minor accidents. And the hasty construction also left its traces. Soon the floor coverings on the ground floor began to come loose on rainy days.

Under extreme pressure, the Coop-Himmelb(l)au pavilion was barely completed for the opening, and had to be presented as a bare and empty space. The structure was plagued for a long time by poor insulation and air-conditioning. The opening of the painting collection had to

The New Museum

Male hinausgeschoben – nicht zuletzt, weil eine Hängung der
Gemälde aufgrund der Architektur unmöglich scheint. Nach einer Adaptierung – abgehängte Wände bieten nun Hängeflächen – werden im
Oktober 1995 erstmals die Gemälde im Pavillon präsentiert. Schließlich führen ein Übermaß an Tageslicht und die enorme Höhe der
gehängten Gemälde zur endgültigen Umsiedlung in den einen Stock
tiefer gelegenen „Mendini-Pavillon".

Darüber hinaus hat das Museum auch noch mit Hochwasser-
problemen zu kämpfen. Entgegen Versicherungen, daß ein bestimmter
Wasserpegel nie erreicht werden würde, steht im Sommer 1998 das
gesamte Untergeschoß unter Wasser, die betreffenden Pavillons
müssen ausgeräumt werden.

Nach den Renovierungsarbeiten kehrt die Sammlung Archäologie
und Geschichte der Region nicht mehr in ihre Räume zurück. Der Pavillon wird heute für temporäre Ausstellungen genutzt. Auch eine Neugestaltung des Kunsthandwerk-Pavillons wird überlegt.

Jedenfalls erweist sich das neue Museum als Publikumsmagnet. Ein
Jahr nach Eröffnung zählt man bereits 400.000 Besucher. Auch die
Skepsis innerhalb der Bevölkerung schwindet. 1995 gewinnt das
Museum bei einer Architekturumfrage einer Zeitung den Publikums-
preis. Die Fachjury kommt jedoch zu einem anderen Ergebnis:
Obwohl städtebaulich ein Gewinn für die Stadt, wird das Museum
schlicht als „schlechte Architektur" bezeichnet.[20]

Das Museum bestätigt auch die Hoffnungen, einen positiven Impuls
auf den Tourismus und damit die wirtschaftliche Expansion der Stadt zu
haben. Die Straßenverbindungen zwischen Museum und Stadtkern entwickeln sich in den folgenden Jahren zu florierenden Einkaufsstraßen.

Der Erfolg gibt dem Konzept recht, auch wenn es nicht jedermanns
Gechmack ist.

be postponed a number of times, not least because the architecture itself made it impossible to hang the paintings. After some modifications – suspended walls were installed to provide surfaces for attaching frames – the paintings were presented in the pavilion for the first time in October 1995. In the end, excessive daylight and the extreme height at which the paintings had to be hung made it necessary to move this collection to the "Mendini Pavilion" on the floor below. On top of all this, the museum also had to deal with problems of flooding. In spite of assurances that the water level would never rise above a certain mark, the entire basement was flooded in the summer of 1998, and the pavilions affected had to be cleared out. The Regional Archaeology and History section was never returned to its previous venue after the renovation. These days the pavilion is used for temporary exhibitions. And a renovation of the Arts and Crafts pavilion is also under consideration.

Still, the new museum has turned out to be a major attraction: 400,000 visitors were counted in the first year alone. Public opinion, too, began to change. In a 1995 newspaper poll on architecture, the general public voted the museum its favourite. The professional jury, however, reached another verdict, declaring that, although of benefit to the city, the museum itself could only be described in plain terms as "bad architecture."[20]

The museum has fulfilled the hopes of stimulating the city's tourism and contributing to its economic expansion. In the ensuing years, the streets that link the museum to the city centre have developed into flourishing shopping areas. Success has legitimized the concept, even if it is not to everone's taste.

Fußnoten

MuseumsQuartier Wien
1: Pseudonym des Wiener Architekten Gustav Peichl
2: Gustav W. Trampitsch zitiert Bernd Lötsch, in: TOP, November 1994
3: Ulrich Zerbs zitiert Bernd Lötsch, in: Neue Kronen Zeitung, 8.9.1992
4: Karlheinz Roschitz: „Endlich gesund geschrumpft!", in: Neue Kronen Zeitung, 21.5.1993
5: Bernhard Görg: „Ich sage ‚Nein', weil ich ein Museumsquartier will", Inserate in: Der Standard und Die Presse, 22.1.1993; und Roland Kopt: „Nur noch SP-Politiker für Museums-Monster", zit. Görg, in: Neue Kronen Zeitung, 27.9.1992
6: Karikatur von Dieter Zehentmayr: „Kleinkariert is bjutifull!", in: Kurier, 30.9.1992
7: Aurelius: „Sieg der Vernunft", in: Neue Kronen Zeitung, 2.10.1992
8: Ulrich Zerbs und Roland Kopt: „Monsterprojekt zerstört Wien", in: Neue Kronen Zeitung, 24.8.1993
9: Ein von der Museumsquartier-Errichtungsgesellschaft 2000 organisiertes Projekt, Plakate von Künstlern zum Museumsquartier entwerfen zu lassen.

Sydney Opera House
1: Malcolm Brown: Utzon given final say, and the crowd loves it, in: The Sydney Morning Herald, 26.10.1998
2: Mitglieder: S. Haviland (Vorsitzender); Roy Hendy, Oberstadtdirektor, Sydney; Sir Charles Moses, CBE, General Manager, Australian Broadcasting Commission; Sir Eugene Goossens, Direktor, Musik-Konservatorium; Professor H. Ingham Ashworth, Dekan, Faculty of Architecture, University of Sydney
3: Françoise Fromonot: Jørn Utzon, The Sydney Opera House. Electa/Gingko, Milan 1998, S. 25
4: Einer anderen Version folgend, wählte Saarinen aus den zehn in die engere Wahl gekommenen Projekten jenes von Utzon aus.
5: Sunday Morning Herald, 30.1.1957
6: Interview mit Harry Seidler in der Dokumentation „The Edge of the Possible"; Co-Autor und Regisseur Daryl Dellora; © 1998 Film Art Doco Pty Ltd & the Australian Film Finance Corporation
7: Jørn Utzon: Sydney National Opera House. Atelier Elektra, Copenhagen 1958
8: Brief Utzons an Ashworth, datiert vom 27.November 1961; Ashworth Papers, Box 1, Folder 10, aus: Françoise Fromonot: Jørn Utzon, The Sydney Opera House, S. 85
9: Interview von Françoise Fromonot mit Mogens Prip-Buus, Nizza, Juni 1994; aus Françoise Fromonot: Jørn Utzon, The Sydney Opera House, S. 89
10: Die Regierung bewilligte im „Sydney Opera House Act" 1960 den Bau der Oper und ein Budget in der Höhe von 4.880.000 Australischen Dollar plus 10 Prozent.
11: Werbebroschüre für die „Sydney Fliesen-Serie", herausgegeben vom Hersteller Partek Höganäs AB, 1990
12: In: Utzon and the Sydney Opera House. Rare Limited Edition. 1st edition 1967. 2nd limited edition 1998. Morgan Publications, Sydney 1967. (Republished by Elias Duek Cohen. Sydney 1998)
13: In: TELE., 5.7.1962
14: Aus dem Film „The Edge of the Possible"; Co-Autor und Regisseur Daryl Dellora; © 1998 Film Art Doco Pty Ltd & the Australian Film Finance Corporation
15: In: Michael Baume: The Sydney Opera House. Thomas Nelson Ltd., Sydney 1967, S. 84
16: In: Michael Baume: The Sydney Opera House. Thomas Nelson Ltd., Sydney 1967, S. 84ff.
17: In: Michael Baume: The Sydney Opera House. Thomas Nelson Ltd., Sydney 1967, S. 85
18: 1.095.106 AUD an bezahltem Honorar, in: Sunday Morning Herald, 1.3.1966
19: John O'Hara: „Angry clash on fees reported", in: Sunday Morning Herald, 1. 3.1966
20: Brief von Utzon an Arup, vom 10.2.1966, zitiert in: Françoise Fromonot: Jørn Utzon, The Sydney Opera House, S. 181

Footnotes

MuseumsQuartier Wien
1: Pseudonym of the Viennese architect Gustav Peichl.
2: Gustav W. Trampitsch quotes Bernd Lötsch, in: TOP, November 1994.
3: Ulrich Zerbs quotes Bernd Lötsch, in: Neue Kronen Zeitung, September 8, 1992.
4: Karlheinz Roschitz: "Endlich gesund geschrumpft!", in: Neue Kronen Zeitung,
   May 21, 1993.
5: Bernhard Görg: "Ich sage 'Nein', weil ich ein Museumsquartier will", advertisements
   in Der Standard and Die Presse, January 22, 1993 and Roland Kopt: "Nur noch
   SP-Politiker für Museums-Monster", quotes Görg, in: Neue Kronen Zeitung,
   September 27, 1992.
6: Cartoon by Dieter Zehentmayr: "Kleinkariert is bjutifull!", in: Kurier, September 30,
   1992.
7: Aurelius: "Sieg der Vernunft", in: Neue Kronen Zeitung, October 2, 1992.
8: Ulrich Zerbs and Roland Kopt: "Monsterprojekt zerstört Wien", in: Neue Kronen
   Zeitung, August 24, 1993.
9: A project organized by the Museum Quarter Development and Operation Co. Ltd. 2000
   that had artists design posters with the Museum Quarter as theme.

Sydney Opera House
1: Malcolm Brown: Utzon given final say, and the crowd loves it, in: The Sydney Morning
   Herald, October 26, 1998.
2: Members: S. Haviland (chairman), undersecretary of regional government; Roy Hendy,
   town clerk, Sydney; Sir Charles Moses, CBE, general manager, Australian Broadcasting Corporation; Sir Eugene Goossens, director, conservatory of music;
   Professor H. Ingham Ashworth, dean, faculty of architecture, University of Sydney.
3: Françoise Fromonot: Jørn Utzon, The Sydney Opera House. Electa/Gingko,
   Milan 1998, p. 25.
4: According to another version, Saarinen selected Utzon's entry from ten proposals that
   had been chosen for final selection.
5: Sunday Morning Herald, January 30, 1957.
6: Interview with Harry Seidler in the documentary: "The Edge of the Possible";
   Co-written and directed by Daryl Dellora; © 1998 Film Art Doco Pty Ltd & the
   Australian Film Finance Corporation.
7: Jørn Utzon: Sydney National Opera House. Atelier Elektra, Copenhagen 1958.
8: Letter by Utzon to Ashworth, dated November 27, 1961; Ashworth Papers, Box 1,
   Folder 10, as quoted in Françoise Fromonot: Jørn Utzon, The Sydney Opera House, p. 85.
9: Françoise Fromonot in conversation with Mogens Prip-Buus, Nice, June 1994;
   in Françoise Fromonot: Jørn Utzon, The Sydney Opera House, p. 89.
10: With the "Sydney Opera House Act" of 1960, the government approved the construc-
    tion of an opera house and a budget of 4,880,000 million Australian dollars, plus 10%.
11: Brochure for the "Sydney tile series," published by the manufacturer Partek Höganäs
    AB, 1990.
12: In: Utzon and the Sydney Opera House. Rare Limited Edition. 1st edition 1967. 2nd
    limited edition 1998. Morgan Publications: Sydney 1967. (Republished by Elias Duek
    Cohen. Sydney 1998.)
13: In: TELE., July 5, 1962.
14: From the documentary: "The Edge of the Possible"; Co-written and directed by Daryl
    Dellora; © 1998 Film Art Doco Pty Ltd & the Australian Film Finance Corporation.
15: In: Michael Baume: The Sydney Opera House. Thomas Nelson Ltd, Sydney 1967, p. 84.
16: In: Michael Baume: The Sydney Opera House. Thomas Nelson Ltd, Sydney 1967, p. 84f.
17: In: Michael Baume: The Sydney Opera House. Thomas Nelson Ltd, Sydney 1967, p. 85.
18: 1,095,106 Australian dollars of fees paid; in: Sunday Morning Herald, March 1, 1966.
19: John O'Hara: "Angry clash on fees reported"; In: Sunday Morning Herald, March 1, 1966.

21: In: Michael Baume: The Sydney Opera House. Thomas Nelson Ltd, Sydney 1967, S. 41ff.
22: In: Michael Baume: The Sydney Opera House. Thomas Nelson Ltd, Sydney 1967, S. 43ff.
23: In: The Arup Journal, Vol. 8, Nr. 3, Oktober 1973, London
24: In: Utzon and the Sydney Opera House. Rare Limited Edition. 1st edition 1967. 2nd limited edition 1998. Morgan Publications, Sydney 1967. (Republished by Elias Duek Cohen. Sydney 1998. S. 77f.)
25: „The Edge of the Possible"; Co-Autor und Regisseur Daryl Dellora; © 1998 Film Art Doco Pty Ltd & the Australian Film Finance Corporation
26: Peter Hall/Public Works, Lionel Todd/Hanson Todd and Partners, David Littlemore/Rudder Littlemore and Rudder
27: In: The Sydney Morning Herald, 1.3.1967

Le Grand Louvre

1: Der Cour Napoléon hat eine Grundfläche von 2,8 ha – das ist zweimal so groß wie der Markusplatz in Venedig.
2: Peter Rice arbeitete für Ove Arup & Partners an der Verwirklichung der Sydney Oper.
3: Bernini hatte seinerzeit große Projekte für den Louvre geplant, wurde jedoch durch Intrigen französischer Architekten aus dem Land vertrieben.

Kultur- und Kongresszentrum Luzern

1: Interview der Autoren mit Franz Kurmeyer, damaliger Stadtpräsident von Luzern, am 1.12.2000
2: Luzerner Neueste Nachrichten, 5.12.1990
3: Luzerner Neueste Nachrichten, 5.12.1990
4: Gleichzeitig wird dabei aber der 6,3-Millionen-Schweizer-Franken-Kredit für den Umbau der Boa-Fabrik angenommen.
5: In: Der Architekt Armin Meili und das Kunst- und Kongresshaus Luzern, 1993
6: Karl Lüönd: „Der Besuch bei der alten Dame", in: Die Weltwoche, 23.3.2000
7: Thomas Held in einem Vortrag anläßlich eines Symposions im Architektur Zentrum Wien, 1995
8: Im Sommer 1994 trennen sich Jean Nouvel und Emanuel Cattani.
9: In: KKL – die Geschichte seines Werdens, die Zukunft seiner Idee, Zürcher Druck und Verlag AG, Zürich, 1998
10: Das Bourbaki-Panorama-Gebäude wird 2000 fertiggestellt und beherbergt neben dem Panorama-Gemälde auch die Stadtbibliothek, drei Kinosäle und eine Galerie für junge Kunst aus der Innerschweiz.
11: Interview von Hugo Bischof und Urs Mattenberger mit Michael Wittwer (und anderen) „Das Signal ist da, jetzt beginnt das Gespräch", in: Neue Luzerner Zeitung, 18.6.1998
12: In: KKL – die Geschichte seines Werdens, die Zukunft seiner Idee, Zürcher Druck und Verlag AG, Zürich, 1998
13: Walter Schnieper: „Tourismusprofi an KKL-Spitze", In: Luzerner Neueste Nachrichten, 12.5.2000
14: Konzertsaal mit 1.840 und Luzerner Saal mit 900 Sitzplätzen
15: Das Dach ist 107 m breit und 112 m lang

Museum Mönchengladbach

1: Im Frühjahr 1970 zeigt Cladders eine Ausstellung über Hans Hollein (Hans Hollein. Alles ist Architektur – Eine Ausstellung zum Thema Tod. 25.1.–1.3.1970), wobei sich die ersten Diskussionen zum Thema Museumsbau anbahnen.
2: Interview mit Prof. Hugo Borger, in: Rheinische Post, 6.6.1974
3: In: Rheinische Post, 5.10.1974
4: In: WZ, 5.12.75
5: Hans Rudolf Hartung, in: Rheinische Post, 4.9.1976
6: Schlagzeile der Rheinischen Rost, 10.12.1976
7: Leserbrief von Hans Hollein an die Frankfurter Allgemeine Zeitung, 28.1.1977

20: Letter by Utzon to Arup, February 10, 1966, quoted in: Françoise Fromonot: Jørn Utzon, The Sydney Opera House, p. 181.

21: In: Michael Baume: The Sydney Opera House. Thomas Nelson Ltd., Sydney 1967, p. 41f.

22: In: Michael Baume: The Sydney Opera House. Thomas Nelson Ltd., Sydney 1967, p. 43f.

23: In: The Arup Journal. Vol. 8, No. 3, October 1973, London.

24: In: Utzon and the Sydney Opera House. Rare Limited Edition. 1st edition 1967. 2nd limited edition 1998. Morgan Publications, Sydney 1967. (Republished by Elias Duek Cohen. Sydney 1998, p. 77f.)

25: "The Edge of the Possible"; Co-written and directed by Daryl Dellora; © 1998 Film Art Doco Pty Ltd & the Australian Film Finance Corporation.

26: Peter Hall/Public Works, Lionel Todd/Hanson Todd and Partners, David Littlemore/Rudder Littlemore and Rudder.

27: In: The Sydney Morning Herald, March 1, 1967.

Le Grand Louvre

1: The Cour Napoléon covers an area of 2,8 hectares – twice the size of St. Mark's Square in Venice.

2: Peter Rice worked for Ove Arup & Partners on the Sydney Opera project.

3: Bernini had envisioned plans for the Louvre on a grand scale, but he was forced to leave the country as a result of intrigues by French architects.

Kultur- und Kongresszentrum Luzern

1: The authors in conversation with Franz Kurzmeyer, then mayor of Lucerne, December 1, 2000.

2: Luzerner Neueste Nachrichten, December 5, 1990.

3: Luzerner Neueste Nachrichten, December 5, 1990.

4: The Boa factory conversion is simultaneously financed through a loan of CHF 6.3 million.

5: In: Der Architekt Armin Meili und das Kunst- und Kongresshaus Luzern, 1993.

6: Karl Lüönd: "Der Besuch bei der alten Dame", in: Die Weltwoche, March 23, 2000.

7: Thomas Held in a lecture at a symposium at the Architektur Zentrum Wien, 1995.

8: Jean Nouvel and Emanuel Cattani go their separate ways in the summer of 1994.

9: In: KKL – die Geschichte seines Werdens, die Zukunft seiner Idee, Zürcher Druck und Verlag AG, Zurich, 1998.

10: The Bourbaki-Panorama-building is completed in 2000. In addition to the panorama, it houses the municipal library, three movie theatres and a gallery for emerging artists from central Switzerland.

11: Hugo Bischof and Urs Mattenberger in conversation with Michael Wittwer and others. "Das Signal ist da, jetzt beginnt das Gespräch", in: Neue Luzerner Zeitung, June 18, 1998.

12: In: KKL – die Geschichte seines Werdens, die Zukunft seiner Idee, Zürcher Druck und Verlag AG, Zurich, 1998.

13: Walter Schnieper: "Tourismusprofi an KKL-Spitze", In: Luzerner Neueste Nachrichten, May 12, 2000.

14: Concert hall with 1,840 seats and Lucerne Hall with 900 seats.

15: The roof is 107-m-wide and 112-m-long.

Museum Mönchengladbach

1: In the spring of 1970 Cladders shows an exhibition on Hans Hollein (Hans Hollein. Alles ist Architektur – Eine Ausstellung zum Thema Tod. 25.1.–1.3.1970), which initiates the first discussions on the topic of building a museum.

2: Interview with Professor Hugo Borger, in: Rheinische Post, June 6, 1974.

3: In: Rheinische Post, October 5,1974.

4: In: WZ, December 5, 1975.

5: Hans Rudolf Hartung, in: Rheinische Post, September 4, 1976.

6: Headline of Rheinische Post, December 10, 1976.

8: Leserbrief von Dr. Dohmen, im Auftrag der SPD-Fraktion Mönchengladbach in: WZ, 3.12.76
9: Panza war außerdem mit der Stadt Düsseldorf im Gespräch. Dabei ging es um einen zweiten Sammlungsteil, den Panza dem geplanten Erweiterungsbau des Kunstmuseums am Ehrenhof angeboten hatte.
10: Moderator: Reiner Assion; Hörfunksendung: „Zwischen Rhein und Weser"; Thema: Museumsneubau Abteiberg; Westdeutscher Rundfunk, 29.7.80
11: In: Rheinische Post, 30.1.1979
12: 1984 verkauft Graf Panza di Biumo seine Sammlung der fünfziger und sechziger Jahre an das Museum of Contemporary Art, Los Angeles. 1990 verkauft er den zweiten Teil seiner Sammlung der Minimal Art und Concept Art an das Guggenheim Museum, New York.
13: 1996 zog die Sammlung Erich Marx vom Museum Mönchengladbach in das neu eröffnete Museum für Gegenwartskunst in Berlin, Hamburger Bahnhof, um.

Groninger Museum
1: Henk Weulink über Frans Haks in einem Interview mit den Autoren am 24.11.2000 in Amsterdam
2: Im Wendebecken erreicht der Verbindungskanal seine maximale Breite und ermöglicht Schiffen eine Wendung.
3: Als positives Beispiel für die perfekte Verbindung von Kultur und Natur nennt er das Kröller-Müller-Museum in Otterlo.
4: Ypke Gietema in einem Interview mit Marijke Martin und Cor Wagenaar, Sommer 1994, in: Mendini, Starck, De Lucchi, Coop Himmelb(l)au in Groningen. Hrg. Marijke Martin, Cor Wagenaar, Annette Welkamp, S.119
5: Nieuwsblad van het Noorden, 17.11.1988
6: Corien Ligtenberg: A new policy for a new museum. A conversation with Frans Haks, in: Mendini, Starck, De Lucchi, Coop Himmelb(l)au in Groningen. Hrg. Marijke Martin, Cor Wagenaar, Annette Welkamp, S. 48ff.
7: Frans Haks: Een calculerende Terrier-Logboek van het Groninger Museum, Uitgeverij de Arbeiderspers, Amsterdam 1997
8: Johannes Cladders ist Gründungsdirektor des städtischen Museums Mönchengladbach. Er setzte seinen Wunscharchitekten Hans Hollein in allen politischen Gremien durch.
9: Henk Weulink über Frans Haks in einem Interview mit den Autoren am 24.11.2000 in Amsterdam
10: Frans Haks: ebd.
11: Frans Haks: ebd., Eintragung 7.-8.2.1990, S. 163
12: Frans Haks: ebd., Eintragung 20.-22.9.1992, S. 262
13: Henk Weulink über Frans Haks in einem Interview mit den Autoren am 24.11.2000 in Amsterdam
14: Wolf Prix in einem Interview mit Maijke Martin und Cor Wagenaar, Sommer 1994, in: Mendini, Starck, De Lucchi, Coop Himmelb(l)au in Groningen. Hrg. Marijke Martin, Cor Wagenaar, Annette Welkamp, S. 124ff.
15: Flaubert in einem Brief an Louise Colet am 20. Juni 1853
16: Bund: 3 Millionen Gulden; Provinz: 500.000 Gulden; Gemeinde: 1,5 Millionen Gulden; Gasunie: 500.000 Gulden; Museum: 1 Million Gulden; verschiedene Fonds: 500.000 Gulden
17: Corien Ligtenberg: A new policy for a new museum. A conversation with Frans Haks, in: Mendini, Starck, De Lucchi, Coop Himmelb(l)au in Groningen. Hrg. Marijke Martin, Cor Wagenaar, Annette Welkamp
18: Hans Fuchs: „Groninger Museum ist mehr Design als Architektur", in: Rouwwefeld; Januar 1995
19: Ed Mellet: „Eine kontrollierte Explosion", in: de Architect; Nr.1, 1995
20: Groninger Gezinsbode, 3.7.1995

7: Letter to the editor by Hans Hollein to Frankfurter Allgemeine Zeitung, January 28, 1977.
8: Letter to the editor by Dr. Dohmen, on behalf of the SPD faction of Mönchengladbach in: WZ, December 3, 1976.
9: Panza was also negotiating with Düsseldorf with regard to another part of the collection, which he had offered for the planned expansion of the Kunstmuseum am Ehrenhof.
10: Moderator: Reiner Assion; radio programme: "Zwischen Rhein und Weser"; topic: the new museum on the Abteiberg; Westdeutscher Rundfunk, July 29, 1980.
11: In: Rheinische Post, January 30, 1979.
12: In 1984 Count Panza di Biumo sells his collection of 1950s and 1960s art to the Museum of Contemporary Art, Los Angeles. In 1990 he sells the remainder of his Minimal and Concept Art collection to the Guggenheim Museum, New York.
13: In 1996 the Erich Marx collection was relocated from the museum in Mönchengladbach to the newly opened Museum of Contemporary Art in Berlin, Hamburger Bahnhof.

Groninger Museum

1: Henk Weulink on Frans Haks, in conversation with the authors on November 24, 2000, Amsterdam.
2: Where the canal reaches its greatest width, permitting ships to turn around.
3: He cites the Kröller-Müller Museum in Otterlo as a positive example of an ideal combination of culture and nature.
4: Ypke Gietema in conversation with Marijke Martin and Cor Wagenaar, summer 1994, in: Mendini, Starck, De Lucchi, Coop Himmelb(l)au in Groningen, Marijke Martin, Cor Wagenaar, Annette Welkamp, eds., p. 119.
5: Nieuwsblad van het Noorden, November 17, 1988.
6: Corien Ligtenberg: A new policy for a new museum. A conversation with Frans Haks, in: Mendini, Starck, De Lucchi, Coop Himmelb(l)au in Groningen, Marijke Martin, Cor Wagenaar, Annette Welkamp, eds., p. 48ff.
7: Frans Haks: Een calculerende Terrier-Logboek van het Groninger Museum, Uitgeverij de Arbeiderspers, Amsterdam 1997.
8: Johannes Cladder was the founding director of the Municipal Museum Abteiberg in Mönchengladbach. He successfully championed the architect of his choice, Hans Hollein, against all political bodies.
9: Henk Weulink on Frans Haks, in conversation with the authors on November 24, 2000, Amsterdam.
10: Frans Haks: op.cit.
11: Frans Haks: op.cit., entry on 7 – 8 February, 1990, p. 163.
12: Frans Haks: op.cit., entry on 20 – 22 September, 1992, p. 262.
13: Henk Weulink on Frans Haks, in conversation with the authors on November 24, 2000, Amsterdam.
14: Wolf Prix in conversation with Maijke Martin and Cor Wagenaar, summer 1994, in: Mendini, Starck, De Lucchi, Coop Himmelb(l)au in Groningen, Marijke Martin, Cor Wagenaar, Annette Welkamp, eds., p. 124f.
15: Flaubert in a letter to Louise Colet on June 20, 1853.
16: State: 3 million guilder; province: 500,000 guilder; community: 1.5 million guilder; Gasunie: 500,000 guilder; museum: 1 million guilder; various funds: 500,000 guilder.
17: Corien Ligtenberg: A new policy for a new museum. A conversation with Frans Haks, in: Mendini, Starck, De Lucchi, Coop Himmelb(l)au in Groningen, Marijke Martin, Cor Wagenaar, Annette Welkamp, eds.
18: Hans Fuchs: "Groningen museum is more design than architecture", in: Rouwwefeld, January 1995.
19: Ed Mellet: "A controlled explosion", in: de Architect, No.1, 1995.
20: Groninger Gezinsbode, July 3, 1995.

Bildnachweis/Credits

Wir haben uns bemüht, alle Fotorechte zu recherchieren und anzugeben. Für den Fall, daß einzelne namentlich nicht angeführte Fotografen Rechtsansprüche haben, ersuchen wir diese, mit dem Herausgeber Kontakt aufzunehmen.

We attempted to research all copyrights and to name them. In the case that any individual photographer not cited by name own legal rights, please contact the editors.

MuseumsQuartier Wien

Seite/page 22: Melanie van der Hoorn; Seite/page 23: Robert Newald; Seite/page 24: Kunsthistorisches Museum der Stadt Wien; Seite/page 25: Thomas Kussin; Seite/page 32: Archiv Manfred Wehdorn; Seite/page 36–39: Rupert Steiner; Seite/page 40: Archiv D.M. Steiner; Seite/page 41: Archiv Manfred Wehdorn; Seite/page 42: Archiv Ortner + Ortner; Seite/page 43: H. Schwingenschlögl; Seite/page 44–45: Archiv D.M. Steiner; Seite/page 46–47: Archiv Ortner + Ortner; Seite/page 48–49: Gebäudeteile Stand 1994 Archiv Ortner + Ortner, Gebäudeteile Stand 1999 Julia Oppermann; Seite/page 50: H. Schwingenschlögl; Seite/page 51: Gerald Zugmann; Seite/page 52–53: Rupert Steiner; Seite/page 54–55: Rupert Steiner, Lagepläne Archiv Architektur Zentrum Wien

Sydney Opera House

Seite/page 60: Archiv Max Dupain; Seite/page 61: „The Arup Journal", Oktober 1973 (Plan/plan); Film Art Doco (Skizze/scetch); Seite/page 63: Image Library, State Library of NSW; Seite/page 64–65: Archiv Max Dupain; Seite/page 66–67: im Uhrzeigersinn/ clockwise: Film Art Doco, Image Library, State Library of NSW (2), Film Art Doco, Archiv Max Dupain (3); Seite/page 68: Image Library, State Library of NSW; Seite/page 70: aus „The Arup Journal", Oktober 1973; Seite/page 72: Thomas Kussin; Seite/page 73: aus „Architecture in Australia", Dezember 1965; Seite/page 74: Image Library, State Library of NSW; Seite/page 75: Claudia Czech; Seite/page 76–77: Thomas Kussin; Seite/page 79: Thomas Kussin; Seite/page 80: Archiv Max Dupain; Seite/page 81: Thomas Kussin; Seite/page 82–83: Thomas Kussin

Le Grand Louvre

Seite/page 87: EPGL; Seite/page 88: EPGL; Seite/page 88–89: Sasha Pirker; Seite/page 90: Yves Chaudouët; Seite/page 91: EPGL; Seite/page 92: EPGL; Seite/page 94–95: EPGL (P. Astier links/left); Seite/page 96: Le quotidien de Paris, 31.1.1985; Le Figaro, 14.10.1988; Seite/page 97: AFP (4), EPGL „Pyramide du Louvre", Arch. I.M.Pei; Seite/page 98–99: EPGL; Seite/page 100: Sasha Pirker; Seite/page 101: EPGL; Seite/page102: EPGL; Seite/page 104: EPGL, „Pyramide du Louvre", Arch. I.M.Pei, Yves Chaudouët, Sasha Pirker; Seite/page 105: EPGL, „Pyramide du Louvre", Arch. I.M.Pei, (S. de Luigi); Seite/page 107: Yves Chaudouët; Seite/page 108–109: Yves Chaudouët

Kultur- und Kongreßzentrum Luzern

Seite/page 112–113: Bourbaki Panorama Verein; Seite/page 114: Trägerstiftung (Priska Ketterer); Seite/page 115: Vincent Lafont; Trägerstiftung (Stadtarchiv Luzern); Seite/page 116: Luscher Architects; Seite/page 117: Archiv Jean Nouvel (Gaston), Archiv Luzerner Neueste Nachrichten; Seite/page 118: Trägerstiftung (Theo Müller); Seite/page 119: Trägerstiftung (Emanuel Amman/AURA); Seite/page 120–121: Trägerstiftung; Seite/page 122: Trägerstiftung (Eggerrmann&Eichenberger (2); Priska Ketterer); Seite/page 126–127:Trägerstiftung (Eggerrmann& Eichenberger), P. Ruault (unten/below); Seite/page 129: Trägerstiftung, P. Ruault (2); Seite/page 131: Trägerstiftung, P. Ruault (2); Seite/page 132–133: Trägerstiftung (Nique Nager: links unten/left below); Seite/page 135–137: P. Ruault

Museum Mönchengladbach

Seite/page 141: Marlies Darsow, Sasha Pirker; Seite/page 143: Archiv Hollein; Seite/page 144–145: Marlies Darsow, Archiv Hollein; Seite/page 146: Archiv Hollein; Seite/page 147: Jerzy Surwillo; Seite/page 148: Jerzy Surwillo, Archiv Hollein; Seite/page 149: Archiv Hollein; Seite/page 150–151: Franz Hubmann; Seite/page 152–156: Archiv Hollein; Seite/page 157: Franz Hubmann; Seite/page 158–159: Archiv Hollein; Seite/page 160: Marlies Darsow; Seite/page 162–163: im Uhrzeigersinn/clockwise: Archiv Hollein, Marlies Darsow, Archiv Hollein, Franz Hubmann; Seite/page 164: Sasha Pirker; Seite/page 166: Archiv Hollein, Marlies Darsow; Seite/page 167: Archiv Hollein

Groninger Museum

Seite/page 171: Pez Hejduk; Seite/page 172: Archiv Alessandro Mendini; Seite/page 172–173: Margherita Spiluttini; Seite/page 176: Groninger Archieven; Seite/page 178: Archiv Groninger Museum; Seite/page 179: Archiv Alessandro Mendini; Seite/page 180–181: Archiv Groninger Museum; Seite/page 182–183: Groninger Archieven; Seite/page 184: Archiv Alessandro Mendini, Archiv Groninger Museum (Portraits); Seite/page 185: Archiv Alessandro Mendini; Seite/page 186–187: Archiv Alessandro Mendini; Seite/page 188: Archiv Alessandro Mendini, Archiv Groninger Museum (unten/below); Seite/page 189: Archiv Alessandro Mendini; Seite/page 190: Groninger Archieven; Seite/page 191: Groninger Museum, Pez Hejduk; Seite/page 192: Margherita Spiluttini; Seite/page 193: John Stoel; Seite/page 194: Margherita Spiluttini, Archiv Alessandro Mendini (2); Seite/page 195: Archiv Alessandro Mendini, Margherita Spiluttini

Bibliografie/Bibliography

Allgemeine Literatur /
General literature

Fliedl, Gottfried (Hg.): „Museum als soziales Gedächtnis? Kritische Beiträge zu Museums-
wissenschaft und Museumspädagogik", Klagenfurter Beiträge, Bd. 19., Kärntner Druck- und
Verlags GmbH, Klagenfurt 1988.

Fliedl, Gottfried (Hg.): „Die Erfindung des Museums. Bürgerliche Museumsidee und
Französische Revolution", Publikationsreihe Museum zum Quadrat, Bd. 6, Verlag
Turia+Kant, Wien 1996.

Frehner, Matthias: „Wie Mr. Krens die Museumswelt auf den Kopf stellt", in: Neue
Zürcher Zeitung, Folio, am 14.10.2000.

Hoffmann, Hilmar (Hg.): „Das Guggenheim Prinzip", Verlag DuMont, Köln 1999.

Hollein, Max: „Kunst boom", Böhlau Verlag, Wien 1999.

Karp, Ivan; Kraemer, Christine Mullen; Lavine, Steven D.: „Museums and Communities.
The Politics of Public Culture", Smithsonian Institution Press, Washington and London
1992.

Klotz, Heinrich: „Architektur der Zweiten Moderne", DVA, Stuttgart 1999.

Lampugnani, Vittorio Magnago; Sachs, Angelika: „Museen für ein neues Jahrtausend",
Verlag Prestel, München, London, New York, 1999.

Mack, Gerhard: „Kunstmuseen. Auf dem Weg ins 21. Jahrhundert", Birkhäuser Verlag,
Basel, Boston, Berlin 1999.

„Museum galore", in: The Economist, 19.2.2000, Seite/page 82ff.

Newhouse, Victoria: „Towards a New Museum", The Monacelli Press, New York 1998.

Peressut, Luca Basso: „Musées. Architectures 1990–2000", Verlag Actes Sud/Motta,
Mailand 1999.

Preiß/Stamm/Zehnder: „Das Museum. Die Entwicklung in den 80er Jahren", Festschrift
für Hugo Borger zum 65. Geburtstag, Klinkhardt & Biermann, München 1990.

Rieger, Andrea: „Die Museums-Macher", in: Architektur, Nr. 3/4 2000, Seite/page 32ff.

Schneede, Uwe: „Museum 2000 – Erlebnispark oder Bildungsstätte", Verlag DuMont,
Köln 2000.

MuseumsQuartier Wien

〉 Publikationen / publications:
„Ortner & Ortner. 3 Bauten für europäische Kultur", Verlag Walther König, Köln 1998.
Ortner, Laurids; Waechter-Böhm, Liesbeth; Zohlen, Gerwin: „Wörterbuch der Baukunst",
Verlag Birkhäuser, Basel, Boston, Berlin 2000.

〉 Fachzeitschriften (Auswahl) / periodicals (selection):
„Museumsquartier Wien", in: Wettbewerbe, Jahrgang 17, Nr. 119/120, Januar, Februar
1993, Wien, Seite/page 22ff.

Wailand, Markus; Zinggl, Wolfgang (Hg.): „Zur Sache Museumsquartier", Zeitschrift für
Kunst- und Kulturpolitik, Jahrgang 1, Nr 0, Wien 1995.

„Museumsquartier Wien", in: Architektur Aktuell, Nr. 175/176, Januar, Februar 1995,
Wien, Seite/page 20ff.

Waechter-Böhm, Liesbeth: „Museumsquartier Wien", in: Architektur Aktuell, Nr. 211/212,
Januar, Februar 1998, Seite/page 108ff.

Interview Franziska Leeb mit Laurids Ortner, in: Achitektur, Nr. 3, 4/2000, Seite/page 39ff.

Weh, Vitus H.: „Museumsquartier Wien", in: Kunstforum, Band 150, 4–6/2000, S./p. 450ff.

Walden, Gert: „Museumsquartier Wien", in: Baumeister, März 2001, Seite/page 16ff.

„Museumsquartier Wien", in: de Architect, Jahrgang 32, März 2001, Seite/page 30ff.

〉 Fernsehsendung des ORF 1992, Kulturfrühstück vom 18.10.1992 mit den Gästen
Gustav Peichl, Bernd Lötsch, Karlheinz Roschitz, Laurids Ortner.
〉 Gesammelte Tagespresse ab 1961 / collected daily press since 1961.

Sydney Opera House

〉 Publikationen / publications:
Baume, Michael: „The Sydney Opera House Affair", Halstead Press, Sydney 1967.
Rice, Peter: „An Engineer Images", Ellipsis, London 1994.

Sommer, Degenhard; Stöcher, Herbert; Weißer, Lutz: „Ove Arup & Partners. Ingenieure
	als Wegbereiter der Architektur", Verlag Birkhäuser, Basel, Boston, Berlin 1994.
Fromonot, Françoise: „Jørn Utzon, The Sydney Opera Hose", Electa/Gingko, Milan 1998.
„Utzon and the Sydney Opera House", Statement in the public interest, Morgan
	Publications, Sydney 1967; republished by E. Duek-Cohen, Marrickville 1998.
Czarnetzki, Jolanda; Voit, Miriam: „Jørn Utzon. Wohnungsbau", Technische Universität,
	München 1999.
Nieto, Fuensanta; Sobejano, Enrique (Hg. der Originalausgabe): „Jørn Utzon", Katalog,
	Verlag Pustet, Salzburg 1999.
> **Fachzeitschriften (Auswahl) / periodicals (selection):**
„Sydney Opera House Competition", in: the Builder, 1.3.1957, Seite/page 399ff.
„Sydney Opera House", in: Architecture in Australia, Vol 54, No. 3, 12/1965, Seite/page 72ff.
„Uproar over the opera house", in: Engineering, No. 33 1966, Seite/page 731ff.
Baume, Michael: „Who are the guilty men?", in: The Bulletin, 2.4.1966, Seite/page 18ff.
Parsons, Philip: „Radical versus Conservative Architecture: The ruin of Utzon's audacious
	vision", in: Meanjin Quarterly, 9/1967, Seite/page 339ff.
Power, John: „The Continuing Story of the Opera House Affair", in: Quadrant, 1967,
	Seite/page 65ff.
Power, John: „Opera House, outrage and objectivity", in: Quadrant, 1967, Seite/page 5ff.
McCulloch: „Tritons and mermaids: a retrospective view of the Sydney Opera House", in:
	Meanjin Quarterly, no. 110, 1967, Seite/page 347ff.
Baume, Michael: „The Utzons and me", in: Quadrant, 1/2 1968, Seite/page 5ff.
„Sydney Opera House", in: Architecture in Australia, Vol 57, No. 3, 6/1968, Seite/page 462ff.
Duek-Cohen, Elias: „Two and a half years without Utzon", in: The Bulletin, 30.11.1968.
Utzon, Jørn: „Additive architecture", in: Arkitektur, no. 1, 1970, Seite/page 1ff.
Hughes, Robert: „Australia's Own Taj Mahal", in: Time, 8.10.1973, Seite/page 48ff.
„Sydney Opera House", in: The Arup Journal, Vol. 8, No. 3, 10/1973.
Ruhen, Olaf: „The Sydney Opera House: an exquisite abstraction", in: Australia Now,
	1973/74.
„Sydney Opera House", in: db- deutsche bauzeitung, Nr. 9, September 1996, Seite/page 98ff.
> **Dellora, Daryl (Director): „The Edge of the Possible", Film Art Doco Pty Ltd. &
	the Australian Film Finance Corp. 1998.**
> **Gesammelte Tagespresse ab 1955 / collected daily press since 1955.**

> **Publikationen / publications:**   **Le Grand Louvre**

Bezombes, Dominique: „Le Grand Louvre. Histoire d'un Projet", Le Moniteur, Paris 1994.
Boehm, Gero von: „Conversations with I.M. Pei. Light is the Key", Verlag Prestel,
	München, London, New York 2000.
Chaslin, François: „Les Paris de François Mitterrand: Histoires des Grands Projets
	architecturaux", Ed. Gallimard, Paris 1985.
Daufresne, Claude: „Louvre et Tuileries: Architecture de Papier", Ed. Mardaga 1987.
Foucart, Bruno; Loste Sébastien; Schnapper, Antoine: „Paris mystifié – La grande illusion
	du Grand Louvre", Ed. Julliard 1985.
Holland, Yngve Jan: „Grand Arche und Louvre-Pyramide. Zwei Pariser Staatsprojekte
	unter François Mitterrand", punctum ed. scaneg. 1996.
Mission de Coordination des grandes opérations d'architecture et d'urbanisme (Hg.):
	„Architectures capitales – Paris 1979–1989. Les grands projets de l'Etat à Paris",
	Ed. Electa Moniteur 1987.
Rice, Peter; Dutton, Hugh: „Transparente Architektur. Glasfassaden mit Structural
	Glazing", Birkhäuser Verlag, Basel, Boston, Berlin 1995.
Schmid, Erik: „Staatsarchitektur der Ära Mitterrand in Paris", S. Roderer, Regensburg 1996.
Schüle, Klaus: „Paris. Vordergründe/Hintergründe/Abgründe", Verlag Aries, München 1997.
> **Fachzeitschriften (Auswahl) / periodicals (selection):**
Allain-Dupré, Elisabeth: „Pyramide du Louvre: Les Structures de l'Invisible",
	in: L'architecture d'aujourd'hui, 10/87, Seite/page 63ff.
Chaslin, François: „La Marque du Sphinx", in: L'architecture d'aujourd'hui, 4/88,
	Seite/page 14ff.

Interview von Philip Jodidio mit I.M. Pei: „Le Louvre selon I.M. Pei", in: Connaissance des Arts, 2/89, Seite/page 84ff.

Chaslin, François: „Grand Louvre", in: L'architecture d'aujourd'hui, Nr. 263, 7/89, Seite/page 8ff.

Fitoussi, Brigitte, in: L'architecture d'aujourd'hui, Nr. 263, 7/89, Seite/page 198ff.

Sergent, Jean-Claude: „Archi Pei. Naissance d'une Pyramide", in: Beaux Arts, 1989, Seite/page 62ff.

„Le Grand Louvre", in: Le Moniteur Architecture, Nr. 1, 1990, Seite/page 33ff.

Campbell, Barbara Ann: „Light Periscope", in: Architectural Review, Nr. 1163, 1/94, Seite/page 18f.

„Inverted Pyramid", in: Architectural Design, Vol. 65, 9-10/95, Seite/page 59f.

> Gesammelte Tagespresse ab 1981 / collected daily press since 1981.

Kultur- und Kongreßzentrum Luzern	> **Publikationen / publications:**

Bernfeld, Dan; Bourgarel, Gerard; Gerosa, Pier Giorgie; Schmidt, Urs P.: „Wem gehört die Stadt? 50 schweizerische Bürgerinitiativen stellen sich vor", Editions du Ciedart, Venise 1980.

Drews, Isabel: „Kultur- und Kongresszentrum Luzern. Von der Vision zur Realisierung. Eine Chronologie", Verlag DIE REGION, Emmenbrücke 1998.

Bühlmann, Karl (Hg.): „KKL Kultur- und Krongresszentrum Luzern. Die Geschichte seines Werdens, die Zukunft seiner Idee", Zürcher Druck und Verlags AG, Rotkreuz 1988.

„Kultur- und Kongresszentrum am See. Architekturwettbewerb in zwei Stufen", Stadt Luzern 1989/1990.

„Ver-rücktes Luzern. Stadt und Landschaft als Ereignis", Ausstellungskatalog der BSA Ortsgruppe Zentralschweiz, Luzern, 1997.

Architektur Zentrum Wien (Hg.): „Der leere Raum 94 – Der öffentliche Raum 95", Vortrag von Thomas Held anläßlich des Symposiums, Verlag Springer, Wien 1996.

Boissiere, Olivier: „Jean Nouvel", Verlag Birkhäuser, Basel 1996.

„Bericht vom Bau. Kultur- und Kongresszentrum Luzern", Trägerstiftung Luzern 1997.

Architekturgalerie Luzern (Hg.): „Jean Nouvel – Luzern. concert hall – konzertsaal – salle de concert", Ausstellungskatalog der Architekturgalerie Luzern (26. September bis 25. Oktober 1998), Luzern 1998.

„Kultur- und Kongresszentrum Luzern – Das Jahrhundertdach", Broschüre der Alusuisse Allega AG, Niederglatt ZH; Elektrowatt Engineering AG, Zürich; Carl Spaeter AG, Basel; Tuchschmid Unternehmungen, Frauenfeld und Meggen, 1998.

„Kultur- und Kongresszentrum Luzern. Das Architekturprojekt", Pressedienst 1998.

> **Fachzeitschriften (Auswahl) / periodicals (selection):**

Capol, Jan: „Die Farben des Klangs", in: Hochparterre, 6-7/1996, Seite/page 25ff.

„Pour Lucerne. Centre Culture et Congres", in: Techniques & Architecture, Nr. 440, 10-11/1998, Seite/page 16ff.

„Jean Nouvel. Concert hall", in: a+u, Nr. 339, 12/1998, Seite/page 52ff.

Valda, Andreas: „Jean Nouvel. Das Dach der Dächer", in: Architektur aktuell, Nr. 221, 10/1998, Seite/page 46ff.

„Jean Nouvel. Centro Cultural de Congresos de Lucerna", in: El Croquis, Nr. 88/89, 1998, Seite/page 124ff.

„Jean Nouvel. Centro Cultural de Congresos de Lucerna", in: El Croquis, Nr. 92, 1998, Seite/page 84ff.

Deon, Luca: „Voir et etre vu. Le centre de la culture et de congrès de Lucerne", in: Faces, Nr. 46, Sommer 1999, Seite/page 22ff.

> Gesammelte Tagespresse ab 1980 / collected daily press since 1980.

Museum Mönchengladbach	> **Publikationen / publications:**

„Städtisches Museum Abtei Mönchengladbach", Ausstellungskatalog der Galerie Ulysses (24. Oktober bis 24. November), Wien 1979.

Pehnt, Wolfgang: „Hans Hollein. Museum Mönchengladbach", Fischer Verlag, Frankfurt 1989.

„Hans Hollein", Ausstellungskatalog des Historischen Museums der Stadt Wien, Eigenverlag der Museen der Stadt Wien 1995.

„Sonderschau Städtisches Museum Abteiberg Mönchengladbach", in: Internationaler Kunstmarkt Düsseldorf, Ausstellungskatalog 29.11.–4.12.1978, Hatje Verlag, Stuttgart 1978.

Inventory of the Giuseppe Panza Papers, 1956–1190, Quelle: Getty Research Institute for the History of Art and Humanities.

> **Fachzeitschriften (Auswahl):**

„Städtisches Museum, Abteiberg, Mönchengladbach", in: Baumeister, Mai 1975.

Cladders, Johannes: „Mönchengladbach: Der Modellfall eines Museums", in: Transparent. Manuskripte für Architektur, Oktober 1975, Seite/page 229ff.

„Städtisches Museum Mönchengladbach", in: Kunst Bulletin, Nr. 9., September 1975.

„Städtisches Museum Abteiberg Mönchengladbach", in: Bauwelt, Nr. 25, Juli 1979.

Claddders, Johannes: „Museum Abteiberg Mönchengladbach", in: Architektur Wettbewerbe, Nr. 101, 1980.

Engelhard, Günter: „Die Wiedergeburt des Museums. Das Projekt Mönchengladbach des H. Hollein", eine Sendung des NDR am 19.3.1975.

Pomsel, Horst: „Museumsneubau Abteiberg Mönchengladbach", eine Sendung des WDR am 29.7.1980.

> **Gesammelte Tagespresse ab 1972 / collected daily press since 1972.**

> **Publikationen / publications:**   Groninger Museum

Newhouse, Victoria: „Towards a new Museum", The Monacelli Press, New York 1998.

Martin, Marijke; Wagenaar, Cor; Welkamp, Annette (Hg.): „Mendini! De Lucchi! Starck! Coop Himmelb(l)au! In Groningen!", Groninger Museum, Groningen 1996.

Lootsma, Bart; Damen, Hélène: „Groningen – A Star is born. The City as a Stage", Thoth, Bussum 1996.

Haks, Frans: „Een Calculerende Terriër. Logboek van het Groninger Museum. 16.1.1986 –31.12.1995", Uitgeverij de Arbeiderspers, Amsterdam 1997.

Pearson, James: „Frank Stella. From Minimalism to Maximalism", Crescent Moon Publishing 1994.

> **Fachzeitschriften (Auswahl) / periodicals (selection):**

Radziewsky, Elke von: „Schwärmen jetzt alle für Kitsch?", in: Architektur & Wohnen, 4-5/1991, Seite/page 115ff.

Scharfenorth, Heiner: „Bunte Fähre für die Kunst", in: Architektur & Wohnen, 6/1994, Seite/page 120ff.

Lootsma, Bart: „Frans Haks und das Groninger Museum", in: Bauwelt, Jahrgang 86, Heft 3, 20. Januar 1995, Seite/page 106ff.

Wortmann, Arthur: „Zarathustra in Groningen – the spirits of the museum. Alessandro Mendini's Groninger Museum", in: Archis, Januar 1995, Seite/page 18ff.

„Coop Himmelb(l)au. Video Clip Folly", in: Architectural Design, Vol 65 No 1/2, January, February 1995, Seite/page 30ff.

„Groninger Museum", in: architecture créé, Nr. 264, February, March 1995, Seite/page 52ff.

„Groninger Museum", in: Techniques & Architecture, Nr. 419, April, Mai 1995.

Synghel, Koen van: „In quest of architecture. Fourteen architects in Groningen", in: Archis, June 1995, Seite/page 2ff.

„Coop Himmelb(l)au, Groninger Museum, the East Pavilion", in: Architecture and Urbanism, No. 310, July 1996, Seite/page 94ff.

> **Auswahl der Tagespresse ab 1987 / selection of the daily press since 1987.**

WITHDRAWN-UNL